Hell, No, We Didn't Go!

Hell, No, We Didn't Go!
Firsthand Accounts
of Vietnam War
Protest and Resistance

Eli Greenbaum

 University Press of Kansas

© 2024 by Eliahu Greenbaum LLC
All rights reserved. No part of this book may be reproduced in any form or by any electronic or mechanical means including information and retrieval storage systems, except in the case of brief quotations for reviews, without written permission from the publisher.

Published by the University Press of Kansas (Lawrence, Kansas 66045), which was organized by the Kansas Board of Regents and is operated and funded by Emporia State University, Fort Hays State University, Kansas State University, Pittsburg State University, the University of Kansas, and Wichita State University.

Library of Congress Cataloging-in-Publication Data

Names: Greenbaum, Eli, 1945– author.
Title: Hell, no, we didn't go! : firsthand accounts of Vietnam War protest and resistance / Eli Greenbaum.
Other titles: Firsthand accounts of Vietnam War protest and resistance
Description: Lawrence, Kansas: University Press of Kansas, 2024 | Includes bibliographical references.
Identifiers: LCCN 2023033977 (print) | LCCN 2023033978 (ebook)
  ISBN 9780700636297 (cloth)
  ISBN 9780700636303 (paperback)
  ISBN 9780700636310 (ebook)
Subjects: LCSH: Vietnam War, 1961–1975—Draft resisters—United States. | Vietnam War, 1961–1975—Conscientious objectors—United States. | Vietnam War, 1961–1975—Protest movements—United States. | Draft resisters—United States—Biography. | United States. Selective Service System. | United States—Armed Forces—Recruiting, enlistment, etc. | Greenbaum, Eli, 1945–
Classification: LCC DS559.8.D7 G74 2024 (print) | LCC DS559.8.D7 (ebook) | DDC 959.704/31—dc23/eng/20231206
LC record available at https://lccn.loc.gov/2023033977.
LC ebook record available at https://lccn.loc.gov/2023033978.

British Library Cataloguing-in-Publication Data is available.

Printed in the United States of America

The paper used in this publication is acid free and meets the minimum requirements of the American National Standard for Permanence of Paper for Printed Library Materials Z39.48–1992.

Some names, locations, and other identifying factors have been changed to protect the privacy of individuals who appear in this book. Any resemblance of those names and characteristics to real persons living or dead is entirely coincidental and not intended by the author.
The Women Against Daddy Warbucks statement is reprinted with permission from *Sisterhood Is Powerful*, compiled and edited by Robin Morgan, copyright 1970 by Robin Morgan, all rights reserved.
The excerpt from Aaron Lansky's *Outwitting History* (Chapel Hill, NC: Algonquin Books of Chapel Hill, 2005) is reprinted by permission from Aaron Lansky, copyright 2004 by Aaron Lansky, all rights reserved.

This book is dedicated to the men and women who chose not to serve in the Vietnam War and extends a heartfelt thank you to those who did.

Contents

Author's Note   ix

Introduction   1

1   Setting the Stage   15
    Carol

2   First Impressions   29

3   Meet the Bureaucracy   38
    Mike, Joseph

4   Noise and Numbers   56
    Bert, Stan, Ed, Mark

5   Better Information, Better Decisions   71
    Jim, Alix, Michael

6   Bend Over and Crack a Smile   87
    Jason, Ray, Bert, Mark, Larry, Rick

7   Do What You Gotta Do   103
    Sid, Carey, Daniel

8   Hiding in Plain Sight   113
    Al, Larry

9   Questions of Conscience   122
    Bert, Erick

10   Choice versus Chance   135
    Alan, George, Lance, Budd, Paul

viii   Contents

11   Go North, Young Man   156
     David, Bob, Tim, Tom, Alan, Leo

12   We Could Complicate Things   187
     RJ, Richard, John, Steve

13   Connections   203
     Ernest, Paul, Lou, Psylvia, Barry, Jürgen

14   Facing Jail Time   218
     Dylan, Howard, Tom, Jim

15   Perspectives   247

Acknowledgments   257

Appendix 1: Selective Service System Statistics, Classifications, and Chain of Events   259

Appendix 2: Items Received from the Selective Service   266

Selected Bibliography   273

For Further Reference   275

Author's Note

This book presents firsthand accounts by men and women who opposed the Vietnam War and its military draft. It is not intended to be a comprehensive history of the Vietnam War era, I am not a historian. However, I have attempted to provide context for that time period by using widely known and easily available and supported historical information.

For readers interested in learning more about the war, the draft, and pertinent cultural, political, and military issues of the time, there is an abundance of information available in bookstores, libraries, and on reputable websites. The "For Further Reference" section on page 275 includes works readers may find to be of value.

For easier reading and flow of content, I have minimized footnotes and incorporated selected source and reference material into the narrative. The book has been fact-checked by the publisher's representative. If there are inaccuracies, they are inadvertent, and I apologize for them.

Introduction

Draft dodging runs in my family. My father avoided being drafted into the Polish Army in 1929 by crossing the border into what was then Czechoslovakia. He had just turned eighteen and received a notice to appear for a preinduction physical examination. If my father passed the physical, he would be called into the military service in a matter of weeks. The family was thrown into a panic. They didn't want him going into the army. This was not unusual: this was Dinov, a small village, a shtetl, in the southern part of Poland. Our family was Jewish and viewed the soldiers in the Polish Army as being anti-Semitic and treacherous.

As my father told me many times when I was a boy, being a Jew in the Polish Army barracks could be more dangerous than being on the battlefield. He said that being a Jew in the Polish Army was essentially an invitation to be bullied, belittled, and beaten by your comrades in arms. True or not, there weren't a lot of Jews enlisting voluntarily. While many Jews did serve honorably in the Polish Army and didn't encounter anti-Semitism, it wasn't out of the question for a Jew, or anyone of any faith for that matter, to look for a way out of being conscripted.

My grandfather was initially distraught—no way did he want a son in the army—but kept a cool head and took a pragmatic and usually effective step to help my father avoid conscription: he offered a generous monetary bribe to the doctor administering the physical exam. Working through go-betweens, the bribe was accepted, and it was arranged that my father would show up for the physical and make a simple coded statement: "I have a heart condition," identifying himself to the doctor, whom he had never met. The doctor would go through the motions of an exam—a poke here, a jab there, fiddle with a stethoscope—and declare my father unfit for service. That would be that. My father would be home in time for dinner with the family.

However, things didn't go as planned. As Yiddish fatalism has it, *Man tracht und Gott lacht*—"Man plans and God laughs." At the last minute, the army switched doctors. When my father said, "I have a heart condition," the unbribed doctor said, "No, you don't. You're healthy and strong, and you'll make a fine soldier." My father's thought was, "So long, Poland. Hello, Czechoslovakia." Within twenty-four hours, he said his goodbyes and stealthily crossed the border into Czech territory. He then quickly moved on to Vienna, where his two brothers—who had left Poland before they could be conscripted—had already settled.

Discard the notion that my father was a coward and afraid of military service. In due course, he traveled on to what is now Israel, joined the Haganah (as did my mother)—the precursor to the Israel Defense Forces—and fought (as did my mother) without hesitation in the Arab-Israeli War following Israel's declaration of independence in 1948. That war was a matter of survival, and it was all hands on deck, nothing like what was happening in Poland in 1929, and certainly nothing like the Vietnam War. After immigrating to the United States and settling our family in Detroit, my father worked in some of the city's roughest neighborhoods without fear. He was physically strong and did what he needed to do when he needed to do it.

This anecdote is not unique to my family. Ever since men have been subject to military conscription, many have found ways to avoid it—often with good reason, sometimes not. Sometimes it worked; sometimes it didn't. Avoiding conscription is a cat-and-mouse game, with elements of hide-and-seek and tag thrown in. It's been played all over the world in every war that has dragged unwilling men into battle. For me, and many men of my generation, the Vietnam War gave us a chance to play dodge-the-draft. It wasn't fun. Nor was it a game we were eager to play. My turn to be "it" came in 1968, with the escalation of US involvement in Vietnam.

Like my father, I wanted to avoid being drafted, not because the US Army practiced institutional anti-Semitism (I don't believe it did then or does today), but simply because I didn't understand why the United States was in Vietnam in the first place. It didn't seem to be "our" war. And I didn't want to be shot or killed in what appeared to me to be a conflict for the Vietnamese to sort out. Unlike my father, I didn't have to bribe anyone, and I didn't have to run away. I had other options. And I used them. So did plenty of other guys.

A few years ago, my wife and I were visiting a high school friend in Pittsburgh, an accomplished university professor well-known in the global academic community for his writings on risk analysis, a man who travels in Nobel Prize circles. At dinner, we began, as guys often do, reminiscing about our school days. The conversation eventually came around to brushes with the local Selective Service System draft board during the Vietnam War and how we fared. We traded stories about our draft resistance adventures—tales about friends and relatives who avoided the war and stories of others who were not so fortunate. We had the advantage, at that time, of an almost fifty-year perspective—the chance to reflect on what we did to avoid the draft and what our country did to try and get us into uniforms.

On the drive home to Detroit, in response to her questions, I began to tell my wife more about the draft and how it affected my friends and me. Most of this was new to her. I hadn't really talked about it before. She, being fifteen years younger than me, was not part of America's Vietnam War–era convulsions. Listening, and clearly intrigued (she's in the publishing industry and interested in everything), she asked a lot of questions. The more we talked about it, the more I realized that even though much had been written about that war, there was still a lot more to tell: personal stories by individuals—the hows and whys of men avoiding the Vietnam War draft. She encouraged me to write about it.

I began to think more about military conscription, often referred to as a draft—a system of selecting individuals to serve in their country's armed forces, particularly in times of war, a practice as ancient as war itself and still in effect in many countries today.

Men have often been drafted into armies to fight someone else's battles. Slaves have been pushed into combat, and men have been kidnapped to fill a king's or a general's ranks. The United States has used conscription six times: in the Revolutionary War, the Civil War, World Wars I and II, the Korean War, and the Vietnam War. In our own civil war, some Irish, German, and other European immigrants were pressed into service upon their arrival in the United States; others enlisted from overseas and had their passage paid. Still others were paid to take the place of someone who'd been conscripted, didn't want to go, and could afford to pay for a stand-in. Some nations today have laws in place calling for conscription in the event of a national crisis or military emergency. However, whether in the service of an ancient or modern king, feudal lord, fascist dictator, or democratically elected president, conscription is rarely popular except, perhaps, when it is implemented for national defense and the populace is motivated. The very concept of a draft suggests involuntary or indentured service, perhaps even slavery. Consequently, avoiding conscription is also as ancient as war itself. But *how* is always the question.

It also struck me that my generation—the baby boomers—was the last to face conscription in the United States. We were the last American generation in which lives and careers were interrupted and placed on hold, redirected, overturned, damaged, or even ended by the whims of a local draft board operating semiautonomously under the distant direction of a remote Congress and a White House administration fixated on war.

While subsequent generations have certainly had their share of life-changing issues to address, no generation since the Vietnam War has had to deal with the reality of having life upended by a military draft—and for an ultimately unpopular war, no less. Yes, we have had to deal with seemingly perpetual wars in the Middle East, classified military missions and skirmishes that we'll never know about, and the tragedies they all have inflicted, but we rationalize that the terrible consequences of post-Vietnam conflicts have involved people who chose to serve, men and women who volunteered to enter the military and agreed to accept the risks of warfare.

Once the draft ended in 1973, members of succeeding

generations of Americans often had little idea of how deeply the war and the draft affected the lives of previous generations. They may have heard or read about the Vietnam War draft, had friends or relatives who served or resisted, knew people who were damaged by it, and as a result had some level of understanding about it, but they didn't live it, participate in it, and weren't directly subject to it. Young men and women today don't have to be concerned with donning a military uniform involuntarily. We did. There's no question that voluntarily enlisting and waking up under fire in Afghanistan or Iraq or anywhere else in the world does not make for an easy day and can certainly have lasting effects, but complaining about it has its limits: *you enlisted; you knew what you were getting into; you made your choice.*

For many of us who had our sights set on a nonmilitary life and career and opposed the Vietnam War, we knew that we didn't want to go into the armed forces. Once the possibility of being drafted entered our brains, it burrowed in, made itself comfortable, and disturbed our thinking and behavior. The Selective Service System that administered the draft made us crazy.

What the Vietnam War did to our nation has been well documented by historians, scholars, social scientists, psychologists, activists, military veterans, politicians, novelists, the media, and Hollywood. As is the case with any war, too many servicemen and women—and civilians—suffered and died. Some returned from duty with chronic physical and psychological damage that affects them to this day. Some were held as prisoners of war, and some simply disappeared: MIA—missing in action. Thankfully, many did return intact with nary a scar of any kind.

Most men who were called to serve accepted the summons and submitted to the demands of their local Selective Service System board either by being inducted into the military or, seeing that they had no choice, enlisting in one of the armed forces in an attempt to retain some degree of control over their destiny. The National Archives indicates that between 1964 and 1973, approximately twenty-seven million American men were eligible for military service.

Around 15.4 million men were deferred, exempted, or disqualified because of student status, mental and physical conditions, marital and parental status, critical occupations, family hardships, conscientious objection, or other legitimate reasons.

Statistics for the exact number of men actually harvested for military duty from the start of the Vietnam War until the last man was inducted on June 30, 1973, vary depending upon historical references and sources. The Selective Service System website points out that from 1960 (when US military involvement in Vietnam increased) until the last draft call, 2,247,153 men were inducted. The website also shows that if August 2, 1964, is considered to be the start of the war (because of the Gulf of Tonkin incident on that date that resulted in the expansion of the president's war-making powers), then 1,857,304 were drafted. And according to John Prados, respected historian and author of *Vietnam: History of an Unwinnable War*, other accepted induction numbers are 2.1 million and even 2,709,918.

It was also said that there were more than 300,000 accused draft evaders and deserters in total, of which approximately 209,000 illegally resisted the draft, while some, about 100,000, deserted after being inducted. After fact-checking this book, Prados pointed out that such statistics can vary: "Problems of dating, periodization, definition and more—and confusion about what was, or was not covered, by amnesty programs offered by Presidents Ford and Carter—complicate the issue. It's impossible to be precise in these instances. . . . Just to illustrate how difficult this is, a position paper from the Association of the United States Army states that only 1,800 deserted while 4,000 more were 'lost' by changes in program. Similarly the Ford and Carter amnesty programs were rife with definitional difficulties."* In addition, of the 209,000 men charged with draft offenses, about 8,700 were convicted and fewer than 3,300 went to prison. About 197,000 cases were dropped or not pursued for one reason or another.†

---

* John Prados, November 2022, in a University Press of Kansas fact-checking review of this book.

† Laurence M. Baskir and William A. Strauss, *Chance and Circumstance: The Draft, the War, and the Vietnam Generation* (New York: Knopf, 1978), 5.

Among the resisters, it's estimated that from 1966 to 1972, twenty thousand to one hundred thousand men opted to go to Canada. Many chose to remain in Canada even after President Gerald R. Ford's conditional amnesty and President Jimmy Carter's pardon took effect (addressed in chapter 11).

It's important to understand what this book is and what it isn't. This is not a textbook history or detailed analysis of the war. It is not a scholarly or authoritative tome intended to be the last word on an issue that still roils my generation. It is not a "We were right, they were wrong" political accusation. It is certainly not an indictment of the men and women who served in Vietnam. All told, more than fifty-eight thousand American men and women died in Vietnam; the wounded and disabled numbered thousands more. They should all be honored, as should the men who had the courage to resist the draft.

One of the most moving moments in my life was standing in front of the Maya Lin-designed Vietnam War Memorial in Washington, DC, in 1982, shortly after it was dedicated, trying to comprehend how many young lives were lost in that unnecessary conflict. It made me sad and angry. It made me even sadder and angrier to watch the families of the men and women whose names were etched into the memorial touch the wall and stoically stand tall or break down and allow their grief to show.

Some resisters at the time found it quite fashionable to disparage those who did serve, but my group of friends did not denigrate, defame, or insult the men and women of the military. Many served because they believed it was the right thing to do—a patriotic duty, an opportunity to do some type of good—or a means to a personal end: an education, a vocation, or a career. Those who served deserve respect for putting themselves in harm's way for what they saw as their responsibility or desire to serve America's interests.

While we often disagreed with the mission of the men and women in the armed forces, we recognized what they did for us. I recall watching an episode of the hit television comedy series *Taxi* in 1979, as one of the cab drivers, Tony, a Vietnam War veteran, angrily points out to his ever-befuddled, acidhead colleague, Jim Ignatowski, that it was the guys fighting in Vietnam that allowed men like Jim to stay home, protest, and smoke dope. Tony asks, "What do you say to that?" And Jim, in his goofy, stoned manner, says, "thank you." I, too, say thank you.

This book is not an anti-war treatise. Regrettably, I believe there are circumstances that can justify war (although in the minds of many, the Vietnam War was not such a conflict). Nor does this book pretend to present a universal viewpoint or what every man subject to the draft was thinking or should have thought. There is no intent here to judge the individuals with whom I spoke or to criticize men who enlisted or accepted the draft.

This book also does not make a substantial distinction between draft resisters, avoiders, and evaders, all often referred to pejoratively as draft dodgers. There are distinctions between the terms—*avoiding* suggests finding a legitimate way out, *evading* implies using tactics that are perhaps a little shadier, and *resisting* connotes a general opposition to the entire concept of the draft (and, perhaps, war). An argument can be made for delving into the distinctions between the terms, but for the purposes of this book, I treat them as synonymous. All three categories refer to men who opposed the Vietnam War and did not want to be drafted into the army. Period. They were all resisters, and each found his way to resist. Those who attempted to avoid the draft one way or another are all part of that umbrella category. We all said, "Hell, no, we won't go!" And we didn't.

This book comprises firsthand accounts by individuals who were confronted with the draft and chose not to passively comply. It's about what we were thinking when we sang anti-war songs, marched in protest, held sit-ins and teach-ins, turned in or burned draft cards, and refused to buckle under the orders of what we believed to be misguided and often disingenuous American leadership.

The narrative here is about why we opted out and the lengths we went to in order to avoid serving. It's about what we were thinking about patriotism, sacrifice, and duty. And what we think about those subjects now.

The Vietnam War became part of the "America. Love It or Leave It" bumper-sticker cultural divide churning throughout the country at the time. Many people viewed opposition to the war as unpatriotic, as hating America, as shirking your duty to your country. But that wasn't the full picture. It took great courage back then to say no to the draft. For those of us who did so, protesting the war was actually a demonstration of faith in America, a belief that our democracy was strong enough to accept, listen to, or at least tolerate a broad spectrum of political and social views, including ours. We learned, painfully in some instances, that this wasn't necessarily the case.

The information provided here is anecdotal. These are oral histories I gathered in interviews and personal essays that are tied together with my own experience. The men and women I interviewed spoke openly. Everyone had a story to tell. Their thoughts varied and didn't always coincide with my opinions. They were often emotional: angry and bitter at how they and their motives were sometimes misperceived or misunderstood; anguished at times about the decisions they had to make; irate that they had to make the decisions at all. Others were finally at peace with the decisions they made and have kept that part of their lives in the past. They spoke of their contact with their draft boards, the preinduction physical exams, their applications for conscientious objector status, the reactions of friends and family, flirtations with law enforcement authorities, and the risk of jail time for their beliefs. Several of the men and women provided documents and photographs—from then and/or now. Their accounts are personal and, to my knowledge, not documented elsewhere, with the possible exception of archived records of local draft boards or personal diaries and journals. I asked my contributors to be honest and candid, and I believe they were. Each person I spoke with has attested to the veracity of his or her account and given me permission to use their information. Interviews in some cases have been lightly edited for clarity, and if there are inaccuracies in an individual's recollections or events are not related in chronological order, it is simply a matter of having too much to remember over fifty-plus years of post–Vietnam War life.

I spoke with dozens of men and women across the United States, in Canada, and in Europe. There were many more I could have approached; almost every man who avoided the draft has a story to tell. I knew many of the men from growing up in Detroit; some were friends I had stayed in touch with over the years and now were living around the country; others I hadn't had contact with in decades; and some were complete strangers to me when I interviewed them. The ones I knew were part of my community as we went through school, chose careers, and made life decisions. And we all had some degree of that gritty Detroit blue-collar, working-class "chip on my shoulder, don't mess with me" attitude, no matter what our individual backgrounds. I had thought the Detroiters' stories might be different, more defiant, from those of the men from other parts of the country, but as it turned out, I encountered diverse stories with underlying similarities that had little if anything to do with geography.

By way of background, I attended Mumford High School in Detroit, at the time academically one of the city's best. I believe about 80 percent of my graduating class went on to college. The student body was about 85 percent White and 15 percent Black. Most of us had comparable backgrounds: we were middle class, lived in comfortable homes, and had hardworking parents. Some of our dads were professionals with college and postgraduate degrees. Others were merchants or skilled tradesmen. My father and mother owned a dry goods store. Our moms tended to be either the stay-at-home variety or employed in traditional women's roles of the time—that is, as teachers, nurses, librarians, office staff, or sales personnel (remember, this was the 1950s and 1960s). But we, the students, were not all alike. Some of us were conventional replications of our parents—at least for a while; others leaned differently.

I spoke with other men and women whom I met in college— Wayne State University in Detroit, the University of Michigan in Ann Arbor, and other midwestern schools—or wherever I worked in Michigan, New York, and California in advertising or law. I was referred to others by friends, acquaintances, and third parties. As word got around that I was gathering these accounts, people started contacting me. They all had something to say about how and why they resisted the draft and wanted their thoughts preserved. Some offered in-depth explanations of their moral views and political skepticism; others kept it light, focusing on the draft interfering with their life plans, or told hilarious stories about what went on at their draft physicals. Some wanted to explain or justify their actions. Others wanted to reinforce their opinions and rant against the politicians of the time—or our current crop. A couple of them wanted to attest to the "sins" they had committed to stay draft-free. One even told me that his account, by inclusion in this book, might be the only way his children and grandchildren would ever understand what he went through. Everyone had a reason for telling their story.

It should be noted that the men and women I spoke with were not part of the celebrity roster of anti-war protestors. With the exception of distinguished authors Alix Kates Shulman and Esther Broner, they were not the headliners or recognizable names holding press conferences, leading rallies, or making themselves visible to the media. The people I interviewed were ordinary people, regular folks, the guys and gals who make our nation work. A cross section of our society is represented—educators, scientists, attorneys, doctors, musicians, therapists, financial advisers, artisans, writers, civil servants, technology gurus, and skilled tradesmen. All industrious folks.

The people I saw were generally among those who had access to the resources—knowledge, money, or connections—that could help keep them out of the draft and the military. Frankly, it was difficult for me to find men from minority groups who evaded the draft. I knew that one of the more effective Black anti-war groups was the National Black Antiwar Antidraft Union (NBAWADU) founded by Gwen Patton in 1968. Patton, now deceased, maintained that the White-led Vietnam War peace movement would work to end the war but would leave racism and US imperialism untouched and do little to change the situation of Black men being drafted for the war: Black people needed their own group to represent them. The NBAWADU activists organized anti-war marches in Washington, DC, and hosted an anti-war conference in New York City in 1968 that, according to the April 13 edition of that year's *New York Times*, about three hundred activists attended. I tried to find individual Black men who might have tried to avoid the draft and would talk to me, but I met with no success. I managed to speak with only one man, and he curtly stated, "I was crazy. They didn't want me. I don't want to talk about it." I was told, however, by Black friends that despite a man's chances of being shipped off to combat, the military could be an appealing career choice for those who might not be able to break into other civilian careers for any number of reasons. Latino friends and acquaintances who enlisted echoed the same thoughts about their own situations. I understand the point: a military career with benefits such as the GI Bill and skills training could offer a pathway to better socioeconomic status and serve as an attractive option, especially when other career avenues were not readily available.

Of the men I approached, quite a few declined the interviews, preferring, for whatever reasons they had, not to raise old demons and memories. One longtime friend, a former attorney and top amateur athlete, told me directly that he simply could not discuss that time in his life. He shut me down quickly, saying that the prospect of being drafted had caused him exceptional distress and that even my casual request for an interview was bringing back all the fears and anxieties he had experienced then. I could feel his tension and unease as he spoke. I backed off. Several other men I spoke with later told me that my questions dredged up similar apprehension.

I posed the same questions to everyone. I asked for their thoughts about the war, their reasons for avoiding the draft, and what they did to achieve that objective. I asked what role, if any, patriotism played in their decisions, and if they had any regrets about their actions. Some of the men and women responded directly to my questions and started conversations that surprised me and often went further than I had anticipated into unforeseen, yet relevant, tangents. Others chose to write of their experiences and thoughts in essay form. Most of the men referred to themselves as war resisters, not draft dodgers. Almost all of them said the war was "stupid" or "immoral." Almost everyone also said they had no intention of serving as "cannon fodder"—and they used that specific term emphatically and repeatedly. It was a common theme.

For those unfamiliar with "cannon fodder," the term denotes soldiers who are often considered to be expendable in battle. According to the *Oxford English Dictionary*, it dates back to 1847 and is defined as "soldiers regarded simply as material to be expended in war." The expression comes from fodder, as food for livestock, making soldiers the "food" for enemy fire (i.e., cannons). It is generally used in situations in which soldiers are forced to fight against hopeless or overwhelming odds. The trench warfare of World War I and the war's unsuccessful Allied landing at Gallipoli are sometimes used as examples. You'll never hear a commanding officer in any war refer to his men as cannon fodder—not if he wants to stay alive; nevertheless, soldiers fit that role all too often. The term may also be used to distinguish the military pecking order: low-grade soldiers are often regarded as cannon fodder when compared to officers.

Quite a few men also talked about the guilt they felt—either for not protesting enough or for the fact that their resistance may have resulted in someone else going to fight in their place. No one expressed regret for not going.

Some of the interviewees asked that their names be withheld. I respected such requests and changed their names, locations, professions, and other identifying characteristics in order to protect their privacy. Here they were, more than fifty years after the war, and the stigma of being called a draft dodger or being identified by name was still a significant concern for them. This was not because they were embarrassed or ashamed of avoiding the draft, but, as each of them explained, they didn't want to make themselves a target for anyone who felt differently about the war. When I asked a man in an affluent California town if he would agree to identifying himself, his wife jumped in before he could respond, saying, "Are you kidding? In no time some nut will be at our door trying to hurt us." I heard much the same from others. There was even some paranoia about the federal government coming after them. One man told me he still carries his draft card because he's afraid that getting rid of it could be considered a crime for which he could be prosecuted. Most of these men are established and successful in their fields. They have families. Grandchildren. Most are also retired. They have made their contributions to society. They would not be called hippies or activists or rebels or dropouts or societal misfits these days. They are long past their vulnerable days when youthful politics, philosophies, and legal and social missteps could compromise their careers, and still they are cautious about revealing their identities and views for fear of the reactions of the people around them. Yet there were others who pushed their names to the forefront, fully prepared to let the world know what they thought of that war. As one man said, "You can use my real name. I'm not ashamed in any way—especially at my age."

I have included women too—the abovementioned Alix Kates Shulman and Esther Broner, both accomplished authors, feminists, and humanists, and both opposed to the war. Shulman's comments appear later in the book. Broner was considering writing the foreword for this book when she died unexpectedly. She was the author of several noteworthy books, including *The Red Squad*—a fictionalized account of faculty life at an unnamed midwestern college campus à la Wayne State University, where Broner taught for several years (and was my creative writing instructor). Students and instructors on the fictitious campus were caught in the upheaval and fallout of the peace, love, and anti-war climate of the 1960s. The book's protagonist is involved in aiding draft resisters to reach Canada, perhaps drawing from Broner's real-life sentiments. Carol Gold-Lande and Psylvia Gurk also had something to say about those years.

I have tried to group contributors' accounts into chapters by subject. However, there is considerable topic overlap, since every account touches on several aspects of the Selective Service System (hereafter referred to as the Selective Service) process. Careful readers will note that while this book depicts real events and dates, some portions of the narrative timeline have been taken out of chronological sequence or condensed for simplicity and flow.

The Vietnam War was a defining period for many of us who were vulnerable to the Selective Service. The draft was not a spectator sport. All of us had some skin in the game, and a lot of people were hurt playing. People's lives were dramatically changed on the battlefields of Vietnam, just as they are changed on any battlefield in any war. And in this war, lives were also considerably changed in draft board offices across the country.

Chapter 1

Setting the Stage

There is a lot to take in concerning the Vietnam War era from the mid-1950s until the mid-1970s. It was a highly complex period that included, as with any war, multifaceted military and political strategies, tactics, policies, secrets, and players. US societal dynamics also had an impact. Detailed historical data is extensively available, but highlighting some of the key military and political events and cultural shifts is helpful to better understand the tone and tenor of those years.

France's colonial rule over Vietnam ended on May 7, 1954, when French troops were defeated at Dien Bien Phu by the forces of the Viet Minh, a Vietnamese Communist independence and nationalist movement led by Ho Chi Minh. Shortly thereafter, in the same year, the Geneva Conference produced an agreement that marked the 17th parallel as a provisional military demarcation line partitioning Vietnam into northern and southern zones, in effect creating two entities that would come to be known as North Vietnam and South Vietnam. Each zone would have its own government. Ho Chi Minh's Communist government, supported by the Soviet Union and China, would lead North Vietnam. French-educated emperor Bao Dai and subsequent president Ngo Dinh Diem would rule South Vietnam with the backing of the United States. While the 17th parallel was a temporary line and not intended to serve as a political border, it functioned as such between the two territories. A referendum was scheduled to be held by 1956 to reunite the two zones under a unified national government. Leaders of the two territories sought reunification, but the North wanted a Communist nation while the South pushed for a Western economic and cultural model. The election was never held. In 1958 the Viet Cong—Communist South Vietnamese guerrillas opposed to the Diem regime—initiated an insurgency that marked the onset of the Vietnam War between the two entities.

The United States believed that if South Vietnam fell to the Communists, a chain reaction across Southeast Asia would result, with country after country—possibly Laos, Cambodia, Burma, Thailand, and others—falling in a row, succumbing to a Communist wave. This was known as the domino theory. President Dwight D. Eisenhower used this argument in 1954 to justify American involvement, which at the time comprised a small number of military advisors, in helping defend South Vietnam.

President John F. Kennedy continued the commitment to the region during his administration and expanded the flow of military personnel and equipment to South Vietnam to assist in operations against North Vietnamese armed forces and Viet Cong guerrillas. Then came a critical turning point in the war. In early August 1964, President Lyndon B. Johnson told the nation that two US Navy destroyers had come under fire by North Vietnamese gunboats in the Gulf of Tonkin. Reports stated that on August 2, the USS *Maddox* was attacked by North Vietnamese torpedo boats in the gulf. Two days later, on August 4, also in the Gulf of Tonkin, the *Maddox* and the USS *Turner Joy* reported coming under torpedo attack. While the August 2 attack was real, there was confusion as to whether the August 4 attack actually took place (the reported events later proved questionable). Johnson told the nation that these were unprovoked acts of aggression by the North Vietnamese; however, he knew the ships were involved in covert intelligence operations supporting South Vietnamese commandos raiding North Vietnamese targets. Nevertheless, the president used the two events as justification to ask Congress for an increase in US military actions and to allow retaliation against North Vietnamese aggression. While historians and military experts question the incidents as initially reported, the two episodes, embellished or not, gave President Johnson an excuse to escalate the war. Reportedly, just hours after the alleged attack, Johnson called for retaliatory air strikes and US troops were readied for deployment to Vietnam. Congress passed the Gulf of Tonkin Resolution on August 7, 1964, authorizing Johnson to take all necessary measures against any aggressor in a US conflict with North Vietnam. Within a year, about 180,000 troops were on the ground in Vietnam, with more on the way. It's worth noting that while Congress passed the resolution, the United States never formally declared war on North Vietnam.

On October 21, 1964, just a few months later, in a campaign speech—"Remarks in Memorial Hall, Akron University"—President Johnson stated that "we are not about to send American boys nine or ten thousand miles away from home to do what Asian boys ought to be doing for themselves." Then, in July 1965, to ensure sufficient US troop levels, Johnson upped the military draft quota from seventeen thousand men per month to thirty-five thousand men, contradicting his pledge.

By 1966 there were approximately four hundred thousand US troops in Vietnam. Peace talks between the United States and North Vietnam began in Paris in 1968, but with neither the talks nor the war going as well as he had hoped and his public support eroding, Johnson chose not to run for reelection. Richard M. Nixon won the presidential race that year, and the conflict continued under his watch, with the number of US troops in Vietnam peaking to 549,000 in 1969 before the United States began to gradually pull out troops later that same year. By the time the Paris Peace Accords were signed in 1973, there were fewer than seventy thousand troops in Vietnam. When Vice President Gerald R. Ford became president following Nixon's resignation on August 8, 1974, US military activity in Vietnam ceased; however, US troops were still there until the city of Saigon fell in 1975, and the remaining US forces evacuated along with approximately one thousand American civilians and seven thousand South Vietnamese refugees.

While the war was raging in Vietnam, there was plenty going on at home. The mood of the United States from 1963 to 1974 was, at times, in a word, *tense*. *Restive*, *turbulent*, and *tumultuous* also come to mind. All these words could be tucked under another word that can be frightening to many people: *change*.

Indeed, change was coming. Swiftly. Back in 1961, in his farewell address to the nation, President Eisenhower had warned of the strength of the military-industrial complex:

> We must guard against the acquisition of unwarranted influence, whether sought or unsought, by the military-industrial complex. ... We must never let the weight of this combination endanger our liberties or democratic processes. ... Only an alert and knowledgeable citizenry can compel the proper meshing of the huge industrial and military machinery of defense with our peaceful methods and goals, so that security and liberty may prosper together.

The message regarding the military-industrial complex was clear, yet there was something else Eisenhower might have been implying that was equally, if not more, important: his language about an "alert and knowledgeable citizenry" suggested that to be good citizens, we had an obligation to stay informed, ready to speak up against the military-industrial machine when a situation called for it. The implication was that citizens should speak their minds and have their voices heard. Throughout the Vietnam War era, we did just that—and cranked up the volume.

The 1960s brought a groundswell of broad and fast change to the United States, as a new generation—my generation—focused on sex, drugs, rock and roll, free speech, and political activism. We were making our presence felt. College campuses became thought-incubators and gathering places for new ideas, attitudes, and protests. Students were making statements, asking questions, and demanding answers. We were questioning the "Establishment," even attacking it as we looked more closely at societal values. America's young people were moving away—some faster than others—from their parents' sleepy, conformist years of the Eisenhower administration.

The formation in 1960 of the Students for a Democratic Society (SDS) by an activist group of college students at the University of Michigan also had an impact. In 1962 the group held its first national convention in Port Huron, Michigan, and issued what came to be known as the Port Huron Statement. Its chief author was Tom Hayden, SDS cofounder, who would go on to become a dominant voice in the anti-war movement and eventually elected to the

California state legislature. The statement was a critical assessment of America's social and political systems, as well as US foreign policy. Issues of racial discrimination, economic inequality, business practices, and the United States' role on the world stage were at the forefront. It was one of the first discordant notes my generation struck.

As we were growing up, we had a few shocks along the way. President Kennedy was assassinated in Dallas, Texas, on the afternoon of November 22, 1963. At forty-three, he had been the youngest man ever to assume the presidency. He was an inspiration for many of the nation's youth who celebrated his establishment of the Peace Corps. His assassination caused many of my generation to wonder about the fabric of America—was it fraying? There were more such shocks to come.

Student activism was growing, but universities were not always receptive to student concerns. School administrations were often resistant to change, reinforcing or imposing campus restrictions on political and social activities. However, students would not back off. In 1964 activist Mario Savio led five hundred students at the University of California, Berkeley campus to the school's administration building and called for the elimination of restrictions on free speech rights throughout the University of California system. It was the launch of the Berkeley Free Speech Movement (FSM). National television coverage served to further spread the word, and soon other activist groups were born. The FSM had made its mark.

The era also witnessed a significant generation gap, as many parents couldn't understand what their kids were doing while young people couldn't accept their parents' long-standing conformity and complacency. Bob Dylan expressed the overall cultural shift in his 1964 song "The Times They Are A-Changin'." The song's perceptive lyrics declared that the times were, indeed, changing, and in one stanza pointed out to parents that their sons and daughters were no longer under their command.

And there was the war. Oh yes, the war. Young people across the country were becoming aware of and disheartened by the Vietnam War. Of course, not every young person was opposed to the war, and not every young person was an activist, but many of those who believed it was wrong began to take action. In Ann Arbor, students, faculty, and SDS members put together the first teach-in on the war. The daylong affair—educating attendees about Vietnam and the war—on March 24, 1965, drew more than three thousand students and faculty. The event created an educational template that was ultimately applied at colleges and universities from coast to coast during the war years.

Less than a month later, on April 17, 1965, the March on Washington to End the War in Vietnam took place. Cosponsored by the SDS and Women Strike for Peace and with support from other anti-war groups, the march was, at the time, the largest peace protest in American history. It marked the emergence of SDS as a national anti-war force. A crowd estimated at up to twenty-five thousand picketed in front of the White House, heard anti-war speeches, listened to singers Joan Baez and Phil Ochs, and delivered a petition to the Capitol to stop the war. SDS cofounder and president Paul Potter gave an impassioned speech calling out frustration with American international and domestic policy. The following are excerpts from the speech, the entirety of which can be found at the SDS Document Library online.*

> Most of us grew up thinking that the United States was a strong but humble nation, that involved itself in world affairs only reluctantly, that respected the integrity of other nations and other systems, and that engaged in wars only as a last resort.... The incredible war in Vietnam has provided the razor, the terrifying sharp cutting edge that has finally severed the last vestige of illusion that morality and democracy are the guiding principles of American foreign policy.... What kind of system is it that justifies the United States or any country seizing the destinies of the Vietnamese people and using them callously for its own purpose? We must name that system. We must name it, describe it, analyze it, understand it and change it. For it is only when that system is changed and brought under control that there can be any hope for stopping the forces that create a war in Vietnam today.

* Paul Potter, "Naming the System," speech delivered during the March on Washington, April 17, 1965, Washington, DC, available at Students for a Democratic Society website, https://www.sds1960s.org/sds_wuo/sds_documents/paul_potter.html.

Potter pointed out that the war was hurting America's image globally and that the march was not only about Vietnam but also an effort to help the United States build a better society. In addition, he questioned whether the war was genuinely undertaken to defend the Vietnamese or if there were other, more self-serving reasons.

Anti-war momentum kept growing. In May 1965 campus activists at Berkeley, including counterculture representative Jerry Rubin, formed the Vietnam Day Committee (VDC) and held Vietnam Day, a thirty-six-hour Vietnam teach-in. More than thirty thousand people attended. Guests included noted war opponents Dr. Benjamin Spock, comedian Dick Gregory, and writer Norman Mailer.

The VDC also organized protest marches to the Berkeley draft board and the Oakland military induction center. Similar marches and protests sprang up across the nation. At some of the demonstrations, young men would burn or destroy their draft cards as a symbolic statement of protest. The practice was highlighted in the 1967 rock musical *Hair*, when one of the lead characters sets his card afire (although it was actually his library card). Burning one's draft card—or a piece of paper that looked like a draft card—was an emphatic and visible symbolic war protest that didn't require a more extreme or risky action such as actually leaving the country, or getting involved in a possibly destructive or violent protest that could result in jail time. But destroying a draft card was also an illegal act: all men who were registered with the Selective Service were required by law to carry their cards with them at all times. If you burned your card, you obviously couldn't very well comply with the law, and therefore you could face charges. In response to a growing number of such acts, on August 30, 1965, Congress passed an amendment to the Selective Service Act making it a crime to mutilate or destroy a draft card. The Draft Card Mutilation Act of 1965, as it was known, provided for a penalty of a fine up to $10,000 and five years in prison. The law was challenged as unconstitutional in a Supreme Court case titled *United States v. O'Brien*.* However, by a seven to one decision issued on May 27, 1968, the court upheld the law, saying that destruction of a draft card interfered with the

---

* United States v. O'Brien, 391 U.S. 367 (1968).

smooth and effective function of the Selective Service. With their decision, the justices blocked a form of perceived free speech, but they also noted that there were other ways to object to the war.

In the early '60s, as the Beat Generation (the "beatniks") of poets and writers—including Jack Kerouac, Allen Ginsberg, Lawrence Ferlinghetti, and others—became more visible, counterculture ideas were slowly making inroads into the mainstream. Communal living, environmental consciousness, political awareness, sexual liberty, recreational drugs, and rebellion against the norm were all fringe concepts that would expand in good time. In the San Francisco Bay Area, the hippy phenomenon was growing. In 1967 along came the Summer of Love.

San Francisco was a magnet that attracted young people from across the United States and even Europe. The Human Be-In at Golden Gate Park in January of that year is often credited as the catalyst for that pivotal period. The scene involved music, speeches, poems, plenty of drugs, and lots of hormones gone wild. The words *psychedelic* and *tripping* were introduced to conventional vocabularies as LSD—acid—became commonplace. More than one hundred thousand flower children rebelling against their parents' values came to the nearby Haight-Ashbury district—or Hashbury, as it came to be known—that summer. It was a hallucinogenic landscape, filled with "flower power," free love, peace signs, hippies, long hair, and a firm anti-war vibe that was catnip to the media. Music was a vital component. John Phillips, a member of the Mamas and Papas group, wrote the song "San Francisco (Be Sure to Wear Some Flowers in Your Hair)," which served as the musical heartbeat of the summer. Appearances by top bands and singers, including the Grateful Dead, the Who, Jimi Hendrix, Jefferson Airplane, and Janis Joplin, lit up area pop festivals. The mood continued into 1968.

Chicago-based former advertising copywriter and creative director Carol Gold-Lande recalled her time in the Bay Area and her thoughts about the war.

> I turned twenty in 1968 and spent the summer with my brother in Berkeley. The war was in the background. I had my coming of age in those years, that one especially. It was an unforgettable experience.

I remember it as violent, exciting, disturbing, exhilarating, a time of so much change in the world and in me. The marches, the music, the miniskirts! The protests, the blood, the tears, the war, the drugs, and the craziness; it was a wild ride. And that Buffalo Springfield song "For What It's Worth" with the line "There's something happening here . . . what it is ain't exactly clear." I always felt that song captured the mood, though there were so many others. A time of great lyrics and stoned melodies. I could wax endlessly about 1968. I was under its spell. Still am.

I wasn't politically tuned into the Vietnam War. I didn't understand deeply enough why we were fighting it. But the draft was a different story. I at least knew the war was wrong, and therefore the draft was wrong. It was a vile menace that hovered over every mother's son, and every mother, and every family, every friend. We lived on tenterhooks. It was such an uneasy time.

Also, it hurt to see how dissed the boys were who made it home. I dated a couple of them, was engaged to one. They didn't believe in the war. They just didn't have the luck to lick the draft. If not injured physically, certainly the war traumatized them. Changed them. And those who dodged it had to give up hearth and home—for a war we shouldn't have been fighting. I can't offer an intelligent, philosophical diatribe about Vietnam because I never formed one. I just adopted the opinions of the people whose opinions I respected. I guess you could say I dodged the war.

The party continued on the opposite side of the country. For three days in August 1969, the Woodstock Music and Art Fair, known simply as Woodstock, was held in Bethel, New York, on Max Yasgur's farm and drew an estimated five hundred thousand young people. It was a seminal music festival that saw a who's who of musical artists thrill the crowd with their performances. The Grateful Dead, Carlos Santana, Richie Havens, Credence Clearwater Revival, Joe Cocker, Jimi Hendrix, Janis Joplin, Blood, Sweat and Tears, and the Who were just a few of the all-star acts that maintained the beat over those days. And with the music came a strong undercurrent of anti-war energy.

In the midst of this time of change, the underground, or

alternative, press sprang up as the voice of the counterculture. The *Fifth Estate* out of Detroit, the *Los Angeles Free Press*, the *Berkeley Barb*, and New York City's *East Village Other* were just a few of the newspapers that bucked the mainstream media and published anti-establishment articles focused on young people and their concerns. Anti-war and draft resistance–related articles took up a lot of space. In 1967 San Francisco-based *Rolling Stone* magazine launched its first issue touting rock and roll music and ultimately incorporating politics and culture into its editorial offerings.

Life was dramatic in America: feminism was rising; the birth control pill was allowing greater sexual freedom; the civil rights movement—and resistance to it—was on the front page; and Vietnam War protests weren't going away.

While a great many Americans at first either supported the war or had no opinion about it, things were changing there too. A Gallup poll conducted in August 1965 showed that only 24 percent of Americans thought the United States had made a mistake sending troops to Vietnam. By August 1968 another Gallup poll found that a majority of Americans—53 percent—thought the war was a mistake; by November 2000 that had increased to 68 percent.*

Television had brought the Vietnam War into the nation's homes, and news shows were airing war footage. Americans had been fed the story that the war was going well, but dissent was building. In an attempt to show that the war effort was making progress, President Johnson called General William Westmoreland, commander of US forces in Vietnam, to Washington to report on events on the front. In 1967 Westmoreland told Congress in April, and the National Press Club in November, that victory was coming. However, that prediction proved wrong, because just two months after his second appearance, the North Vietnamese launched the Tet (Vietnamese Lunar New Year) Offensive on January 31, 1968.

The Tet Offensive caught American and South Vietnamese armed forces off guard, despite some intelligence warnings. In a

---

* Gallup polls conducted from August 27, 1965, through November 13, 2000: "The Vietnam War Statistics," Shmoop.com, accessed November 1, 2023, https://www.shmoop.com/vietnam-war/statistics.html.

coordinated effort, seventy thousand Communist troops attacked approximately one hundred towns and cities throughout South Vietnam. Allied troops ultimately repelled the attacks, and the North Vietnamese forces took significant losses, but the surprise, scope, and intensity of the initial assaults—including one on the US Embassy in Saigon that was particularly humiliating—shook US public confidence in the war. The fallout was considerable. CBS news anchor Walter Cronkite, returning from Vietnam after the Tet Offensive, declared the war to be at a standoff, and, in an editorial on the CBS Evening News broadcast of February 27, 1968, said, "For it seems now more certain than ever, that the bloody experience of Vietnam is to end in a stalemate. To say that we are closer to victory today is to believe in the face of the evidence, the optimists who have been wrong in the past." It was said that a beleaguered President Johnson wondered if by losing Cronkite, he had also lost Middle America.

Anti-war noise was getting louder. The Smothers Brothers were politicizing their popular CBS variety show with anti-war references and outspoken and well-known guest stars such as singer-activists Pete Seeger and Harry Belafonte. CBS censors cut controversial segments, notably Seeger's incisive song "Waist Deep in the Big Muddy," a metaphor for the war and President Johnson's strategy (although it did air at a later date). Johnson was also the target of angry chants at protests—"Hey, hey, LBJ, how many kids did you kill today?"

As noted earlier, on March 31, 1968, Johnson announced he would not run for reelection. The news was completely unexpected and stunned the nation. With that announcement, some of us naively thought Johnson's prospective exit might bring the war to a quick end. It didn't.

Five days later, on April 4, there was another shock: the Reverend Martin Luther King Jr. was assassinated in Memphis, Tennessee. His death set off riots in more than one hundred American cities. The civil disturbances were nothing new. We had witnessed full-blown uprisings in more than 150 cities, including Newark, Detroit, Atlanta, New York, and Cincinnati during what was dubbed "the long, hot summer" of 1967.

Then in June 1968 Senator Robert F. Kennedy, a presidential

candidate, was assassinated in Los Angeles, another tragic and demoralizing event that threw the Democratic presidential campaign into confusion. Yet, there was more to come: at the 1968 National Democratic Convention held in Chicago (August 26–29), more than ten thousand protesters demonstrating their opposition to the Vietnam War and promoting civil rights and other social causes were met head-on by members of Mayor Richard Daley's police force, Illinois National Guard troops, and other state and federal officers—approximately twenty-five thousand in all. It was a confrontation that spun out of control and into some of the most brutal and ugliest moments in American history—the "Battle of Michigan Avenue." The protestors chanted, "The whole world is watching" as televised bloody action on the streets upstaged the convention. More than six hundred protestors were arrested, including prominent political activists Rennie Davis, Tom Hayden, Abbie Hoffman, Jerry Rubin, Lee Weiner, David Dellinger, and John Froines, who became known as the Chicago Seven when charged by the US federal government with conspiracy, crossing state lines with intent to incite a riot, and other anti-war protest offenses. Bobby Seale, cofounder with Huey P. Newton of the revolutionary Black Panther Party, was also arrested and charged with the others, but was tried separately.*

In November 1969 the My Lai Massacre of March 16, 1968, surfaced after a cover-up by US Army officers. American soldiers killed more than five hundred civilians—including women and children—suspected of being Viet Cong guerrillas or sympathizers. The revelation of atrocities by US troops—and the cover-up—sparked international and domestic outrage that contributed to growing opposition to US participation in the war.

With popular support for the war dropping off, on June 13, 1971, the *New York Times*, in a front-page article by reporter Neil Sheehan, brought the Pentagon Papers to the attention of the American public. Formally known as the *Report of the Office of the Secretary of Defense Vietnam Task Force*, the Pentagon Papers were a study of US military and political involvement in Vietnam from 1945 to 1967 and the

---

* Much has been written about the Chicago Seven and Seale trials. Please see "For Further Reference," page 275, for resources.

actions of Presidents Harry S. Truman, Eisenhower, Kennedy, and Johnson in misleading the public. The document was commissioned in 1967 by US Secretary of Defense Robert McNamara and was labeled Top Secret, drawing on classified material from the archives of the Department of Defense, State Department, and the CIA. Daniel Ellsberg, a former marine and Department of Defense analyst who had worked on the study, believed the public had a right to know what it contained, copied the documents, and turned them over to Sheehan. The Pentagon Papers revealed that the United States had secretly expanded the war with the bombing of Cambodia and Laos, raids on North Vietnam, and marine attacks. None of this had been reported by the major American media outlets. The US Department of Justice under President Nixon attempted to enjoin the publication of the Pentagon Papers but lost in the courts, and publication continued. Ellsberg was subsequently charged with conspiracy, espionage, and theft of government property, but the charges were later dismissed.*

The Paris peace talks that had begun in 1968 concluded five years later on January 27, 1973, with an agreement between North Vietnam, South Vietnam, and the United States establishing peace in Vietnam and ending the war—on paper. But that didn't end the conflict between the North and South. Fighting between the two sides continued, with North Vietnam expanding its control. On April 30, 1975, North Vietnam conquered South Vietnam, and on July 2, 1976, the country was reunited as the Socialist Republic of Vietnam.

The Vietnam War era in the United States saw political assassinations, urban riots, flower power and hippies, and mass protests against a hated war, almost all of it on prime-time television. In this period of flux, one thing was definitely clear: my generation had

---

* An abundance of information from numerous sources is available about the Pentagon Papers and Daniel Ellsberg. Noteworthy examples include John Prados and Margaret Pratt Porter, eds., *Inside the Pentagon Papers* (Lawrence: University Press of Kansas, 2004); Neil Sheehan et al., *The Pentagon Papers: The Secret History of the Vietnam War* (New York: Racehorse, 2017); and Daniel Ellsberg, *Secrets: A Memoir of Vietnam and the Pentagon Papers* (New York: Viking Books, 2002).

learned how to say *no* to college administrators, politicians, and our parents. Enough blind obedience. We had a voice. If we could say no to all those people, we could certainly say no to the draft board. So that's what we did.

Chapter 2

First Impressions

I was eight years old in 1954 when I first heard the word *Vietnam*. I had a cold and didn't go to school that day. On sick days, my mother would stay home from work and bundle me up in flannel pajamas, wrap me in a quilt, and park me on the living room sofa where I would watch a small-screen black-and-white television as she puttered around the house. There were only the three major networks on the air—ABC, NBC, and CBS, although in Detroit we could also pull in Canada's CBC at the end of that year. It was the old days when television reception was iffy, as network connections frequently broke and broadcasts were often interrupted.

That particular morning, sometime during the first week of May, I was watching the *Today* show on NBC—Channel 4 in Detroit. Dave Garroway was the host, and I was hoping to see him and J. Fred Muggs, the show's chimpanzee mascot, drive each other crazy. Eventually, I did, but when the TV finally warmed up and the picture appeared, the first images I saw were newsreel shots of a place in Vietnam called Dien Bien Phu and soldiers in army vehicles and on foot. The news announcer was saying that the town had been overrun by the Viet Minh and that the French were being driven out of the country.

As a kid who played with toy soldiers, built model fighter planes, bombers, and battleships, and loved war movies, I found the newsreels fascinating. In terms of my own reality, none of that footage meant anything. I had no idea what they were talking about. The names and places meant nothing. They sounded funny and foreign. When Garroway and J. Fred came on, Vietnam instantly left my mind, and like most young boys of the 1950s, I turned my attention away from world events and to more immediate monkeyshines.

By 1963, my senior year of high school, Vietnam was no longer some distant, imaginary place. It was getting a smattering of news coverage. There was a war on, and it was slowly building. The public was starting to take notice. I began to listen more closely and read more carefully about the war, trying to understand it. There wasn't too much in the local media about it, and I had not yet realized that I could be directly involved. However, as I headed for college and moved through my undergraduate years, the more I knew about the Vietnam conflict, the less I liked what I was learning.

As with many other young men, when the prospect of being drafted became a reality, I realized I didn't want to serve in the Vietnam War. There were any number of reasons for us to decline to serve, including political opposition to the war, personal moral and ethical beliefs, religious convictions, interference with our academic, professional, and personal lives, and, of course, outright fear of combat. We didn't see the connection between what was essentially a Vietnamese civil war and the defense of America. Was there one? We didn't believe that America's involvement in the war—or stake in Vietnam's future—could be worth the potentially high cost of lost lives and valuable resources. We didn't see the possible fall of Vietnam to Communism as an existential threat to the United States. Many of us saw this conflict as an unjust war designed to address special interests and felt we were the pawns in the game. We saw Communism not as a real threat to the country but as an excuse, a justification, for entering into a problematic war. More to the point, we didn't believe this was our nation's war. We saw it as a Vietnamese civil war, and we did not want to take part. We simply didn't want to get shot or blown up for this questionable cause. Nor did we want to shoot or blow up anyone else. No one wanted to die in Vietnam. To be blunt, the draft equaled potential death, and no way would we become cannon fodder. Once we voiced our opposition to the war, the only remaining question was how far we would go to make our stands. What would we do? What could we do to fight induction into the armed forces?

There were a lot of theories about how to stay out of the army, plenty of creative paths to follow to avoid the Selective Service's feared 1-A (available for military service) classification and achieve the much sought-after 1-Y or 4-F (maybe take me later or don't take me at all, respectively) classifications and their accompanying deferment or exemption from service.*

Many of us figured if you caused enough problems, the army wouldn't want you. You'd be out. Others said no, that wasn't the way. The army would view you as just another challenge, take you, and break you. In fact, many troubled young men convicted of petty crimes were often given the choice of jail time or army time. Other suggestions were to go catatonic at your physical, wear a dress, tamper with your urine sample, any of which—it was rumored—would lead to instant rejection. Maybe, but unlikely. There were still more options. We could intensify our actions and maim ourselves to fail a physical, flee the country, or simply refuse induction and risk going to jail. And what sort of a statement would our opposition to being drafted make? Would we even be heard or taken seriously? How would we be viewed? Would we become victims of our escalating domestic culture wars, social pariahs, and easy targets for the America, Love It or Leave It crowd? One thing to keep in mind: we loved our country. We just weren't crazy about our government, and we didn't agree with what it was doing.

While many men opposed the war, many couldn't or didn't avoid the draft—they didn't know they could or they didn't know how. However, some did. Most cases of men avoiding the draft were fully within the law—legitimate deferrals and exemptions; others were questionable. Regardless, we found ways.

Years later, when I glance at old correspondence with my draft board, check tattered documents, or stare at my well-worn draft card, I'm reminded that it was all very real—with a good bit of the surreal blended in. It all started out innocently enough for me. Although I didn't want to go to Vietnam, my draft board had other ideas. Fortunately, I wasn't alone in opposing the war.

---

* Selective Service classifications and their descriptions evolved over time. For a complete list, please see pages 260–262.

* * *

Early on, I was too politically naive to fully grasp what was going on around me—the Vietnam War, the protests, the social unrest, and the rage (on all sides of the political divide) running through the country. I had been in elementary school during the placid Eisenhower years. While I was in high school, civil rights, free speech, the growing presence of drugs, and other forms of personal expression were issues coming to the fore and fracturing the nation. By the time I was in college, I was tuned in. Vietnam was in the mix as President Johnson took us deeper into a war that had grown under President Kennedy's watch. Johnson might have been able to stop the war momentum but did not do so, as the South Vietnamese kept us entangled with their requests for help.

My friends and I agreed this war smelled bad: it appeared contrived, and we didn't want any part of it. We made a lot of noise and took action, some of it extreme. Simple protests and marches sometimes turned violent. Depending on where you stood, you were a hero or a traitor for avoiding the draft, a hero or a traitor for serving in the military. Years later, we learned that the facts surrounding the Gulf of Tonkin incident were not presented honestly to the American public. The Pentagon Papers also confirmed suspicions. Applying Eisenhower's speech, we learned that it was our responsibility to question our federal administrations about statements they make and actions they take. Between the Vietnam War and the later Watergate debacle, my generation's faith in politicians and government was shaken. But back then, as the war was always on our minds, did we have a choice? If you wanted to avoid the war, you couldn't just turn away; you first had to avoid the draft. Of course, that was easier said than done. The good thing was, you didn't stand alone.

At the time, I was angry because of what the war, the draft board, and my country put me through. There was something unfair and opaque about the "selective" service methodology. The system and its process were configured to address the various categories of the population with appropriate deferments and exemptions for individuals in different life situations. The scheme was built to differentiate between students, married men, fathers, men in critical occupations, clergymen, men who were physically compromised, men who were already serving in some approved capacity, men who were fit for service, and men who were not. But *selective* had a whole different meaning in how the system actually operated. It favored those individuals with clout, money, connections, or knowledge of the system—think of George W. Bush, Bill Clinton, Dan Quayle, Dick Cheney, Donald Trump, or the actor George Hamilton and many others who found alternatives to being drafted or minimized their chances of being sent to Vietnam—and let them avoid their local draft board's efforts to call them in. Yet the military needed men to fill the ranks, and the middle class was kicking up a fuss about being drafted. Consequently, in 1966, to help boost the pool of draftable men, Defense Secretary Robert McNamara, serving under President Johnson, initiated Project 100,000, a Department of Defense program that lowered army recruitment standards in order to annually induct one hundred thousand men who would not have been qualified to serve under previous mental or physical standards. This included men whose IQs fell below 91, and some with IQs below 71. By the time the program ended in 1971, 354,000 previously ineligible men were brought into the military. These were men who were the least able to avoid the draft and in most cases the least qualified to serve. As noted by Hamilton Gregory in his book, *McNamara's Folly: The Use of Low-IQ Troops in the Vietnam War*, and his 2016 article "McNamara's Morons: Salvaging the Deficient for the War Effort,"* these troops, sometimes regrettably referred to as McNamara's Misfits or McNamara's Morons, died at significantly higher rates than other Americans serving in Vietnam. The program was ostensibly created to provide these men with career opportunities and training they were unlikely to receive in civilian life. But it was also thought that by drafting these men, it would not be necessary to end college deferments or activate National Guard or Reserve units, which could be politically unpopular moves and intensify anti-war sentiment. The program was initiated at approximately the same time that an

---

* Hamilton Gergory, "McNamara's Morons. Salvaging the Deficient for the War Effort," The VVA Veteran, May/June 2016, https://vvaveteran.org/36-3/36-3_morons.html.

escalating war effort would require an increased monthly draft call of up to forty thousand men.

In an attempt to display draft fairness and tamp down anti-war sentiment, the Nixon administration implemented a draft lottery in 1969. The intention was to level the playing field by making everyone equally vulnerable. The lottery achieved that to some extent, but it didn't solve the problem for those men whose numbers randomly came up and were chosen for induction. The war was still the war, and men were still being called up although in a somewhat different manner. In 1973 the Vietnam draft was suspended. The draft's demise was a cause for celebration—then. In retrospect, that may not have been such a good thing, as several of the interviewees will point out.

Most of the people I knew sat out the war. Whatever it took to do so was deemed acceptable. The objective was not to be drafted. Some guys got lucky and drew a high lottery number. Many of us had legitimate reasons—situations that led to various rightful deferments or exemptions—that allowed us to avoid the draft. Still others were resourceful and created a basis for deferment: I knew of a man who bought a farm and grew corn so that he could claim a critical occupation as a farmer contributing to the nation's food supply. He was a city boy and had never grown anything before in his life. He did not get the exemption. Other men took medications to raise their blood pressure—or to lower it. Some feigned deafness, or madness. Pretending to be homosexual was a common ploy, which generally didn't work—unless, perhaps, you really were gay. Braces, on teeth and legs, became a common sight at physical exams, as did fungal infections in the crotch or anus. Some men defecated and urinated in their underpants and didn't bother changing them for the physical. Others went further or farther, literally, to avoid serving: they left the country. The chant *Hell, no! We won't go!* summed up our position.

Vietnam loomed as a potential death trap for many of us. But if you were determined to avoid the draft and stay out of the army or the marines, there were plenty of imaginative roads to follow to achieve a Selective Service classification that would set you free.

Consider these pathways: A young man in San Francisco hugs

his coconspirator parents, says goodbye, and sneaks off to Vancouver. A man in New York finds a loophole in the Selective Service regulations and laughs all the way to a university in Montreal. A man from Brooklyn leaps across a table and physically attacks an army psychiatrist. Another man pleads his case and writes two book reports that allow him to keep his civilian status. And a man in Michigan meets a Selective Service doctor who believes he should join the Israeli Army, not the US military. All these men avoided the draft and managed to steer clear of the army and Vietnam.

Dodging the draft evolved into a high-stakes game of us versus them, "us" being anybody who wanted to stay out and "them" being anybody who wanted you in—particularly the local draft board and the army. Yet underneath all the maneuvering, there was something else: a question of loyalty and patriotism. If you genuinely believed that the war was not in the best interest of the nation, were you truly disloyal to your country by refusing to join the service? If you accepted the war and became a soldier even though you believed it to be wrong, were you a hypocrite? We questioned whether to blindly participate in the war or fulfill a self-determined obligation to protect the country and ourselves from our nation's misdeeds. We were torn between "following orders"—shades of the Nazi soldiers defending their actions during World War II—and perpetrating the crimes and atrocities those orders could lead to, or defying them. We were compelled to protest faulty, misguided, deceptive, inept, and ambivalent leadership and wondered how far to take those protests. We struggled with our rights, duties, and obligations to take our objections beyond the ballot box and into the streets with civil disobedience tactics or even violence if or when it was justified. In short, we believed that we had a choice: the duty to obey or the obligation to decline the opportunity to serve. Our premise was that we were justified in refusing to comply with the draft and saying, "No, thank you. My country is wrong. The war is wrong." Or, as so many pro-war people, the hawks, pointed out, were we—the doves—just cowards and all the debating merely a cover for faintheartedness?

These were the issues that arose in conversations that took place in apartments, coffeehouses, and bars in Ann Arbor, on the Wayne State University campus in Detroit, and wherever else concerned draft-eligible young men and their friends and families gathered around the nation.

Wayne State University—where I earned my bachelor's and law degrees and later taught as an adjunct professor for two years—was always rife with political activism. Michigan's only urban public research university, it's situated between Detroit's Midtown neighborhood and the Cultural Center embracing the city's major museums, theaters, and music venues. When I attended as an undergraduate from 1963 to 1967, and as a law school student until 1972, it was primarily a commuter school of more than twenty thousand students. For Metro Detroiters, it was—and still is—an affordable high-quality academic alternative to the University of Michigan, forty minutes away, while offering immediate access to everything stirring in the city's corridors of power. Wayne students had their fingers on the pulse of the city, state, national, and world events and made their opinions known. This included labor relations (because of the city's focus on the automotive industry and its unionized labor force), issues of race and civil rights, the Vietnam War, and more—with all sides represented. Wayne was the second campus in the country to protest against Dow Chemical, the makers of napalm, in 1966, and the student paper, the *Daily Collegian*, became the *South End* in 1967, reflecting the working-class area where it was located on campus and its leftist politics. Motown music was born just a short hop away from the university. Hangouts along the popular Cass Corridor on the fringe of the campus were home to students and locals of every color and stripe; this is where folksingers Chuck and Joni Mitchell got their start, where rhythm and blues, funk, and jazz, could be heard every night of the week, and where those political conversations about the war proliferated when someone said, "Let's go grab a beer."

Sometimes those dialogues were the products of too many drinks and too many joints. But piercing, tense conversations also took place when we were all alert and sober. These weren't academic jousts or unfocused bull sessions. There was a war going on, and there was a very real possibility that we could soon find ourselves in uniform in a strange land doing all we could to avoid being killed. That's what preoccupied us. Peaceniks or patriots, we were standing up for our convictions. Through it all, however, we respected those who chose to serve or had to serve. They were brave or hapless. Maybe they were both, but the people in uniform were never the target of our scorn.

We also knew that if we avoided the draft, the military wouldn't simply fold up its tents and fade away. The war machine and its bureaucracy would find others to go in our place: young men who might not know how to evade the draft; others not as well versed in stalling the process; guys who had no access to amphetamines or prescriptive enhancers; boys who lacked affluent parents who knew the right people—sympathetic letter-writing doctors or psychiatrists or lawyers—who could fend off the drill instructors; and, of course, guys who had no qualms about entering the service.

Avoiding the draft was a middle-class activity. It hurt to know that as I paraded through my physical exam wearing only underpants and shoes, nearly all of the well-educated guys walking with me would still be attending classes the next day, while most of the guys who weren't in college would soon be on a khaki green bus to basic training. The Selective Service had created a draft selection system that treated some men as more expendable than others. Did the fact that someone was a celebrity or a college student or a laborer or an athlete or of any particular race make them any more or less human than any other person? Was one man's life more valuable than another's? There was an argument to be made that perhaps either everyone should be drafted or no one should be drafted. There was something guilt-inducing in knowing that because we knew how to game the system, we would remain outside the army's reach. But to us, this was life and death, and nothing was too extreme.

Chapter 3

Meet the Bureaucracy

To register men and maintain a system that, when authorized by the President and Congress, rapidly provides personnel in a fair and equitable manner while managing an alternative service program for conscientious objectors.

—Selective Service System Mission Statement

The Selective Service System was established on May 18,1917, in response to US manpower needs during World War I. In 1940, prior to World War II, the Selective Training and Service Act instituted America's first peacetime draft. Since then, several similar congressional acts have modified and refined the Selective Service System, its deferments and exemptions, and the draft process. Today there is no draft. However, if and when Congress and the president determine conscription is needed, the Selective Service is the agency that will procure, process, and provide men to the US Armed Forces.

For us, the local draft board was where it all began. According to the Selective Service, during the Vietnam War, there were approximately forty-one hundred draft boards among the fifty states, US territories, and US possessions. There was also at least one appeal board per state and one national appeal board. It was at the local draft board that we registered for the Selective Service when we turned eighteen. Men who had to register but were residing outside the United States had to present themselves to the respective country's US Embassy or Consulate to register in person or contact these offices to obtain the Selective Service registration form. Men registering with a residence outside the United States had their records forwarded to Local Board 100 in Washington, DC.

The Selective Service operated as an independent agency. Its director answered to the president. State governors administered Selective Service laws with responsibilities delegated to each state's respective Selective Service director. Local boards comprised citizens representing the community. Boards were assigned quotas depending on military manpower requirements and selected men for induction based on individual cases and with consideration for the needs of the local economy and industry—that is, what the community would lose if the individual was drafted. Those determinations were not always objective.

Failure to register with the local draft board was a violation of the Military Selective Service Act. Conviction for such a violation could result in imprisonment for up to five years and/or a fine of not more than $250,000. Failure to register would also make a man ineligible for a number of federal and state benefits and disqualified for government employment.

Once a man registered, the local board determined his status and assigned him an alphanumeric classification in accordance with regulations and guidance issued from the national office. The most vulnerable classification was 1-A, which indicated that a registrant was available for military service and meant you could be called up at any time for induction into the army. For those of us avoiding the draft, 4-F was the most desired classification; it designated the registrant as not qualified for any military service. A classification of 1-Y was also valued because you would be subject to induction only in a time of national emergency. There were other classifications. Deferments and exemptions were available for students, clergy, conscientious objectors, individuals engaged in occupations that supported the national interest, and those whose induction would cause financial hardship for their family, and included numerous other reasons that categorized men as unqualified, unfit, unsuitable, or unavailable for service. It was the obligation of the registrant to provide the information that local boards required to determine proper classification. If a man disagreed with the classification he received, he had a right to appeal. Each local board had a government appeal agent available to assist a registrant with an appeal, a personal appearance to the board, or any other procedural right. The appeal agent or his representative would provide legal counsel at no charge on Selective Service issues only. However, the appeal agent frequently had a bias in favor of the local board. As the Selective Service acknowledges today, deferments granted at the time lacked nationwide uniformity; and "because the boards determined who would be drafted, there were instances when personal relationships and favoritism played a part in deciding who would be drafted. Today, the Uniform National Call, [designed to provide an equitable draft process in the event conscription is required] ensures that men will be treated the same, no matter which board they are assigned to."*

Since boards were made up of local community members, prominent individuals in the community could have an outsize influence on which men would be called—or not called—to serve. Preferential treatment was not unknown. Although there is no draft today, men still must register when they turn eighteen. Should the need for conscription ever arise, it is hoped that the mechanism in place, the Uniform National Call, operates as intended in a fair manner.

Once we registered, we had to keep our contact information current. We were required to keep the board informed of any change in our lives that could affect our status. Physical or mental health, jobs, residence, marriage, children, education, religious and personal views, and run-ins with the law could have an impact on classification. If you left the city for school or work or wanted to travel outside the country, the draft board wanted to know. Did everybody abide by these rules and regulations? Definitely not. But the intimidation factor and risk of being charged with a federal offense for not adhering to Selective Service rules and regulations were still there, and most of us complied—but not happily. When a man did comply, the person he generally came in contact with at the local office was the receptionist, who was also the secretary and essentially ran the place. She (it was almost always a woman in those days) was perceived (rightfully?) by us to have had a tremendous amount of influence on our status with the draft board. The secretary could make a person's file disappear or move to the bottom of the pile. Conversely, she could make a file rise in priority. You didn't want to get on the wrong side of this person.

In 1963, like most of the guys I'd graduated with in high school, I lived in the area that fell under the aegis of Michigan Selective Service Local Board 179. It was now September. I was eighteen, and

---

* Selective Service System, "Changes from Vietnam to Now," accessed August 2, 2023, www.sss.gov/history-and-records/changes-from-vietnam-to-now/.

I made the mandatory trip to the draft board office to register and have my first encounter with the board executive secretary, Mary Ann Modelski.

Every Vietnam War–era draft-eligible male had a Mary Ann Modelski in his life. She may have had a different name or a different gender, but hers was the face you saw when you walked into your draft board office. She was the one who registered you for the Selective Service, signed your draft card, sent you unwanted notices, and controlled where your file went when it was time to be called up.

My Mary Ann Modelski was a personal nightmare simply because for me she was the face of my draft board. She was inextricably linked with the Vietnam War effort and would have a huge impact on my life, and the lives of many other young men. Miss Modelski was a formidable local legend known for her apparent scorn for the guys in the community. We did not have a good impression of her. We saw her as the key contact that could send us off to Vietnam. She was a force of nature: she had muscle, knew it, and used it. We were afraid of her the same way we were afraid of any bully who had a modicum of authority or power and enjoyed wielding it—a teacher, a cop, a parent, or the big kid at the playground. So we created a politically incorrect image of her as a calculating villain, a brutal woman, an enforcer of unjust Selective Service rules. Because of her totalitarian authority, as we perceived it, she was more than menacing. In fact, she was the person who caused me to add the adjective "dreaded" to every subsequent visit to my draft board. The result was a contentious relationship that inspired (mutual?) suspicion, resentment, and disdain.

The day I went to see Miss Modelski in 1963, there were no major wars on the horizon of which I was aware. Yes, Vietnam was receiving some press, but it was far away. College was a few weeks off, and US military adventurism was nowhere on my radar. I knew we had some military personnel in Southeast Asia, but the teacher in my high school contemporary world affairs class had spent only a few minutes on the subject.

I made the short trip to downtown Detroit and the forty-story Cadillac Tower Building, a neo-Gothic structure filled with law offices, accounting firms, and other sundry enterprises including, on the eleventh floor, my draft board. Utterly impassive, Miss Modelski gave me the requisite forms to fill out and handed me a brochure titled "Selective Service and You" and a two-sided sheet titled "Selective Service Facts." I filled out the forms and left the office, treating the event as nothing more than an inconsequential formality. In retrospect, I think that if I had turned and glanced over my shoulder as I exited, I can imagine Miss Modelski might have been chuckling and thinking about what she could do to me.

Mike Rosenblatt is a retired podiatric surgeon, raised in Detroit and now living in Nevada. He, too, had a distinct impression of Miss Modelski. He saw her only a few times but still has a clear image of her. When Mike graduated Mumford High School, Vietnam was not yet in the headlines; still, since he was eighteen, like every other guy, he was required to register for the draft. While in college full time with a 2-S classification (student deferment, registrant deferred because of activity in study), Mike was unexpectedly—and perhaps inappropriately—reclassified 1-A and called up for a draft physical.

Mike's homelife in Detroit was difficult. His family was not wealthy, and Mike earned money with a weekend bagel delivery route to support his studies. His mother was affected by a bipolar disorder, and there was constant screaming and arguing at home. His brother committed suicide in the driveway of his mother's house. Mike saw a psychiatric social worker for therapy for several years, and at his physical, he noted it on the questionnaire that all prospective draftees receive. He was directed toward a separate group of men to be interviewed by an army psychiatrist. Mike related his experience with Miss Modelski and the physical:

> Vietnam was eventually the five-thousand-pound gorilla for every man in my graduating class. I did not serve in the armed services, but many of my classmates did. A number of them did not come back from Vietnam.
>
> I remember Mary Ann Modelski from my draft board with great clarity—a lady with a permanent scowl on her face. I will never forget her. Her name brings back astonishing memories for me. I had several experiences with her, both directly and indirectly. Even now I

see her visage in a tiny, smelly office in the Cadillac Tower, scowling at the teenagers who nervously entered her private doorway. She was stern, abrupt, and rude. For most of us in those years, she represented a "ghost" who could rear her head at any time and take away your life by simply moving your file up. I'm sure Mary Ann regarded people like me as a privileged minority and that others were going in our place, potentially to die in our place.

I wasn't in therapy to create a basis for dodging the draft; I needed it because of my homelife. I told the shrink I just wanted to finish Wayne State University and go to podiatry school. I was willing to serve my country after my education. "Let me finish Wayne," I said. "I will be of more value to my country." The shrink said nothing. Thirty days later I received a 1-Y classification. After finishing Wayne, I never heard from the draft board again.

If a 9/11 event had happened then, I would've gone. I would've said this is my time. I made a very specific attempt to avoid the draft and was successful. I was able to finish podiatry school. I often ask myself, if Ho Chi Minh had been Osama Bin Laden or if it had been more personal for me, would I have felt the same about the draft?

Mike holds a fatalistic view. He did not want to be drafted or go to Vietnam. He did what he could to avoid the draft by indicating that he had been in therapy and was then prepared to accept the Selective Service's decision. As it turned out, he was deferred. On the other hand, if the United States had been attacked at the time, he said he would have served without hesitation.

One possibility Mike fantasized about: if he couldn't beat the draft, he would have tried to get into an army band. He is an excellent amateur concert pianist and studied with Mischa Kottler, a longtime pianist with the well-respected Detroit Symphony Orchestra. Shortly after our conversation, Mike sent me a recording of him playing "Un Sospiro," an etude in arpeggios by Franz Liszt. It was a pleasure to listen to him play, and in all likelihood, he would have been welcome in an elite army band; he's that good. Mike continued:

A part of me is very, very glad that I did not have to go to Vietnam. Our leaders were ambivalent about the war, and I think that affected

American military performance and sentiment. The war left gashes in our society that still exist. But I also have to tell you that I served a surgical residency at a VA hospital and at Munson Army Hospital at Fort Leavenworth, Kansas, as a podiatrist after I graduated. I encountered many Vietnam War veterans and other military people at those venues.

I like to think that my residency was a kind of sincere thank-you to them for their service because I could help them. In an ironic, prescient way, this contribution to veterans allowed me to actually be of service to them, even though I was not in uniform. But I won't dare suggest that this substituted in any way for the raw courage of real soldiering. It also furthered my education in an extraordinary way; maybe they gave more to me than I deserved. A part of me feels guilty that I did not serve and that others died in Vietnam in my place. I guess the psychologists would call that survivor's guilt.

Through his residency and rotations at Veterans Administration hospitals, Mike treated army personnel, many from Vietnam action, and was familiar with their war injuries and subsequent frailties. That survivor guilt extended to a visit to Washington, DC, when he, like me, cried at the Vietnam Memorial, recognizing classmates' names engraved on the wall.

In recent years, Mike has visited Vietnam twice as a tourist. He went to Ho Chi Minh's office. According to what Mike learned, Ho had opportunities to carry out terrorist attacks in the United States but was firmly against doing so. Ho believed terrorism on US soil would sap anti-war sentiment and firm up American resolve against North Vietnam. Mike adds:

I also wonder how many of us who avoided the draft or escaped it by a lucky lottery number ever protested against the war. Perhaps I should have, but I never did. I was always busy studying. I had to make sure I stayed in undergrad and podiatry school. Is that an excuse? I don't know. I have had a wonderful life. I don't think I would have made a very good soldier, but then again, I never had to prove it. Did I do enough for my country? Mary Ann would say no.

Out of the office, Miss Modelski may have been a different person, perhaps a much kinder and more personable soul than we encountered at the draft board. But that gentler image was hard to fathom. We thought she was killing us. Perhaps she was just doing her job, and maintaining a hard stance was the best way for her to cope with a difficult situation, a complex task she had to perform knowing the impact that her work could have on the men assigned to her office. I certainly don't know. In an attempt at fairness and to give her a chance to recount her views of those days, I tried to contact her and speak with her for this book, only to find out from one of her family members that she died several years ago. I think her perspective could have been informative and enlightening and would have offered some nuance to the difficult situation back then, perhaps even changed our perceptions. My own experiences with Miss Modelski were less than pleasant.

By the winter of 1967–1968, in my first year of law school at Wayne State, I was firmly against the war, but I wasn't one for marches or demonstrations. I held a 2-S classification and maintained a low public profile. I did not feel comfortable drawing attention to myself in any way. However, the war was escalating, there were signs that student draft deferments were going to end, the army was reaching deeper into the middle class for recruits, and there was a good chance the Selective Service would eye me as a viable candidate for the draft. In early 1968, frustrated with our involvement in Vietnam, I took a major step and wrote a letter to President Johnson, expressing in no uncertain terms my feelings about the war: *I don't like it; we shouldn't be there; and I'm not going to participate.* There, I'd gotten it off my chest, I thought. My letter will be filed away somewhere, and life will go on.

I was wrong.

Within two weeks, I received a letter from the Selective Service national office asking me if I wanted to apply for conscientious objector (CO) status. If I did, the letter continued, this would be my only opportunity to do so. I was advised by lawyer friends that having CO by your name was not necessarily a guarantee that you would avoid the service and probably not a plus for your future legal

Chapter Three

Eli Greenbaum during the Vietnam War era (author's collection)

career, since many law firms at the time were not enthusiastic about hiring anyone who could be viewed as a dissident. I did not respond to the letter, but a similar correspondence soon arrived from the Michigan Selective Service office, followed by another from my local draft board. Each letter said the same thing: apply for CO now or your window of opportunity will close. The local draft board's letter, from Miss Modelski, also warned me not to leave the area without informing the office and ordered me to advise them of where I would be over the coming summer. I compared notes with my friends and found that I was the only one in our group to receive such a communication from the local board. Was this the price I would pay for expressing my opinion?

Shortly after I wrote my protest letter to President Johnson, but before I received a reply, I requested permission to travel abroad in a separate letter to the draft board. A friend and I had been planning on backpacking through France and Italy during the summer of 1968. I had saved money for the trip and was looking forward to it. In response, and after advising me of my window to apply for CO status, the local board sent me a second letter saying my travel request was denied and that my file would be reviewed for reclassification. I knew the possibility existed that by requesting travel permission, I would draw the attention of the draft board, but I also naively thought my student deferment would protect me at least through the summer. I now believed that my travel request, combined with my protest letter, had caused my name to move closer to the top of the call-up list. I wondered if I was being punished for protesting the war. Could the draft board do

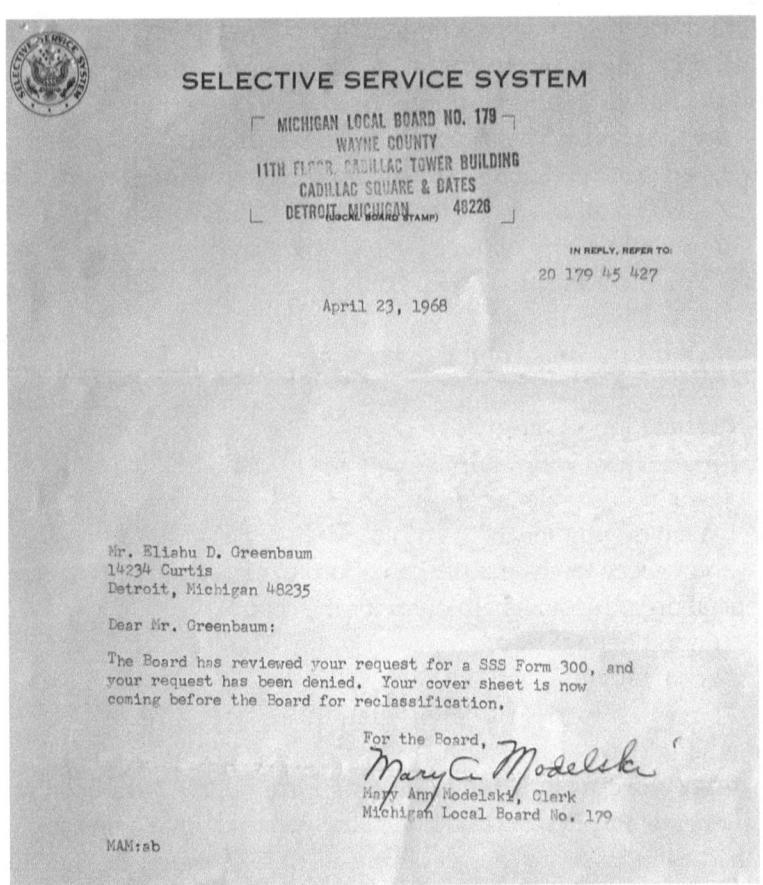

Letter from draft board denying the author's travel request (author's collection)

that? I was still a student, but with travel plans dashed, I had to find summer employment. I opted to work at a nearby sleepaway camp that was affiliated with the Fresh Air Society of Detroit, one of the region's predominantly Jewish community nonprofit organizations. I'd worked at the camp for the past five summers. While plenty of other guys wouldn't bother contacting the board, I was compulsive about doing things by the book when it came to the Selective Service rules. I called the board to give them my summer address information. As it turned out, my board would not accept the information by phone or letter. The person I spoke with insisted I come down to the office. On a warm spring afternoon, I paid the board an unannounced visit.

My file was on Miss Modelski's desk—an ominous sign—when I dropped in. Here's our conversation—interrogation, more accurately—as I recall it, when I told her I would be working and living all summer at a camp outside Detroit.

"Where's the camp?" she asked.

"Near Flint," I said.

"What's the name of the camp?"

"Tamarack."

"What kind of camp is it?"

"It's a sleepaway camp, largely for Jewish kids. It's supported by a Jewish charitable organization."

"What do you mean?"

"Not every Jewish family can afford to send their kids to camp, so social organizations help out with the cost."

"I don't believe you."

"What do you mean?"

"I never heard of a Jewish family not being able to afford something."

Uh-oh. Her comment seemed inappropriate. Alarm bells rang in my head, and I could imagine being reclassified 1-A and my file pushed even closer to the "get this guy" pile. This war was getting personal.

She then told me to make sure that I let them know where they could find me at any time in the coming months. I didn't know if she actually had the legal authority to stop me from going anywhere, but I wasn't about to test her. Her "no" was enough to keep me on a tight leash. That, combined with an intensifying war, scared me. Instead of bopping across Europe, I would spend June, July, and August as a camp counselor. Not bad, but France sounded better. Shortly thereafter, I received notice that I had been reclassified 1-A. The war, the draft, the feeling that I had no control over my life: the nastiness of the whole situation was inside my head and slowly taking over every aspect of my being. I was on hold and didn't know what was going to happen. The only thing I was certain of was that there was no way I would go to Vietnam. This is what we had to deal with. It wasn't just limited to Local Board 179; it was happening everywhere.

I again wondered if my written objection to the war and my request to temporarily leave the country had prompted my 1-A reclassification. After all, about nine months earlier, in October 1967, in response to growing student demonstrations against military recruiting on college campuses, General Lewis B. Hershey, director of the Selective Service, had issued to draft boards Local Board Memorandum No. 85, known as the Hershey Directive, suggesting that men who had mutilated their draft cards be reclassified as 1-A and declared delinquent—a punitive act that set their induction process in motion. He followed up a few days later with a letter suggesting the same treatment to men who violated the Selective Service Act or other regulations, including illegal activities that interfered with military recruiting or draft board functions. This was interpreted to include protests against the war. In fact, Hershey's memorandum and letter served to provoke even more protests. Although I hadn't broken any rules, perhaps the Select Service decided to select me for reclassification simply because I had put myself on their radar.

I then learned about an earlier situation that had taken place in Ann Arbor in 1965, in which sixteen students classified 2-S were part of a group that had staged a sit-in at a local draft board. Because of their sit-in, thirteen of the students were reclassified 1-A as punishment by their draft boards. Two of the full-time students, Peter Wolff and Richard Shortt, were from New York, and their home draft boards saw the sit-in as hindering the work of the Ann Arbor board. The New York boards decided the students had committed a federal crime punishable by a fine of $10,000 and five years in prison. The practical result was that their local boards had essentially charged and convicted them of a crime and, as their punishment, sentenced them to 1-A status and subject to induction—all without a trial or constitutional due process protections. Hershey supported the board's decision when he said that local boards should be able to punish student demonstrators for their actions, "the government would be committing suicide if it deferred students who defied the Selective

Service System."* The two students challenged the draft board's decision and asked the federal district court to nullify the order for reclassification. The court declined, but Wolff and Shortt appealed to the US Court of Appeals for the Second Circuit. Appeals Court Judge Harold R. Medina reversed the lower court and stated that while courts may hesitate to interfere with draft board actions, free speech takes priority.† In his decision, Medina declared, "Here, it is the free expression of views on issues of critical current importance that is jeopardized. On such topics, perhaps more than any other, it is imperative that the public debate be full and each segment of our society be permitted freely to express its views." Medina added that the First Amendment right to free speech does not allow draft boards to "punish these students by reclassifying them 1-A because they protested as they did over the Government's [sic] involvement in Vietnam." He also noted that no draft law specifies what type of protest may precipitate reclassification, thereby creating a situation without a standard of conduct or defined parameters.

As reported in the *Fifth Estate*, at the time of the Ann Arbor sit-in, Colonel Arthur A. Holmes, Selective Service director for the state of Michigan, had announced his intent to use the Selective Service Act "as a device to punish dissent" and called for "the immediate induction" of Vietnam protestors who had violated Selective Service regulations or caused interruption of board procedures. Rolland O'Hare, chairman of the American Civil Liberties Union of Michigan (ACLU), was quoted in the article:

> Until now, no one in any position of responsibility in the government has suggested that the Selective Service Act may be used as a device to punish dissent. If young men who disagree with the government's

---

* "Resistance and Revolution: The Anti–Vietnam War Movement at the University of Michigan," Michigan in the World, University of Michigan, accessed November 2, 2023, https://michiganintheworld.history.lsa.umich.edu/antivietnamwar/exhibits/show/exhibit/draft_protests/international-days-of-protest/the-selective-service-office-s.

† Wolff and Shortt v. Selective Service Local Board No. 16, et al., 372 F.2d 817 (2d Cir. 1967).

policy in Vietnam may be singled out for discriminatory application of the Act today, who can say how the threat may be used to dragoon youth into conformity tomorrow?

The selective service system [sic] which places awesome power in the hands of government administrators must, as a matter of law, treat all who come within its scope fairly and uniformly on the basis of reasonable applications equally applied. The moment it is allowed to deviate from those limitations, we have placed the lives and liberties of a sizable portion of the population of the United States at the unfettered whim of what this or that draft board or functionary considers the national interest to require.

If any person in the course of his protest on the subject of Vietnam or any other matter of public concern transgresses the law, he may obviously properly be made to answer in a court of law for his act and, if found guilty, be punished in accordance with the law. The Selective Service Act itself has provisions for carrying criminal penalties which, however, are to be enforced by a court, not a single administrative office.*

Several other cases involving reclassifications as a response to a man's anti-war or draft protests reached similar conclusions on a First Amendment basis or on the grounds that nothing in the Selective Service Act gave local boards the power to withdraw deferments or exemptions because of a man's political protests. One case out of Cheyenne, Wyoming, *Oestereich v. Selective Service System Local Board No. 11*, escalated the matter to the Supreme Court.† According to the case record, a theological student, James J. Oestereich, held a 4-D (minister of religion or divinity student) deferment. He turned in his registration certificate to express his dissent against US participation in the Vietnam War. The board declared him delinquent and changed his classification to 1-A. Oestereich filed a Selective Service administrative appeal, lost, and was directed to report for induction. He then filed an action in federal district court

---

* "ACLU Blasts Draft as Punishment," *Fifth Estate*, November 19, 1965, 1.

† Oestereich v. Selective Service System Local Board No. 11, 393 U.S. 233 (1968).

to dismiss his induction order and lost there too. He lost again at the federal appeal court level. The Supreme Court then accepted the case for review. After hearing arguments, on December 16, 1968, the court reversed the lower court's decision and remanded the case to the district court. Associate Justice William O. Douglas delivered the opinion of the Supreme Court, including the comment, "There is no suggestion in the legislative history that, when Congress has granted an exemption and a registrant meets its terms and conditions, a [local] Board can nonetheless withhold it from him for activities or conduct not material to the grant or withdrawal of the exemption. So to hold would make the Boards free-wheeling agencies meting out their brand of justice in a vindictive manner."* Bottom line: local boards could not reclassify a man 1-A simply because he protested against the war. Reclassification could not be used as punishment. Local boards did not have that power.

Several federal cases ruled against Hershey's memorandum and voided it. Hershey withdrew it on January 21, 1970. The controversy over the Hershey Directive led to calls for his retirement. On February 15, 1970, President Nixon appointed Hershey as presidential advisor for manpower mobilization, and he vacated the office of director of the Selective Service. He was replaced with Curtis W. Tarr, who served from April 6, 1970, to May 1, 1972.

In retrospect, was my reclassification a punitive action taken by the board? I was still enrolled in law school. Even though student deferments were more difficult to obtain, I might have still qualified, Miss Modelski never inquired as to whether or not I was still in school. And if it was so noble to serve in the armed forces, why was it that for those men who protested, were reclassified 1-A, and subsequently inducted, the army was a punishment?

To sit on a local board, individuals had to meet certain requirements: they had to be US citizens, could not be the spouse of a Selective Service employee, and had to be at least thirty years old.

Not all the people on the draft board were necessarily rude or

---

* Oestereich v. Selective Service System Local Board No. 11, p. 237.

nasty, played favorites, or were in favor of the war. I had the good fortune to speak with Joseph Cabot, DDS, who sat on a draft appeals board on the east side of Detroit.

Dr. Cabot was the chairman of a Michigan Selective Service District Appeals Board. I was friends with his daughter in high school. I didn't know him well, but from the few times I met him, he struck me as a solid-citizen type of guy who recognized that in life, doing the right thing, the ethical thing, was critical. In Yiddish, he would be called a *mensch*, an honorable man.

Dr. Cabot volunteered for military service in 1941 at the start of World War II and entered an army specialist training program. In 1942 he was commissioned as a member of the army reserves in order to enroll in dental school. He was discharged from the reserves when he failed a physical in 1945 and was classified 4-F. Then in 1954, he was ordered to report for another physical as part of the doctor and dentist draft in effect at the time. Medical professionals were a high priority for the military for obvious reasons. Consequently, physical exams for them were not always rigorous. In addition, many men were allowed to finish their education and enter medical practice before being inducted into the service. Dr. Cabot had been deferred until he became a dentist. At that point, he had a wife and three kids and was established in his profession. He somehow managed to be stationed at the Fort Wayne army base in Detroit, close to his family and mother whom he supported financially. At Fort Wayne, he was in a MASH unit (mobile army surgical hospital) and would have gone to Korea if it had been activated. While serving at Fort Wayne, Dr. Cabot often complained to one of his patients, a colonel, about the doctor draft—which he referred to as stupid—that sometimes took men in their forties and fifties out of their lives and parked them in the army without having any particular need for them. One day the colonel got fed up and told Dr. Cabot if he thought the draft job was so easy, he'd give him the chance to do something about it. Dr. Cabot's file was turned over to Colonel Holmes, who appointed him to an appeals board. In effect, Dr. Cabot got drafted into the Selective Service administration.

Dr. Cabot served on a board outside his home area. In his role as appeals chairman in a district far from where he lived, he was unlikely to encounter people he knew and never had any pressure placed on him by young registrants or their families and friends from his local community. He told me there were very few people trying to appeal decisions in his district because, according to Dr. Cabot, the district was not "a hotbed of anti-war activism." He recalled there were five men on the board. Their meetings consisted of reviewing paperwork and considering candidate appeals based entirely on the situational information in their files. He said that a candidate's history of opposition to the war was "not a relevant consideration" in denying or accepting appeals. He also told me that in retrospect he couldn't objectively evaluate the Selective Service and its operations, although it puzzled him at times how board decisions were made. Still, he served. "Being on the draft board was a civic duty," he said. "It was there. Somebody was going to do it."

But Dr. Cabot did have opinions about the war itself that he did not allow to factor in his decision-making. "The Vietnam War, those were bad times," he said. "Why were we there? There was no reason. War stinks, especially when unjustified. Only World War II was justified." In his opinion, the Vietnam War was similar to our recent conflicts in Iraq and Afghanistan. "We were in Iraq for oil," he says. "War is all about greed."

Dr. Cabot offered two anecdotes that illustrated opposite positions. He told me about an acquaintance of his, a man not in his draft board area who wanted to avoid military service at any cost. The gentleman told his board that his wife had cancer and that he needed a deferment in order to care for her, a legitimate basis for a deferment if she was, indeed, ill. He got letters from doctors attesting to her illness and was deferred. It was later found out that his wife did not have cancer. She was fine. The letters were all lies. The doctors were complicit. Dr. Cabot could not hide the disappointment in his friend and the situation he had manipulated.

On the other hand, a young Black man wanted more than anything to join the army and asked the appeals board to overturn his 3-A deferment that was based on economic hardship to his family. The young man had tried to enlist but was rejected because he was the family's sole breadwinner. Dr. Cabot's board turned down his appeal. "You have responsibilities to your family," the board decreed. "Stay home and take care of them."

The young man said, "But I want to get away. This is my only chance."

The young man's statement was in accord with what a few Black people I contacted told me: difficult social economics of the time might have prevented widespread draft resistance in minority communities. In many cases, the military was seen as an opportunity, a chance to train for a career, advance an education, earn some money, and receive post-service benefits. In such cases, when other possibilities were limited, the prospect of a military stint can look good and make sense on many levels.

Chapter 4

Noise and Numbers

Until American military participation in Vietnam accelerated during President Johnson's time in office, the Southeast Asia war had not been high on the list of concerns for most of the American public. But as Johnson cranked up the US entanglement in Vietnam, he effectively contributed to a growing schism in our society.

There was already plenty stirring the domestic pot. People were taking sides on the war, civil rights, and the counterculture—seemingly taking sides on everything. Similar to today, there were two Americas. Peace was fighting with war. Love was opposing hate. Pushback was strong on both sides. Change had been in the air, and it was now on the ground. Underneath it all, a new generation, committed to rejecting the perceived repressive conformist attitudes (*Mad* magazine's April 1957 issue called it "creeping meatballism") of their Eisenhower-era parents, was realizing its own power and insisted on being heard. This was a generation that was well-educated and couldn't be easily pushed around. Protests were becoming ubiquitous. Voices were getting louder.

As the war's rumble got noisier, the peace—or anti-war—movement was matching it, surging forward and incorporating activist groups. It was attracting young people, intellectuals, and parents of vulnerable young men, and eventually crossing societal divides to create a nationwide wave of protests. Televised scenes of bloodied and tear-gassed protestors at the 1968 Democratic National Convention made some viewers wonder where the real war was.

The convention sparked an explosive reaction that had been impatiently waiting to ignite. More Americans came out boldly against the Vietnam War, an adventure that many felt was reckless and turning our boys into sacrificial lambs. The government began to feel the wrath of its citizenry. Protests, some turning violent, became more common as the war escalated. College campuses became intellectual battlefields, sometimes physical battlefields. Activist groups—including the SDS and the Weather Underground (a small, more extreme offshoot of the SDS) along with other groups such as the Student Nonviolent Coordinating Committee that had other social justice priorities but still denounced the war—made their voices heard. On October 15, 1969, a demonstration coordinated by the Vietnam Moratorium Committee centered in Washington, DC, and duplicated in other cities across the United States, mobilized an estimated two million Americans to peacefully march in their hometowns and say no to the Vietnam War. The committee arranged a second demonstration that year on November 15, in Washington, DC, which attracted an estimated five hundred thousand people from across the country. Dozens of my friends and law school classmates drove or rode buses to the Capitol to be heard. There were also anti-American and anti-war protests abroad; however, none of this resulted in visible US military de-escalation in Vietnam. Draft calls did not abate, and campus protests continued. Then came the US invasion of Cambodia.

Cambodia was neutral during the Vietnam War, but North Vietnam was moving troops and supplies through the northern part of the country. In March 1969, President Nixon okayed secret US bombing of North Vietnamese supply lines and camps in Cambodia. This was followed on April 28, 1970, with an invasion by US ground forces. President Nixon waited until April 30 to publicly announce these new developments.

Public reaction to the escalation was swift and strong. Massive anti-war demonstrations immediately spiked on college campuses across the country. More than one hundred thousand people marched on Washington in protest. Then things turned ugly and violent. On May 2, during a demonstration at Kent State University in Ohio, students burned down an ROTC building. Two days later, on May 4, 1970, Ohio National Guard troops, on location at the university, fired toward a crowd of demonstrators, killing four students and wounding nine.

The event was a catalyst: the shooting outraged much (but not all) of the public and united students across the country, setting off a nationwide student strike that intensified protests and closed hundreds of colleges and universities. Returning Vietnam War veterans who were opposed to the war joined with other protestors. As protests became angrier, people were hurt and arrests were made. Undercover cops and federal agents infiltrated anti-war organizations. Paranoia, often justified, ran deep. Anti-war fervor was coming to a head.

In reaction to the killing, folk-rocker Neil Young wrote the protest song "Ohio." It was recorded by the pop supergroup in which he performed, Crosby, Stills, Nash, & Young, and released as a 45 RPM single record, with Stephen Stills's musical tribute to the war's dead "Find the Cost of Freedom" on the back, or "B," side. "Ohio" quickly became a *Billboard* Hot 100 hit, streaking up to number 14, and Crosby, Stills, Nash, & Young took on hero status.

The Kent State killings were fuel on the fire of Vietnam War discord. Bert Torino, a student at Wayne State University, saw what it did on the Detroit campus as opposing sides met head-on in a relatively mild confrontation. This was Bert's experience:

> I was attending classes at Wayne State University. Students were shouting and waving anti-war banners. I never took part in any of the protests against the war even though I agreed with their message. The closest I came was to go out and watch and stand on the periphery of this protest taking place on the university mall, which had a giant flagpole at its center. Apparently, someone had replaced the American flag with the flag of North Vietnam. Then they threw the draw chain about twenty feet up the pole, and it caught on a winding post. This made the act of taking the Vietnam flag down to put the American flag back up almost impossible. More and more students who were outraged against this action were shouting louder and louder for someone to climb the pole and get the chain down.
>
> I did not want to get too involved. I just wanted to be a bystander. I admired people who could act on their convictions, but I felt safe on the sidelines even though I had really strong objections to

the Vietnam War. I felt my reason for being in college was to pursue my career. I didn't want external events to insert control into my life. I followed the path of least resistance.

The football team jocks showed up, and one after another tried to shinny up the two-foot diameter, slick metal flagpole. They could only get about eight feet up, then embarrassingly kept slipping down. This went on for about fifteen minutes with pro-war and anti-war students starting to confront each other. I thought a riot was about to break out. Then a skinny little kid was able to shinny up and release the chain. Everyone started cheering. The American flag was then restored to its former glory in short time.

Stan Roeper, a retired physical education instructor who taught in the Detroit school system for more than thirty years, witnessed several protests while in college. Stan is a hardworking, focused individual, a family guy. Solidly grounded with a keen sense of humor and a warm regard for his fellow man, Stan refuses to suffer fools. As he recalls,

> There were two big protests at Eastern Michigan University (EMU) in Ypsilanti while I was there. There was one in the fall of 1969 and another in May 1970 in response to the Kent State killings. That one was called for late afternoon. The protest was held at the top of the campus near the administration building. There was a very large crowd with a number of speakers.
> The college administration had placed a seven o'clock curfew on all students. At about six thirty, Washtenaw County and university police started to make their presence known. A few incidents broke out between protesters and police, and before anyone knew what was happening, a number of people were being pushed and shoved. The crowd got unruly at this point and started to run through the campus. I remember tear gas was shot into the area. With the curfew approaching, many students didn't have time to return to their dorms or apartments from late classes. The police began arresting people. While the chaos was going on, there was even an incident of tear gas shot into a dorm filled with many handicapped students.

One of my roommates, a protester, was arrested. As he tried to get back to our apartment (quite a distance from the scene), he was chased by a police dog, caught, taken to the Washtenaw County Jail, and charged with a curfew violation. When we found out about this, my other roommates and I went the next morning to see how we could get him out of jail. There was a large group of people already there when we arrived. We were directed to wait across the street from the jail until his name was called. As the day dragged on, two incidents took place. In the first, a car stopped near the crowd, and the driver got out and started to verbally lambaste all the people standing across from the jail. He used all the terms associated with protesters: hippies, long-haired punks, etcetera. He yelled at the crowd for quite a long time with no intervention by the police, which seemed strange to me, as they were right there monitoring the crowd. The second incident involved a man who seemed drunk and showed up near the crowd. He also yelled insults. He hung around for about five minutes before he moved on. We remained at the jail area for approximately five or six hours before we were able to bail out our roommate. A short time later, we learned from a friend—the boyfriend of one of the jail dispatchers was an EMU student—that the two people who insulted and harassed the crowd were actually undercover police sent, in my opinion, to provoke the crowd and get more people arrested.

It was a war that proved to be a major mistake made by our government. The number of military killed and the negative treatment and scorn returning soldiers received stays etched in my mind.

These and other episodes took place daily and served to clearly, and at times brutally, display the rancor of two dissonant Americas, each with contempt for the other. The protests lasted throughout the war.

Some servicemen returning from Vietnam had participated in anti-war protests. Now they stepped up to take the lead in the rallies. For these men, it was too late to say no to the draft, but it was not too late to say *enough*. Vietnam Veterans Against the War, Inc. (VVAW) was formed in 1967 in New York City after six Vietnam veterans marched together in a peace demonstration. The organization's establishment reflected the growing opposition among returning servicemen

Edward Damato aboard the USS Benewah *(courtesy of Edward Damato)*

and servicewomen to the ongoing war in Southeast Asia. Membership fluctuated throughout the war—growing from an estimated fifteen hundred to as high as thirty thousand—as anti-war sentiment increased and included veterans in the United States and active duty GIs stationed in Vietnam.

The group sponsored a number of rallies and protests. One, held in Washington, DC, in April 1971, was called Operation Dewey Canyon III, named after small-scale secret US incursions—Dewey Canyon I and II—into Laos and the US invasion of Cambodia in April 1970. During the Dewey Canyon III protest, veterans threw away their medals to show their disgust with the ongoing war.

Edward Damato, Vietnam War army veteran, was the VVAW's New York State regional coordinator. He took part in Operation Dewey Canyon III and remains active with the organization today. For a returning soldier to be so open about his anti–Vietnam War position at that time was not a common occurrence. I wanted to know more about his opposition. Edward told me that in April 1966, he had received the usual form letter beginning *Greeting* [sic], auto-signed by President Johnson, with a subway token attached to get him to the Whitehall Street induction station in Manhattan, the same induction center made famous in Arlo Guthrie's 1967 song "Alice's Restaurant."* He passed his physical and a month later was drafted into the army.

Edward took his basic training at Fort Riley, Kansas, and was assigned to the Second Brigade, Ninth Infantry Division with the Mobile Riverine Force (MRF), a dual US Army/US Navy group. The

---

* The satirical and popular anti–Vietnam War song/commentary related Mr. Guthrie's experience with the Selective Service process and how his conviction for littering affected his draft status.

62   Chapter Four

Edward Damato (courtesy of Edward Damato)

entire division shipped over to Vietnam between December 1966 and February 1967. He spent a year in Vietnam as a radio/teletype operator in a joint US Army-Navy action patrolling the Mekong River Delta aboard the MRF's ship, the USS *Benewah*. "I was an army guy on a navy ship," he said.

Edward was opposed to the war; however, he served out his obligation honorably. "I didn't actively turn against the war until the Kent State killings in May 1970. That did it. That August, I joined VVAW as soon as I learned there was a Vietnam veterans' organization working to end the war."

Edward was not the only one joining the VVAW. He recalls that the February 1971 edition of *Playboy* magazine featured a free full-page ad for the VVAW. It drew a flood of inquiries. "I remember working to respond to all those mail-ins (long before the email or texting years). The post office delivered at least a sack or two of mail each day. We sent the veterans information about us and then computerized those names. I believe that in addition to our nationwide membership list, we had almost twenty thousand members."

Years after the Vietnam War ended, Edward was able to look back and put his thoughts about the war and the rally down on paper in the Fall/Winter 2000 issue of the *Veteran*, the VVAW newspaper. He explained:

> Returning our medals [at Dewey Canyon III] as we did allowed for two things: It gave each and every veteran the center stage to express his sadness and anger at having taken part in the Vietnam War. It helped cleanse our consciences, and most important, it made for a great, historic action of veterans standing tall and true and expressing our deepest sentiments at a war we believed to be unjust.

We aren't given a choice of wars to be called upon to fight. We can't choose to be at Gettysburg to fight for the Union. We can't choose to be at Normandy to fight against fascism and annihilation. Our time came during the Vietnam War. At Dewey Canyon III we expressed ourselves in just as honest and heartfelt a way as they did when raising the flag at Iwo Jima. We were just as courageous and patriotic as all our fellow veterans from all the wars we are made to fight in.

Edward retains his anti–Vietnam War convictions to this day.

For Mark Greenberg, a retired publishing-industry executive, the protests and demonstrations were a heady time.

I went to school at the University of California, Berkeley, and took degrees in comparative literature. My immediate family members were not especially politically active, just good, solid Democrats. I became quite political, though: a Bolshie for a chunk of my teens so that by the time I got to Cal, I was ready for the fight.

I never for a moment believed that the war should be fought, and by the time the draft board caught up with me, it had become a war that hardly anyone could stomach—and the body bags were piling up. I knew I couldn't serve, and had I not gotten deferments, I would certainly have expatriated, which seemed a better option than shooting off my toe or going to jail. By '65, refusing to sign the loyalty oath, claiming or (in my case) admitting that you were gay, even getting really high on amphetamines and wearing lipstick to the induction were not guarantees to get you out. Only White privilege could do that, it turned out. I don't remember if I talked to my parents about the draft; my guess is that they would have supported, and indeed encouraged, any course I took to avoid being drafted.

What I do remember is being able to watch the war on TV—I didn't own a TV in those days, but older friends of mine did, and scotch and water in hand, we'd watch it on the evening news: it was simply an unprecedented and bizarre way of being "informed." For me, it confirmed a decision that politics (and cowardice?) had already led me to. Being able to tune in and see the war on television must have done a lot to encourage even those who did not have antiwar politics to decide to take a pass on that call from Uncle Sam.

When I applied for the nascent Peace Corps in '63, I don't think a deferment was uppermost in my mind. I just wanted some exotic adventure. Vietnam was still a rather distant affair. Later on, when the war was ratcheting up, I needed a deferment and turned to my academic advisor. I really don't know what she did, but it was Cal, and I think the university would have bent over backward for any student facing the draft. As it was, she encouraged me to pursue graduate studies many times, and we were fond of each other. She knew where the strings were, and she pulled them for me and got me quickly into a graduate program. The draft board, in turn, simply sent me a student deferment notice.

I would have tried expatriation if the grad school option hadn't materialized. Barring that, who knew, but even jail sounded better than a casualty list. As for my friends, I think all of them had student deferments. Of course, I hung on in grad school forever. By the time I left school and took a job, the war was winding down. This was in '72, and in '75, the US pulled out. I suppose I was vulnerable in '72 and after, but I wasn't called and don't remember being very worried about it at the time. I was thirty by then—too old to be trusted by my peers, and far too old to do any fighting.

Of course I joined the protests. There were so many of them! In Berkeley, in Oakland, in San Francisco, and in DC. They all seem a blur now, but I do remember that there was a sort of exuberance in doing what young people always want to do, which is to disobey, shout, and generally cause trouble. And there was a great feeling of comradeship, not only with those marching with you but with young people all over the world (or, at least, the free world) who were on the march as well. We were effective: we brought down a presidency (which, history will note, was followed by a far worse one) and made the war no longer politically viable. And we expressed and inculcated in the national consciousness a distrust of the government and a cynicism about its Cold War policies—a cynicism new to America. We were having fun and acting on principle, but we were also being the rebels and hooligans that movies and literature had told us to admire. We smashed store windows, overturned cars, terrified people who, by and large, were not our enemies. I met the love of my life on the night before a large demonstration in Berkeley, and so our first date was that protest. I remember some jerks throwing rocks through the windows of an old antiquarian bookstore, and even then, I wondered, what are we doing? But politics, love, sex, music, and anger all made us do things that in sober adulthood seem pretty lame.

As the war dragged on, the North Vietnamese actually became "our side," and bitterness evolved toward the government and the boys who were doing the fighting. We might have asked LBJ how many boys he'd killed that day, but when we actually saw them, they seemed to personify the guilt we all shared in prosecuting an unjust war, in committing vile war crimes, in conducting indiscriminate bombing. And they were responsible. But were they guilty? We treated them very shabbily when it was all over.

One afternoon I was in the San Francisco airport with Alex, the small, adored son of friends in Berkeley. The place was, as usual, filled with guys in uniform, and Alex, having no qualms about starting any conversation, turned to a couple of fresh-faced sailors and began to question them about ships and war and guns. They seemed to be enchanted, were perfect gentlemen, and naturally made the whole mess a child's fantasy. Alex was in heaven. Later, I thought that the United States might just possibly get those sailors killed—and for no reason.

Now I go to the Vietnam Memorial on the National Mall, near the Lincoln Memorial, simply to remember what those years cost this country. I try never to think of Vietnam solely in terms of protest and politics but as a kind of national filicide, something we ought never to forget. You ask if I have regrets. How can I not? I'm an American, and these things were done in my name no matter how much I marched and shouted and protested. But I have no regrets whatsoever about avoiding the draft.

Protests aside, newspaper headlines and avuncular CBS television news anchor Walter Cronkite—at the time popularly considered "the most trusted man in America"—and his contemporaries at NBC and ABC brought Vietnam into the nation's homes almost every night. While previous wars were presented through newsreels and newspaper and radio stories, this war was a daily dinnertime reality show—although coverage was not necessarily live—right there in front of you as you were trying eat your dinner. It was the graphic evening broadcast filled with body counts and body bags displaying the ugly realities of combat and military and civilian casualties that caused many Americans to lose their appetite for the war.

More Americans began clamoring for peace and an end to the war. Signs urging "Peace Now" and "Bring the Troops Home" became more visible at protests. The peace talks in Paris were on (they'd begun in May 1968), yet even as the diplomats and politicians were conferring and making snail's pace progress, American soldiers were still fighting and dying on Vietnamese territory. And men were still needed to fill the ranks. The Selective Service was steadily calling in young men and funneling them directly to the army and the marines. Many registrants, seeing they were about to be drafted, preferred the idea of "choice over chance" and opted to enlist, and by joining the army, marines, navy, air force, coast guard, or a variety of National Guard or reserve units, hoped to have a say in their military placement. Judges and courts were also aiding the war effort at times by giving young men charged with petty crimes the choice of either serving jail time or serving in the armed forces. It made for an interesting concept: equating military service with prison, not to mention adding a criminal element to the country's national defense.

For those men who wanted to avoid the draft, there were ways to do it. Deferments and exemptions based on various factors were available if you qualified, and assistance in acquiring those disqualifications was accessible. Draft counseling centers were eager to help and provide information. Anti-war clergy, lawyers, doctors, academics, parents, and other sympathizers helped young men find legitimate—and sometimes not-so-legitimate—ways to escape induction. Even if you didn't qualify for a deferment, just because you received a notice from your draft board to report for induction didn't automatically mean you were going to comply. You could choose not to. For many men, that notice was the wake-up call that sent them on the road to Canada, Europe, or a doctor or attorney's office to find a way to avoid military service.

But why? Why were we so intent on beating the draft, not going to Vietnam, and not fighting for our country? Many of us would not have hesitated to enlist during World War II or to step up if the Vietnam escapade were a genuine threat to the United States. Now, however, with our nation's vital interests supposedly at stake—so the politicians were telling us—why were so many of us looking for an out? Among my friends, it was simply because we doubted the legitimacy of the war and the genuine need for it. Later, we learned we weren't far from the truth.

Selective Service officials finally had a glimmer about how unfair the draft was in seeming to favor and exempt or defer middle-class boys who could go to college. They attempted to fix it with a lottery that was intended to make everyone equal in vulnerability. Men would be called up according to where their priority number fell—based on a random lottery drawing of birth dates. The lottery would also curtail a man's draft exposure to only one year, thereby limiting the uncertainty that comes with being vulnerable for a prolonged period of time. On December 1, 1969, America's first draft lottery since 1942 was conducted at the Selective Service headquarters in Washington, DC.

Because television brought the war into our living rooms, it seemed only proper that it would also bring the lottery into our homes. That evening, across the country, millions of draft-eligible young men eighteen to twenty-six years of age sat in front of TV sets, anxiously watching to see what the lottery held in store for them. There was also radio and film coverage. This event would determine the order of calls for induction during 1970 for registrants born between January 1, 1944, and December 31, 1950. CBS carried the broadcast live, with correspondent Roger Mudd narrating the action.

Three hundred sixty-six blue plastic capsules were placed in a large glass jar. Inside each capsule was a sheet of paper with a birth date imprinted on it. The national Selective Service director, General Lewis B. Hershey, had invited New York congressman Alexander Pirnie, the ranking Republican on the House Armed Services

Committee, to draw the first number. The congressman pulled out a capsule and handed it over to a Selective Service assistant who opened the capsule, extracted the paper, and announced the date written on it—September 14. The number was posted on a large board. Since it was the first birth date drawn, all men born on that date in any year from 1944 through 1950 were assigned lottery number 1. The process continued with 365 more draws and assignments (leap year included).

Nothing involving the draft was without controversy. The randomness of the lottery date selection was questioned. Everything from how the capsules were placed into the container to how many times and for how long the container had been rotated was challenged. Adjustments were made to ensure unpredictability in capsule selection. The whole affair was like a Mega Millions or Powerball lottery, but here there was a real question as to what constituted a lucky number.

Each capsule created its own drama. As each number was called, reactions varied from the men watching. Some let out great sighs of relief as their number was passed over. Others fell silent or into deep despair as their number came up. When Stan Roeper's birth date was called, he did what so many other men in his situation did: "I drew a high number and was no longer threatened by the draft. My friends and I built a bonfire and burned all our draft board notices and documents."

When the lottery concluded, the board showed every birth date with a corresponding lottery number next to it. Projecting anticipated manpower needs for 1970, the Selective Service estimated that those holding lottery numbers in the lowest third would probably be drafted; those in the upper third were probably safe; and those in the middle couldn't be sure of anything. The following chart shows the lottery results. If your number was low or in the middle and you weren't looking forward to military service, you had to make some decisions fairly quickly.

The chart shows the birth dates in a given year and the lottery numbers assigned to those dates. The months of the year are across the top. The dates of the month are at the far left. The numbers in the chart indicate the selection priority. The format displays the random

SELECTIVE SERVICE SYSTEM
1970 RANDOM SELECTION SEQUENCE, BY MONTH AND DAY

	Jan	Feb	Mar	Apr	May	Jun	Jul	Aug	Sep	Oct	Nov	Dec
1	305	086	108	032	330	249	093	111	225	359	019	129
2	159	144	029	271	298	228	350	045	161	125	034	328
3	251	297	267	083	040	301	115	261	049	244	348	157
4	215	210	275	081	276	020	279	145	232	202	266	165
5	101	214	293	269	364	028	188	054	082	024	310	056
6	224	347	139	253	155	110	327	114	006	087	076	010
7	306	091	122	147	035	085	050	168	008	234	051	012
8	199	181	213	312	321	366	013	048	184	283	097	105
9	194	338	317	219	197	335	277	106	263	342	080	043
10	325	216	323	218	065	206	284	021	071	220	282	041
11	329	150	136	014	037	134	248	324	158	237	046	039
12	221	068	300	346	133	272	015	142	242	072	066	314
13	318	152	259	124	295	069	042	307	175	138	126	163
14	238	004	354	231	178	356	331	198	001	294	127	026
15	017	089	169	273	130	180	322	102	113	171	131	320
16	121	212	166	148	055	274	120	044	207	254	107	096
17	235	189	033	260	112	073	098	154	255	288	143	304
18	140	292	332	090	278	341	190	141	246	005	146	128
19	058	025	200	336	075	104	227	311	177	241	203	240
20	280	302	239	345	183	360	187	344	063	192	185	135
21	186	363	334	062	250	060	027	291	204	243	156	070
22	337	290	265	316	326	247	153	339	160	117	009	053
23	118	057	256	252	319	109	172	116	119	201	182	162
24	059	236	258	002	031	358	023	036	195	196	230	095
25	052	179	343	351	361	137	067	286	149	176	132	084
26	092	365	170	340	357	022	303	245	018	007	309	173
27	355	205	268	074	296	064	289	352	233	264	047	078
28	077	299	223	262	308	222	088	167	257	094	281	123
29	349	285	362	191	226	353	270	061	151	229	099	016
30	164	----	217	208	103	209	287	333	315	038	174	003
31	211	----	030	----	313	----	193	011	----	079	----	100

Selective Service System 1970 lottery random selection sequence, by month and day (source: Selective Service System)

selection sequence by month and day. For example, a man with a birth date of March 17 would have lottery number 33, meaning there was almost a certainty that he would be drafted. In contrast, a man born on August 27 would have number 352, and it would be extremely unlikely for him to be called. And a man celebrating his birthday on November 23 with number 182 would be caught in the middle.

There were six more lotteries conducted—one every year from 1971 through 1975—even though the last draft call was on December 7, 1972, and the Selective Service's authority to order induction expired on June 30, 1973. The last just-in-case lottery drawing was held on March 12, 1975. I don't think many people were paying attention by then.

The lottery created a numerical call-up sequence, but it didn't change the attitude toward the war or the efforts or tactics of those men who were still in the Selective Service's sights. All the lottery did was eliminate some men from call-up probability and make those most exposed dodge a little harder and a little faster.

Chapter 5

Better Information, Better Decisions

The voices protesting the war weren't only the voices of men who were vulnerable to the draft. We had support. Plenty of it.

It was now spring 1968, and I knew there was a good chance I would be called in for a physical. As a probable result of my protest letter and simultaneous request to travel outside the United States, my 2-S classification was changed to 1-A. I became proactive. There was no way I would go into the army for this war. I'm not a pacifist, and I hope I'm not a coward, but this war smelled off from the start and was sold to an unsuspecting American public. I began to check out my options.

I was finishing my first year of law school at the time, and I'd received the letters from the Selective Service regarding applying for CO status, had my request for out-of-country travel rejected, and knew that I had to take some steps soon to avoid the draft. The National Lawyers Guild (NLG), a progressive organization with an anti-war stance, had a presence on campus. The tide of protest wasn't quite a tsunami force yet, but because the draft was beginning to intrude on the lives of middle-class White boys in college, opposition to the war was getting louder. I was tuning in to what the NLG's members were saying and learned that anti-draft lawyers were holding counseling and advisory sessions at churches, community centers, meeting halls, and private offices across Metro Detroit. I knew I wasn't going to move to Canada (I was an American, and the United States was still my country), nor was I willing to join the military reserves or the National Guard. I believed if the war got big enough, those units would be in Vietnam in any case. There had to be an alternative. I would find it. I would become a full-fledged draft resister.

I knew that certain medical, physical, and mental conditions could keep me out of the service, and I quickly checked out those possibilities. No luck. My doctor, who'd known me since I was five years old, sympathetic as he was, said there was nothing wrong with me medically, nothing that would generate a 1-Y or 4-F classification. A novice psychotherapist I had seen for counseling through the university health service when I was an undergraduate pronounced me mentally and emotionally sound (a claim my friends jokingly disputed). I was beginning to get nervous. I considered applying for the Judge Advocate General's Corps (JAG), the army's legal branch, but realized that if accepted, I would still be in the army and could be ordered to prosecute soldiers who were AWOL (absent without leave) or deserters with whom I sympathized. I even thought for a nanosecond about going to Israel, where I had family. Yes, there is mandatory military service there, too, but for entirely different reasons and types of wars. After thinking about it for a few days, I rejected the notion. In my heart, I didn't want to run away.

I also heard from friends that in deciding whether you were suitable for induction, the army didn't care what it did to you; it cared about what you would do to it. If you were going to be a troublemaker, a burden to others or the system, a problem in any form, it might not be worth bringing you in. Physically, if you were extremely large or small and would require special uniforms or shoes, or if you couldn't properly fit into a tank or armored vehicle, they didn't want you. If you were going to question every order, ask why, throw a monkey wrench into anything in any way—and kept it up—they didn't want you. If you were a thorn, you were to be pruned. The army wanted compliant guys who fell within certain physical parameters, took orders, and kept their mouths shut. Of course, they would try to break you and force you to fit into their mold, but if they couldn't accomplish that by sticking you in the stockade, through peer pressure, or by making your life miserable through other punitive means, eventually you were out—but not honorably. Rumor had it that it was easier to get out once you were in than to avoid going in altogether. But I didn't want to test that hypothesis. I didn't want to go in at all. Then they started drafting men into the marines, and I really got tense. Having heard about the missions marines are assigned, I figured conscription into the corps would be a potential death sentence.

At that point I decided to consult with the anti-war "radical" lawyers advising prospective draft dodgers. I attended a draft-counseling clinic and met attorney Jim Lafferty. He became the critical factor in my avoiding the draft.

Detroit-based attorney Jim Lafferty was an outspoken and visible opponent of the Vietnam War, actively involved in helping men find ways to resist the draft. Jim's age (he was in his thirties at the time) excluded him from being called up; nevertheless, he was one of the national leaders of the anti-war movement and remains a highly respected voice when it comes to social justice issues.

Jim was at the center of Detroit's anti-war culture and practiced draft law, representing a range of clients who had run-ins with the Selective Service. If he couldn't help an individual avoid the draft entirely, he could certainly find a way to slow down the process, run out the clock so to speak—perhaps even indefinitely—by filing appeals and identifying regulations and administrative loopholes that favored his clients. His methods were legal, contentious at times, and effective. His efforts were diverse: his anti-war attitude crossed racial and economic lines, and he helped everyone who asked for assistance. While working to keep men out of the army, he also worked with groups to get men *into* the army—to try to organize soldiers from within against the war. He helped me find a way around the draft. In fact, he helped several of the men I interviewed.

It's important to appreciate Jim's background. He grew up in a working-class family in Detroit and attended the University of Michigan on a full scholarship. He received a BA and went on to Wayne State University Law School for his law degree. He was the national director of the NLG for several years starting in 1963, and from 1967 to 1969, he held the position of coordinator, Civil Division, Wayne County Neighborhood Legal Services. From 1969 to 1977, he was a partner in the Detroit law firm of Lafferty, Reosti, Jabara, Papakhian,

James, Stickgold, Soble and Smith and specialized in civil rights and Selective Service/military law. During these years, Jim rose to prominence as one of the nation's most effective draft attorneys, actively leading numerous anti-war organizations. In 1969 he founded the group called the Detroit Coalition to End the War in Vietnam NOW! and, at the same time, was a cofounder and a national coordinator of the National Peace Action Coalition, one of the largest anti–Vietnam War organizations of the era. With chapters across the country, the coalition led numerous major anti-war demonstrations in Washington, DC, San Francisco, and other cities to demand the immediate and unconditional withdrawal of US forces from Vietnam. During the same period, he was taking on civil rights work in the Deep South. In short, his street creds and qualifications as a human rights, civil rights, and social justice champion—a compassionate people's lawyer—were and are impeccable. He was exactly the advocate I wanted on my side.

Along with other local and national leaders, Jim felt that providing resources to men who were seeking to avoid the draft would promote the broader anti-war position. Getting the information out to vulnerable men was critical. He decided to hold the nation's first draft counseling conference at which all possible deferments—not just the well-known conscientious objector exemption, for example—would be discussed. He asked then NLG president and fellow Detroit attorney Ernest Goodman to deliver the lecture on how to avoid the draft. But Goodman, an accomplished and well-respected First Amendment and civil rights legal specialist who had argued major cases before the US Supreme Court, declined and, as Jim told me, said, "No, Lafferty, you should learn draft law and do it yourself." Goodman handed Jim the book containing the Selective Service regulations governing the draft. Jim studied them over the weekend and delivered the speech the following week. The conference was held in 1968 at the Central United Methodist Church in Detroit, where the Reverend David Gracie—who had since moved to a position with the Episcopal Diocese of Pennsylvania—had committed the church to a firm anti-war position and provided free draft counseling on Sunday evenings. The national media showed up in droves adding to the publicity. Following that event, Jim set up free draft counseling centers throughout the Midwest.

When advising young men one-on-one and in speaking engagements, Jim spoke in detail about the types of deferments available and how to obtain and use them. Over the years, he built a reputation as a successful and well-respected activist attorney. However, while he may have had success with his individual cases, the draft boards were undeterred. As Jim said more than once, "Despite our efforts, local draft boards still met their quotas. We'd keep ten guys out, they'd find another ten guys to fill in."

Jim also knew about the unfairness of draft physicals: they weren't uniform in process or results. If Selective Service guidelines for physical examinations existed, Jim was not aware of them, and he regularly scrutinized Selective Service regulations to stay on top of any changes. If, in fact, there were standardized qualifications and conditions, they were not being applied consistently at physical examinations. The doctors seemed to have wide parameters and interpretations as to which medical conditions would disqualify a man from the draft. Jim related a couple of key anecdotes illustrating the indifference of the Selective Service to their targets' well-being or suitability for military service. In one case, a young man, accompanied by his wife and child, appeared unannounced at Jim's office seeking assistance. The man was completely blind in one eye, had overall diminished vision, yet had passed his physical. The army doctors were oblivious to his condition. The man eventually made his way to Canada, eluding the draft. In another situation, an army paramedic from Fort Wayne (the Detroit-area induction center), appalled by the incompetent and arbitrary nature of Selective Service induction physical exams, came to Jim and said he was willing to take on a whistleblower role and go public about it. Jim held a press conference and disclosed the information. Colonel Arthur Holmes, head of the Michigan Selective Service and a frequent Lafferty opponent and butt of complaints, promised reform. Colonel Holmes told Jim that he would treat his clients better in the future. Jim asked, "What about everyone else?" To Jim's knowledge, no reform ever came about.

On the other hand, despite or because of Selective Service process inconsistencies, Jim had great success in finding ways to keep men out of the draft. Through administrative maneuvers, including appeals, delays, and various court motions, all legal and part of an effective defense strategy, none of Jim's clients were drafted or sent to jail. However, one came very close. In 1973, as the war was winding down and prosecutions ebbing, some draft evasion cases were still alive in the federal court system. One man found himself facing Federal Judge Robert Edward DeMascio, a Nixon appointee. At the man's arraignment, where he was charged for failing to appear for induction, Judge DeMascio asked him if he was represented by counsel. The man replied that he would represent himself. DeMascio asked him if he understood Selective Service regulations. When the man replied no, DeMascio insisted that he at least speak with an attorney before acting as his own counsel and referred the man to Jim. When they met, the man told Jim he did not want to use any of the legal defenses available to him; instead, he wanted to plead guilty and make a statement about his position on the war. "Will I be able to say anything at my sentencing?" the man asked.

"Yes," said Jim. "But you'll have to let me make a statement first."

On the day of the trial, Jim declared to the court that he had discussed the situation with the defendant, had reviewed the defense options available, and that the defendant had decided to forgo a defense, wanted to plead guilty, make a statement, and was prepared to accept the sentence the court would impose. Jim did this to assure the court that he was not dismissive of the man's rights to a defense but merely respecting and accepting the instructions the defendant had given him. Jim was prepared to offer a vigorous defense if the man would allow him to do so. When Jim finished his statement, the defendant acknowledged Jim's assessment and his guilty plea and asked the judge for permission to speak. His request was granted. He then delivered a fifteen-minute oration about why he was personally opposed to the Vietnam War and why he could not and would not participate in it. Jim described the speech as "eloquent, articulate, and quite moving." As the defendant was speaking, the judge listened carefully but also appeared to be getting irritated at the amount of time the defendant was taking. When the defendant was finished, the judge sat quietly for what seemed like an eternity but was in reality only a minute or two, and then announced his verdict. "You are guilty," he said solemnly. "But I will give you a choice. You can serve two years in federal prison, or (long pause) you can write two book reports—one about *The Best and the Brightest* by David Halberstam and the other on *The Winds of War* by Herman Wouk. What'll it be?"*

Onlookers in the courtroom gallery were astounded, as was Jim, at this unexpected and unorthodox sentencing alternative. Equally stunned, the defendant quickly took the obvious option—the book reports—and was quite relieved. It was a perfect illustration of the power of a persuasive, heartfelt argument.

After listening to Jim at a group counseling session in 1968 and while my file was undergoing review at Local Board 179, I understood what I needed to do and asked him for his assistance. Jim suggested I consider being evaluated to see if I was psychologically a good fit for the military. (As noted, I had already discussed this possibility with a neophyte psychotherapist who declared I was qualified to serve.)

Jim told me about psychiatrist Paul Lowinger, director of Detroit's Lafayette Clinic, a respected psychiatric hospital at the time, who was sympathetic to the anti-war movement, and referred me to him. I made an appointment with Dr. Lowinger and hoped he would be my salvation. When the time came for the interview, I half expected he would give me a letter saying I was crazy, charge a fee, pat me on my fanny, and send me on my way. I couldn't have been more off base.

Dr. Lowinger carried out a comprehensive assessment over several appointments. He explored, probed, asked revealing and uncomfortable questions. I responded truthfully, realizing he would be able to see through any assertions or explanations I could make up to define me as unsuitable for service. By the time I was finished, he had my detailed personal history and had brought several complex issues to the surface. I realized he was an excellent therapist, and I saw him a few more times. Our sessions paid off in more ways than simply avoiding the draft. He made his diagnosis and said I was

---

*The former is a nonfiction work that looks at the origins of the Vietnam War. The latter is a novel based on events leading to World War II.

a candidate for additional therapy and definitely unfit for military service. I asked him to put that in writing, and he did. Jim Lafferty and Dr. Lowinger were my exit ramp.

Jim also pointed out that some men avoided the draft through what was dubbed the George Hamilton deferment—granted to men who were the sole support of their mother. The deferment got its nickname in 1966 when actor George Hamilton was granted a deferment based on potential economic hardships at home. Hamilton informed the draft board that he was the lone financial support of his mother and that he would not be able to support her if he was in the army. Situations of this kind formed a legitimate basis for a 3-A hardship deferment (deferred from military service because service would cause hardship upon his family), but it was difficult to imagine a successful movie star in such circumstances. Such perceived inequities, whether real or not, in the Selective Service process—special treatment for the rich, powerful, or famous—were frustrating to those of us subject to the draft, and one of the factors that led to the lottery.

Jim's viewpoints were not appreciated by everyone: he was summoned before the House Un-American Activities Committee (HUAC) after he and a few other leaders of the anti-war movement returned from a visit to North Vietnam in 1971. The experience just added to his already impressive résumé and accentuated his stance as an activist and peace advocate.

In 2015 Jim retired as the executive director of the NLG in Los Angeles after twenty-five years and became the organization's executive director emeritus. In retrospect, Jim says he has no regrets. His political position created no repercussions in his life. His actions had a real social and political impact. "Looking back, fighting the draft was the right thing to do; it was a matter of civil rights. I believe true patriots speak up when they think their country is doing something it should not be doing."

Not everyone who objected to the draft was subject to it. But there were still plenty of people who were affected by it. There was war resistance from parents, siblings, girlfriends and wives, social justice advocates, and civil rights activists who for one reason or another would never receive a draft notice. Women were not being drafted, but many of those who were opposed to the war were not shy about making their feelings known. Alix Kates Shulman was one of them.

Alix Kates Shulman during the Vietnam War era (photo by Martin Shulman)

A well-respected writer and political activist, Alix is especially recognized for her 1972 million-copy best-selling novel *Memoirs of an Ex-Prom Queen*, which the *Oxford Companion to Women's Writing* declared to be "one of the first novels to emerge from the Women's Liberation Movement." She is also well known for the significant moral stands she took starting in the 1960s—and maintains today—in the civil rights, anti-war, and feminist movements.

Alix grew up in Cleveland, Ohio, where she attended public schools. Her father was a lawyer. He became a labor arbitrator and during World War II served on the local draft board. He was an advocate of justice and viewed it as an ideal to be attained. Alix wanted to be a lawyer but while at Case Western Reserve University, she found another interest—"I got waylaid by philosophy"—and went to New York to study philosophy at the Columbia University Graduate School. She later attended New York University, where she earned a master's degree in humanities.

Alix was opposed to the Vietnam War and served as a volunteer draft counselor for several years in Manhattan. She was trained for counseling at the Quaker Meeting House on East Sixteenth Street and Rutherford Place in New York. Alix is not a Quaker; however, her training was rigorous and followed traditional Quaker pacifist tenets.

Once she completed her training, Alix counseled draft-vulnerable young men at the Quaker Meeting House weekly. She also counseled at Washington Square Methodist Church (the "Peace Church") in New York. While some draft counselors might have openly encouraged young men to resist, Alix's counseling was neutral; she did not advocate dodging the draft. Instead, her approach was designed to provide information about the Selective Service, legal draft avoidance, and the options open to men subject to the draft. She saw her role as providing the critical knowledge that would allow men to make an informed decision about which path to follow regarding the draft.

Conscientious objector status, or alternative service, was a key option. At the time, CO status was limited to men who based their objections on their religious beliefs. However, Alix was ahead of her time and did not think religion should be the critical factor in determining CO status. She firmly believed that "atheists are moral, too." The Supreme Court eventually agreed with Alix's position and ruled in 1970 that CO status could be allowed for personal moral philosophies and principles. (More on CO status in chapter 9.)

Alix's counseling clients represented all branches of society. "They were all kinds, but mostly anxious high school seniors wondering what to do next," she says. "The men were typically ignorant and scared." Sessions usually lasted about an hour. She can't recall ever having a second session with anyone.

She participated in a great number of weekly peace vigils and anti-war protests, including those at which draft cards were burned. She would frequently carry a poster that read "Not my son. Not your son. Not our sons." Eventually, this led to trouble: Alix was arrested on December 12, 1967, at a sit-down demonstration at the Whitehall Street induction center in New York. The story reported by the *New York Times* had a photo of her, self-described as "the woman in front in the big hat." The police rode horses into the crowd of seated protesters, dispersing the throng. This was a dramatic and disruptive tactic the mounted police used more than once in front of induction centers and other government buildings when crowds gathered to protest the war.

Proudly calling herself a "civil disobeyer" and looking back, Alix says, "I wanted to do the most I could do. I am proud of it. I am devoted to it. I was an anti-war counselor before I became a feminist. The war was wrong. I'm happy I had the opportunity to do something good."

In the course of my conversations with her, Alix directed me to look into a 1969 event about women's action against the draft. "This should be of great interest to your readers to see the work of women in opposing the Vietnam draft," she said.

Alix was referring to an anti-war protest held on July 2, 1969, in which five women calling themselves Women Against Daddy Warbucks broke into several New York City draft boards and destroyed the files of men classified 1-A, several thousand files in all. The women also ripped out telephone lines and demolished the number *1* and letter *A* on every office typewriter they could find. Their action caused tremendous disruption to the system.

Two days after their draft board raids, the Women Against Daddy Warbucks publicly turned themselves in for arrest at Rockefeller Center. Before the police and FBI arrived, the group threw the shredded, confetti-like files to the crowd. The women were arrested, but the case was eventually dismissed after witnesses refused to testify and the defendants weren't given a speedy trial (a violation of their constitutional rights) due to numerous delays. The draft board raid was instrumental in rousing female anti-war protests. The following piece, commemorating the event, appeared in one of the earliest anthologies of the women's liberation movement, *Sisterhood Is Powerful*.

OUR STATEMENT
Women Against Daddy Warbucks
We did it.

We interfered with the ability of the 13 uptown Manhattan draft boards to initiate the processing of men into numbers, into killing-machines, into corpses.

We acted together as women against the draft because conscription rests on women's accepted role as insulated comforter and supporter of its violence, as indeed does the violence of American society in general.

Those files were destroyed to decry the incredible continuation of death in Vietnam. Now, we bring file remains to Rockefeller

Center to indict the insidious pattern by which American arms follow capital investment into the Third World.

We are here to make clear the connection between overseas corporate involvement and American military and political intrusions into the affairs of Asia, Africa, and Latin America. Corporations such as Dow, Standard Oil, Shell, and Chase Manhattan—with offices in Rockefeller Center bear as much responsibility for US domination of those areas from which we profit . . .

If our action confuses you, think about what led to our decision. Consider how the draft controls by fear lives that might be inspired by hope. Consider the interdependence between corporation profits and military "protection" overseas. Consider the roles programmed for women by our society, accepted as insulation from social responsibility. Consider the real reasons why resources are wasted in arms competitions while people are starving and homeless . . .

We are saying that profits are not worth lives, that peace does not come through war. Americans, men and women, must confront themselves with what their country is doing.*

This was not the first time such an act had taken place. In an effort to draw attention to the anti-war movement, on October 27, 1967, four men, including Josephite priest Father Philip Berrigan, Catholic artist Tom Lewis, and two Protestants, writer David Eberhardt and Reverend James L. Mengel, entered the Selective Service board office in the Baltimore Customs House and poured blood—a mix of chicken blood and their own blood—over Selective Service records. They were arrested and dubbed the Baltimore Four. Several months later, nine Catholic activists, including Berrigan's Jesuit brother Daniel, walked into the offices of the draft board in Catonsville, Maryland, and removed hundreds of draft files, doused them in homemade napalm, and burned them in a parking lot near the building. The activists were arrested and became known as the Catonsville Nine. In both episodes, all the participants except one

---

* "Women Against Daddy Warbucks," in *Sisterhood Is Powerful*, ed. Robin Morgan (New York: Random House, 1970), 594.

were sentenced to prison terms. Tactics of this kind, however, were often emulated and successful because usually there were no easily accessible duplicate files; while there was a government data bank somewhere, the men whose records were destroyed were suddenly gone—at least for a little while—from local draft board files.

One of the questions draft counselors were often asked was "Why are we in Vietnam?" That was the $64,000-dollar question. If you were buying the government's line, the answer was to save the world from Communism. But was it really? Did we really believe that if Vietnam fell, all those neighboring countries would soon tumble? Could the dominoes fall across the Pacific Ocean? Would Hawaii be next? And before you knew it, would those pesky Viet Cong guerrillas be moving in on Albuquerque? I think more than a few men marched off to protect the nation with that belief in mind.

Michael Klachefsky, a retired insurance executive, agreed with the government line—at first. It turned out that he was not acceptable for induction, but he had definite ideas about the war. He learned more about it and then started counseling draft-eligible young men. This is what he told me:

> My first recollection of the draft is a vague memory of having to register when I turned eighteen in 1965. I remember feeling uneasy about it, but having been brought up during the Red Scare era of Senator Joseph McCarthy, I felt I probably had to keep the world safe from Communism. At the time I was not aware that both my parents, Holocaust survivors, had very good experiences with the Russians during World War II, and my dad had his ass saved by a Communist cell in the Buchenwald concentration camp. My parents were both Commie sympathizers, but it was not something they advertised during the US's Vietnam crusade to prevent all of Asia from going red—remember the domino theory?
>
> I was in college in Detroit when Vietnam caught everyone's attention, so I had a 2-S student deferment. Apparently, the United States did not want any educated men to fight the Viet Cong.
>
> In the summer of 1966, I bummed around Europe and had a

series of really cool adventures. A few times, in Sweden and France, though, young women my age asked me if I supported the Vietnam War. I really wanted to say no so they would like me, but I told the truth, that I did support it. One Swedish girl became indignant and proceeded to ask me if I was a racist, too. Interesting view of the United States from Europe.

During this period, 1966–67, Lyndon Johnson was ramping up our troop commitment, but student deferments still held. Then one day at college, I ran into a friend, Alan, actually sort of a mentor, who was three years older than me. We got to talking about the war, and he was totally against it. I did not want to seem like I had no opinion, so I told him that we really needed to keep the world safe from Communism. He then said, "If you are so anxious to beat the Cong, why don't you go over there and do it?"

That was my turning point. I realized that I was not willing to enlist or be drafted. Alan's thinking influenced me. I wanted to learn more, and I began to read anti-war literature and listen to anti-war speeches. By mid-1967, I realized that there was no way I was going to go over there, and that I would do what I could as an individual to put an end to the war.

After my conversion, I attended a rally where activist lawyer Jim Lafferty was talking about the anti-war resistance at our school, Wayne State University. He told us he was personally training a cadre of counselors to advise young men on how to avoid the draft. I signed up and received the training in the basement of a Baptist church in downtown Detroit.

I soon began to counsel young men, mostly Black, in that church. It was not as satisfying an experience as I might have liked. When I told them about all the things they could do to disrupt the draft process, most of them would get a faraway look in their eyes. It seemed they did not have the anti-authoritarian righteousness needed to resist. Maybe hearing this from a White guy from the university turned them off, but I knew when they got their draft notice, they would go and be inducted.

At one point I visited a draft dodger friend in Vancouver. When his friends found out about my draft counseling background, they asked me to advise a few Americans who were there and considering staying in Canada. It was satisfying talking to these men, because I could see that they were strongly against becoming cannon fodder and would not go to Vietnam. Their only decision was whether to resist in the United States or remain in Canada.

These are some of the techniques we recommended to resisters during counseling:

(1) Don't show up for your physical; tell them you had never been notified. Do this repeatedly;
(2) File for conscientious objector status;
(3) Become a minister (Muhammad Ali did this; he was prosecuted but ultimately won his case); and
(4) Since each draft board was required to retain all documentation you sent them, have two hundred telephone books delivered to the draft board, send a Bible with anti-war sections marked, send childlike drawings of flowers and peace signs, and do these mailings repeatedly.

Another friend, David, was very much his own person and decided he would go to Canada rather than live in the "warmongering" United States as a resister. We'd worked together for several years at a summer camp. He was an outdoorsman, a classic rugged individualist who lived life on his own terms. He came to say goodbye to me as he was on his way out of town. He was one of my closest friends. I took one look at his fully packed car with his student desk strapped to the top and broke down in tears. As he drove away, I wondered how it could come to this: one of my best friends was now a political refugee. I thought of my parents and wondered how this country, which took us in after World War II, could now be producing its own refugees.

As a child, I had been diagnosed with epilepsy and had taken medication for eight years. I had also been seeing a therapist for reasons unrelated to the draft. I was a pretty typical insecure child with a Jewish mother who made Portnoy's mom look like a rank amateur.

Then one day, student deferments became much more restricted, and I no longer qualified. I received a notice to report for

Michael Klachefsky (photo by Larry Zeldner)

a draft physical. Given what I'd learned in my draft counseling training, I was relatively sure that if I presented my mental and physical history as noted above, I would not be drafted. It was also immensely comforting that my mom and dad, with their Commie-lover backgrounds, were completely opposed to me participating in a war against Ho Chi Minh, who was trying to liberate his country from fascism. I was right, no draft for me. But some of my friends, who did not have the same advantages I had, came up with other creative ideas not discussed in draft counselor training.

Thanks to my medical history, I did not get drafted. None of my clever friends did either. Being well educated, middle-class boys paid off for all of us. Instead, uneducated, poor boys became cannon fodder, and many returned home in boxes. I realized someone took my place. I almost wish I knew who. It bothers me to this day.

Michael moved to Winnipeg, Manitoba, in the 1970s *after* the Vietnam War ended. "I moved because I was sick of being American—the war did that to me. I loved Canada, and I had a job offer from the University of Winnipeg," he said.

Today, Michael lives in the Pacific Northwest. An enthusiastic canoeist and backpacker, he managed summer camps and worked as a wilderness tour professional for a number of years. Nothing much intimidates him. He laughs about telling flag-waving Americans that he's a Communist just to see their reactions. I've known Michael since we were seven years old. He was never one to hide his feelings. I admire that.

Chapter 6

Bend Over and Crack a Smile

The military needed bodies, and they were working hard with the Selective Service to procure them. The army wanted us all, and the opt-out routes for avoiding the call were closing. High demand for draftees meant student deferments were disappearing. CO status was elusive and, even if granted, did not promise anything—you could still end up as a medic in a combat zone. Physical and mental deficiencies were suspect. Critical, exemption-worthy occupations and circumstances were becoming less critical. If you didn't want to go in, it was getting harder to stay out. But men were finding a way, as *Time* magazine noted:

> More and more young Americans are being rejected for the draft on physical or mental grounds. From 29.9 percent two years ago, the turndown rate jumped to 46 percent last July. Is the new generation declining in body and mind? Hardly. The young have simply faced up to the cutoff in job and graduate-school deferments and instead have mastered the art of beating the draft with medical or psychiatric excuses. Moreover, they are getting crucial help from a number of psychiatrists and other physicians who write letters attesting to ailments that disqualify the registrants for military service.*

In May 1968 I finally received an invitation from my draft board to attend a preinduction physical in Detroit at Fort Wayne. The big party in Vietnam was getting bigger, and the board wanted me to

---

* "Draft-Defying Doctors," *Time*, November 16, 1970.

attend. There was no RSVP with this invitation, no option to decline. No plus one. I was expected to appear punctually at the appointed date and time for a cursory examination of my physical and mental well-being. I had anticipated receiving the notice. I just hadn't thought it would come so soon. Like many other draft-susceptible young men, I thought I had more time. I didn't. And I was scared. But I would go to my physical armed with the letter I had received from Dr. Lowinger. It was no assurance of rejection or deferral, but at the least it was some sort of weapon or shield.

The physical exam was a critical step in the induction process, perhaps *the* critical step. You could say that this was where it was decided, figuratively and literally, who would stay and who would go. Maybe who would live and who would die. That's how we felt about it. This was also where you got your first taste of what army life would be like, where men in uniform ordered you around, yelling at you, telling you what to do and where to go, ignoring the fact that you were not yet in the army and could pay them no mind. Yes, paying them no mind could lead to some unpleasant consequences during the physical, but you were still within your rights to do exactly that, a fact that only some of us knew. When the physical exam was over, you'd have a pretty good idea of whether or not you'd be wearing army fatigues in the near future.

Comparing the stories of the men I interviewed, there was little consistency in how physicals were administered from site to site across the country. In some locations, individuals were left to their own devices to get to the examination center; in other cases, everyone met at the draft board and took a shuttle bus from there. At some facilities, physicals were all-day affairs with lunch thrown in; at others, it was a half-day experience. Sometimes a man might be transported to the physical site the night before or be kept overnight for further examination after the physical. The physical itself could be brief or involved. Attending doctors and medics could have different priorities. Regardless of the specific procedure, everyone went through an exam of some sort that depended on the mood or nature of the medical personnel involved. It was all very arbitrary.

I had four long weeks in which to build up my anxiety levels for the physical. I was the first in my group of friends to be called in.

I was also starting final exams in law school, had to study, and was in the dark about what to expect at the physical. I did have the letter from Dr. Lowinger, but that was no guarantee. I remembered the arrangement my grandfather had made for my father to avoid conscription into the Polish Army. My parents believed that sometimes war was necessary but that the Vietnam War was insane. They did not want me to participate. They never spoke to me of actively avoiding the draft, but they knew I would do just that and trusted that I would find a way. They did not have the power or the means to assist me, although in my fantasies I saw my mother storming the Selective Service office and telling Miss Modelski to keep her hands off me.

My law exams came and went. I passed my courses but did not do as well as I might have had the draft not been weighing on me. The physical loomed. I drove to my fate on a hot, muggy June morning. Fort Wayne can be intimidating. A huge brick structure built in 1850, it sits on ninety-six acres near the shore of the Detroit River and across from Windsor, Ontario. The river is about a half-mile wide at this point, a half-mile to perceived freedom. The fort had been the main induction center for Michigan troops entering battle in US conflicts since the Civil War.

When I reached the fort, I saw a lot of high school buddies. Some were wearing braces (dental and leg), others limped or used canes, and a few were hyper and twitched or were spacey stoned. I saw Mike Fulton from my law class carrying a letter from his dentist and sporting dental braces. I asked him when he'd started wearing them. "Yesterday," he said. He assured me they'd be off the minute he was rejected. There was also my pharmacist friend Jason Van Winkl, who had tried to join the Coast Guard Reserve but was rebuffed because he was color-blind and could not read naval flags. But the unit's physician told him the army wasn't quite as picky: they would want him specifically because he was color-blind. At his physical, the medic said, "When a Cong sniper is hiding in the tree, you'll lead the platoon because you'll be able to see him; he won't be camouflaged to your eyes." But Jason was prepared for this possibility; being a pharmacist, he had easily acquired medications to raise his blood pressure. His reason for downing the pills was obvious. "I didn't want to get shot," he said. "I had access to drugs, so I took them." Jason also helped out a close friend, providing him with amphetamines to help fail his physical. Friends helping friends avoid the draft whenever possible was standard practice.

Then there was my pal Ray Serafin, with his genuinely bad knee that was repeatedly and painfully twisted and manipulated by a suspicious army doctor even though Ray had a thoroughly vetted letter and X-rays from his personal physician. Ray was rejected, but proactive measures didn't always work. The Asian American boyfriend of one of my colleagues was unsuccessful in his attempt: he had no disqualifying doctor letter, no access to drugs, and apparently, in some sort of Hail Mary effort, drank several quarts of high-sodium soy sauce the night before his physical, hoping it would do something to his blood pressure. All it did was make him sick. He passed the physical but eventually succeeded in gaining CO status. He became a medic.

Almost every guy I knew had a doctor's note. We were all trying to find a way out. A good letter could serve as a "Get out of the draft" card, but you had to know about the note in order to get one. There were also plenty of noncollege White, Black, and Hispanic kids who weren't holding letters from doctors, weren't wearing braces. They were just there, going through the process. I wondered if they were resigned or opposed to being drafted; if they saw the army as an opportunity or a chance to get out of the house. I wondered if these guys knew that they might have options. I wondered if their thinking was anything like mine. I talked to a couple of them and found that a few were taking the physical voluntarily in order to enlist. For some, the military was their dream. Maybe they could fill my board's quota. And shamefully, I hoped that if any of us were taken, it would be them and not me.

For the first step in the day's agenda, we all sat at school desks in a large room and were handed what the army called an aptitude test and a personal questionnaire. I finished the test part quickly in a few minutes. I recall that the questionnaire asked about subversive groups I might have been active with and if I'd ever participated in civil protests, been arrested, taken drugs, or had a homosexual experience. I can't remember all the questions, but I do remember thinking they were asinine. Who would respond honestly if the answer could affect your preferred status? You'd answer the questions to your advantage. If I recall correctly, there was also a loyalty oath. I don't remember if I signed that. I do know that I thought of myself as completely loyal to my country, but I questioned whether or not our government was loyal to its citizens.

Then came the physical.

Entering the exam area, we presented our letters to a medic. I presented mine; it was acknowledged, and I was told that it would be addressed and that I'd be interviewed at the mental health station. I then went with the rest of the sheep. We marched around wearing only shoes, socks, and underpants, carrying our valuables in a paper bag. We also carried our Selective Service files. I went through all the medical stations and was questioned, probed, and fingered by doctors at the various stops. We were taken in large groups into a big room and lined up in rows. We were ordered to drop our briefs, bend over, and spread our cheeks. A medic marched up the rows checking us out, looking for . . . what? Hemorrhoids? (We all took great pleasure in mooning him.) A few stops later and it was drop your drawers again, as the doctors checked us for hernias: two at a time using both their hands, all the while discussing their new cars, movies they'd seen, baseball scores, oblivious to our physical discomfort, their findings noted on our charts. Then, for me, came the psychiatric interview.

The psychiatrist was a cliché right out of a *New Yorker* cartoon. He appeared to be in his fifties, sporting longish salt-and-pepper hair, wearing a Harris Tweed jacket, and obsessed with a pipe he could not keep lit. We sat in his little office with its government-issued metal desk, two chairs, a filing cabinet, and a lamp. He took my file and read the letter from my shrink. "This guy again," he muttered. Then he looked at me, and in the most serious, pseudo-sincere, reaching-out-and-let's-be-intimate-pals voice I've ever heard, he said, "What does the expression 'People in glass houses shouldn't throw stones' mean?"

The question took me aback, and I had to work hard to suppress a reflexive guffaw, but after a brief pause, I responded with, "Don't you know? Glass is so expensive, so expensive! You don't want to break those glass walls and windows." I went on about the danger of glass shards, installation costs, and accused him of being insensitive to the plight of people who could not afford to replace glass easily. He put up his hand, told me to stop, wrote something in my file, and dismissed me. I stepped out of his office, opened my file, and saw he had marked me as "1-Y—deferred for a year, to be reexamined at that time." Free until July 1969. Cloud nine, baby.

I sailed through the rest of my physical, left Fort Wayne, stopped at a pal's house to report on my adventure, and went home to tell my parents. They were quite pleased.

The 1-Y classification was a huge relief. It meant that I did not have to immediately return to law school. The 1-Y gave me a chance to explore other career possibilities. I could work at camp for the summer and then make some decisions. For a long time I had toyed with the idea of working in advertising and thought this would be a perfect time to give it a try. I elected not to return to law school, and in November 1968, I was hired as a copywriter at the Detroit ad agency Young & Rubicam to work on the Chrysler-Plymouth account. I was there for a year and then moved to Los Angeles, where I joined another agency. And then, as expected, I was called up for another physical.

My second invitation came in the summer of 1970. I was working and living comfortably in Los Angeles and had realized the value of therapy. I was seeing a psychotherapist in Beverly Hills, and lest you think I was some kind of rich kid, this was when health insurance generously covered mental health services. When I told the shrink I had to go through another draft physical, he asked about my feelings regarding the war, the draft, the army, and whether I wanted to go into the military. We had never really discussed the subject before, and I explained that I believed there were just wars for the United States to be involved with, but the Vietnam War did not fall into that category. This was a war for the Vietnamese people to sort out and it was immoral for the United States to send its sons to fight and die in someone else's conflict. I believed that in this case, soldiers were pawns for questionable interests, that the government itself was ambivalent about the war, and that there were questions about US military capabilities for this kind of guerrilla warfare. In addition, I thought that the government of South Vietnam was suspect and that a high number of credible and well-respected people from all walks of life had condemned or questioned the conflict. I said that if we, the people, didn't do something about it, things would just get worse. I also asked if he would write a letter to extend my 1-Y classification.

He told me that he felt I was a rational, mature, adult male and, therefore, completely unsuitable for involuntary army life. He had been a major in the US Army Medical Corps during World War II and said he would be happy to write a strong disqualifying letter.

I hadn't notified the draft board that I was living in Los Angeles because I wanted to minimize contact with Miss Modelski. Consequently, my second physical was set for Detroit in June. I could've had it changed to California, but that would have delayed it, and I just wanted to get it over with. On the appointed date, I was back at Fort Wayne. It was déjà vu as I was taking the same test, filling out the same questionnaire, and about to enter the physical examination process again. This time things went differently. At the first station, where medical letters are initially reviewed, I handed mine to a doctor whose name I cannot recall. He looked at my file, noticed my Jewish-sounding name, and said familiarly, "You shouldn't be here. You should be in the Israeli Army." I was surprised, but I couldn't tell if he was serious or sarcastic. I responded with, "Maybe you could do something about that." He said nothing, and I went on to the next station.

As I went through the physical, things got interesting. I was sent to the mental health station. A doctor reviewed my letter, made no comment—didn't appear to recognize my California psychiatrist's name—and marked something in my file. When I left his office, I looked and saw he had indicated I was 4-F. Deferred forever. Exempt. Free. I was elated. Still, I had to go through the rest of the examination and the hoops that were created for all of us to jump through. As it turned out, I flunked my hearing test (I was not faking) and had high blood pressure (news to me). The medic said they were going to hold me for three days and recheck my blood pressure because they suspected I had taken drugs to boost it. (I hadn't.) Three days at Fort Wayne? No way! Were they out of their minds? I asked the medic to mark my blood pressure as normal, since I'd already been disqualified. He refused and directed me to a bench to wait to be transported to the fort's barracks. I sat and thought, "This is crazy." I got up and moved on to the last station. No one stopped me. I was herded through checkout along with other men and randomly wound up with the same doctor who had checked me in. He reviewed my file and mumbled something about a good letter from my shrink. Neither of us said anything about the blood pressure reading. He then told me I could leave and asked me again if I would consider Israel.

I shrugged. "Maybe."

And he actually said, "Have a nice life."

I walked out of the building. In the parking lot, as I was getting into my car, I looked back and knew that I was lucky. Not too many guys were walking out as early in the day as I was. I believed that the draft process was now behind me forever, and I was right. I never heard from my draft board again.

My adventures at Fort Wayne were not unique. Bert Torino told me about his experience.

> Whenever I hear the song "Alice's Restaurant," my mind instantly conjures up the scene from the movie with the same name. The scene when Arlo (Guthrie) had to go down to get a physical, and everyone was exchanging urine samples to botch up everyone's urine test for drugs. This surreal scene was something that could only happen in movies. Right?
>
> Well, that happened to me. I got the letter in the mail that said I had to report for a physical. I went down and stood in long lines to get processed. When it was time for the urine sample, I was handed a small paper cup to bring into the men's room. As I stepped into the large area with all the urinals, some guy was coming around the corner and immediately dumped part of his urine sample into my cup. This was happening en masse. It was really chaotic. I think every guy in the place had his urine sample tainted with someone else's disease or drug levels. I figured there was not too much I could do. It felt like I, too, was in some kind of movie set.

We were all shuffled into a very large room with rows and columns of desks, like we had in grade school. The room was so large, it had extra columns evenly spaced in the open area to support the large expanse of ceiling. There was, it seemed, about a dozen columns and about fifteen rows of these desks with apprehensive young men like myself, not knowing what was to happen next.

Back about that time, there were various ways to get out of service. A good doctor's letter was one way, and I had thought that I was going to be one of a select few with a convincing letter. Some uniformed men came into the room and made a loud announcement. "Does anyone have a doctor's letter?" With a huge outburst of noise, about 80 percent of the hands went up into the air, including mine. Apparently, a majority of the potential draftees had all taken the time to find a doctor who was willing to write such a letter. Then a second of silence, and another large outburst. This time it was laughter with the military officer yelling for everyone to shut up.

A student deferment was another way, although you could only do this for so many years, and you had to be going to school full time. Another accepted way at the time was to get married. Most of these deferments were wiped out when the draft lottery came in. There was also the conscientious objector deferment. That was a possibility for me. Especially when I found out I passed the physical.

My final exposure at the draft physical that day was when they had us all march upstairs. There we were, seated on benches in the center of a long rectangular room. The benches ran the length of the room with large windows on either side. We all waited nervously, not knowing what was to happen next. Then an officer entered the room and began to shout derogatory statements about how we were now property of the US government. He ranted on and on for about five minutes. He called us every name in the book. We were scum of the earth. Didn't he know we were not enlistees? We were normal citizens required to show up for a physical. I found this to be extremely insulting, humiliating, and uncalled-for. I did not enlist in the service, but he treated every single one of us in the room as if we had just joined.

There was a small percentage of enlistees in the room with us. One young man, who was sitting next to me on the bench, nervously raised his hand with a question. He asked the officer, with a trembling voice, if there was any way he could change his mind. Apparently, he had volunteered to enlist. The officer fired back with a loud voice and said the only way he could get out of it was to jump out the window of this second floor at that very moment. The officer then left the room.

I am not knowledgeable about what constitutes a nervous breakdown, but I think I was witnessing it with this young man. He broke down in tears and began sobbing loudly while bending over with his head between his knees. I felt embarrassed. I didn't know what to do or say to this boy. Everybody tried real hard to ignore what was happening. I don't know what happened to him next because we were all excused, leaving the enlistees in the room behind us. Many were shouting yippee as we left quickly and scurried for the exit doors with no sensitivity to the guys we left behind.

Sharing draft stories with friends over the years, I was struck by how spotty the physical exams were and how seemingly irrelevant factors could have a mighty impact on the results.

Attorney friend Mark Gantz told me that he had reported at five a.m. as required to his local draft board on the day of his scheduled physical, along with other prospective inductees. They were to be transported by bus to Fort Wayne for their examinations. They filled six buses and caravanned across Detroit that morning. Mark's bus was involved in an accident, which delayed his arrival at Fort Wayne by several hours. He had a doctor's letter attesting to a benign heart murmur that placed him in the gray area between acceptance and rejection—it would depend on how much weight the doctor would give the letter. By the time he got to the reviewing doctor, it was after seven in the evening. A very tired doctor read the note, looked at Mark, and asked, "Do you want to go in or not?" Surprised at being given a choice, Mark quickly said no. While some of us knew on the spot whether we had passed or failed the exam, others had to wait for the verdict. Mark did not get an immediate answer. A few weeks later, Mark received notice of a 4-F classification. Would the result have been different if the bus had delivered him to the physical on time? If the doctor wasn't so tired? Hard to say. Sure, Mark was relieved to be rejected, and the doctor's exhaustion may have worked in his favor, but how many times did it go the other way? How many times did other young men get accepted because a doctor or medic was too tired to carefully read a letter or examine them properly and just wanted to move them along?

The failure of the Selective Service and the armed forces to maintain consistent physical exam standards for draft prospects left a lot of guys wondering why one man's high blood pressure kept him out while another man's was shrugged off. Larry Dubin is a professor emeritus at the University of Detroit Mercy School of Law. He has lectured extensively on evidence, professional responsibility, and legal ethics, among other topics. He's a highly intelligent, perceptive individual with exceptional communication skills. He has produced law-related documentaries, delivered lectures, written articles and books, and served as an on-air legal "talking head" for several Detroit-area television and radio stations.

I have known Larry since the 1970s when we were both providing free legal advice at Common Ground, a walk-in crisis clinic in affluent, suburban Birmingham, Michigan, just north of Detroit. Most of the people who came in were young, high school or college students, and almost all of the legal questions we addressed were about drugs, petty crimes, evictions, and the draft. When I asked Larry if he would contribute something about his experience with the Vietnam draft, he gave it some thought and then provided me with the following.

> Even though events concerning the military draft during the Vietnam War era occurred a half century ago, the memories remain vivid. I was in my senior year of law school at the University of Michigan. My career seemed bright except for the uncertainty of my possible future participation in the military activities in Vietnam.
>
> My student deferment was coming to an end upon graduation, and my options were not well thought through. I was having a recurring nightmare of being on the battlefield, filled with unimaginable fear. I would wake up in a sweat during the night. If

Chapter Six

Larry Dubin (photo by Kitty Dubin)

drafted, would I be willing to be a soldier in a foreign land that represented an American foreign policy that made no sense to me? Or would I flee to Canada, willing to leave my own country out of principle, or fear, or perhaps both?

I tried joining the Judge Advocate General's Corps and becoming an officer and lawyer in the army, but too many law students had the same idea, and the requirement became a minimum five-year commitment. Even under those conditions, getting in as an officer was impossible under a supply-and-demand theory. However, in making my application for JAG, I was required to take an army physical. I was told to report to my draft board to be bused to Fort Wayne for the physical.

I showed up at Fort Wayne and saw about twenty other young men who had received induction notices. What struck me was that a majority of these men were either using crutches or canes, or carried big envelopes with medical information explaining why they were not suited to fight in our armed forces. When I saw what was going on and how ill-prepared I was to prove that I, too, was unsuitable for battle, I felt naked and vulnerable. That feeling became a reality when I was told to strip and go through this car-wash-type operation that tested our physical condition to be soldiers. I had to raise my arms and legs, bend over and spread cheeks, and comply with other orders given by the attending medical personnel. After an hour of this routine, I was convinced I was not well suited for army life. Yet when I came to the end of the line, all the people who had those crutches, canes, and envelopes were sent to a station to discuss their medical condition, while I was waved on to the line where I was presumed to have no predisposition that could keep me out of the armed forces. Shortly thereafter, I received my classification of 1-A.

The National Guard was also impossible to get into unless your last name was Bush (or its equivalent) and your father was in politics or you had the right connections. So where did that leave me? I got a teaching job in the business department of a state university in Ohio. My hope was that by delaying my job at the law firm that had hired me and was willing to postpone my starting date, I would get a deferment for being a college professor. After a year, I would be twenty-six and no longer eligible to be drafted.

I was shocked when President Johnson, in his buildup of the troop strength in Vietnam, ordered the elimination of many of the deferments, and I became a casualty of my own planning. I didn't get a deferment and found myself teaching under a one-year contract instead of practicing law. My plans had failed to accomplish their intended goals.

As I was finishing my year of teaching, I got another notice to come for a preinduction physical. My worst fears were now becoming a reality. I had no deferment, I was classified as 1-A, and I was one medical exam away from becoming a soldier.

I feared my return engagement with the medical examination would lead me to war, so I decided I needed to bring some medical data to help me go to the left at the end of the exam rather than to the right. My problem was that I was in good health and didn't have any legitimate medical reasons for getting a deferment. I did, however, remember that as a second-year law student, I had once gone to the school's health clinic because I was feeling anxious, and I was told that I had borderline high blood pressure. I went back to that health clinic and got a half-page report about my visit. The report didn't seem nearly as flashy as the crutches or big envelopes filled with medical reports the other guys had.

Nevertheless, I did the best I could with the little I had. I went for my medical exam with great trepidation. I remember getting to the end of the line and seeing some young men arguing with officials about how they wanted to get into the service in spite of their medical issues or their failing scores on the intelligence exam. These men gave me some hope. If I didn't want to be inducted, perhaps there were some who did.

Because of my report, I was permitted to see a medic after the physical exam. I showed him my letter, and based upon its content, he took my blood pressure. It was borderline high but not high enough to automatically get me a deferment. I was told to rest for about an hour and be retested. Nothing much changed when I was subsequently examined. I then met with another medic. He mumbled about how I was twenty-five years old and finishing law school. I could tell he wasn't sure what to do with me. Induct me then and there or exercise discretion and perhaps save my life. He finally said that he would give me a deferment that would permit me to be called for service only in the case of a national emergency. I wanted to kiss this man, but then my deferment—if I got one—would have been based on sexual preference. My blood pressure must have significantly dropped when I heard that I was a free man. I could live my life without government intervention. My life had been spared.

It's clear to me why there is no draft today. Our wars are no longer scrutinized because of the volunteer army. Although I would have liked a volunteer army when I faced the draft, I also realize that I, along with millions of other concerned college students, wouldn't have protested the war without the consequence of the draft. College students today do not have to worry about the political underpinnings of why we are going to war.

Rick Mandell was an administrative law judge in Minnesota for thirty-six years. He finished his career as the chief judge in the state's Department of Employment and Economic Development. Rick was a law student at Wayne State University with me at the height of the Vietnam War. We got to know each other through our study group and when we all played basketball together to relieve the stress of law school. While in school, he, too, was a member of the National Lawyers Guild. He opposed the war and actively protested against it, participating in demonstrations in Detroit and Washington, DC. He was trained as a draft counselor and served as such during his time as a law student.

Rick was called in for a physical in 1968. He went to the exam and presented a letter from his doctor. Rick had the classic basis for exemption: flat feet. The doctors at the physical agreed, and he received a 1-Y deferment. When the Selective Service implemented the lottery, Rick drew a high number and was not at risk. He did not hear from the draft board again until January 28, 1972, when, without asking for it, he was reclassified as 4-F. Because he failed the physical, Rick never had to create a plan B, but he recalls a conversation with his parents about possibly going to Canada "just in case." His parents were supportive and agreed that if being drafted was imminent, he should leave the country. Once Rick's flat feet were documented, he was no longer susceptible to the draft. It was over. Failing his physical gave him the freedom to visit Sweden and, while traveling there, to meet the woman who would become his wife. Had he passed his physical, a trip to Sweden would have taken on a whole different context. But to this day, Rick carries his draft card in his wallet. Why? As Rick lightheartedly answered:

> The reasons are probably multiple. For one, it has been in my wallet a long time, and I have never bothered to remove it. Another would be that it is sort of a historical document memorializing the time. A third reason would be that just in case I receive a draft notice, I can show them I'm 4-F. Of the three, the second is the most sincere.

Rick can make light of it now. Back then, it wasn't so funny. Like Rick, Larry, and so many other men, when I was found to be unqualified for military service, I was relieved, but I was also angry. I remember most of the events related to the physical exam, but I remember even more vividly the feelings of anxiety, fear, and depression over the possibility of being drafted and the unfairness of the process. I remember thinking how I—because I knew where to turn, and how to locate the resources that would help me avoid the draft—was privileged. What happened to the kids who didn't know their options or outs, the kids who would wind up serving as cannon fodder for some president's war? I was uncomfortable with the inequality and inconsistency of the draft process. Yet I know some of those boys saw the army as an opportunity, a career, a chance for an education, for learning a marketable trade, or even as a patriotic move. It was all good, unless you died in Vietnam. Was I angry because of what the war and my draft board put me through? What my country was putting me and my friends through? That people I knew, and strangers I'd never met, were getting killed because of this war? Probably yes to all of the above and a lot more.

Chapter 7

Do What You Gotta Do

Staying out of the draft sometimes meant working a little harder to make the odds more favorable. My cousin Sid Greenbaum was in a situation similar to mine. His parents, especially his mother, didn't want him anywhere near an army unit and certainly nowhere near Vietnam. Sid and I grew up together. Our parents were close (our fathers were brothers), and when we were little, we'd play together, chasing each other, watching television cartoons, or squabbling over Monopoly. Sid has always been outgoing and personable, a warm and generous individual. He's physically active, loves to hike, and is an experienced traveler. He is also very bright, with a self-deprecating sense of humor—and a raconteur par excellence. He can always make me laugh. Sid is a retired attorney and well-schooled in the art of confrontation. He has a strong personality and, as he states below, was determined to avoid conscription.

> My first awareness of the war was in my junior year at Michigan State; prior to that, I had no real knowledge of it. In my senior year, I started hearing people talking against the war. I had already registered for the draft when I turned eighteen, but I knew I was going to law school. At that time, at least the first year of school would be a deferment. I remember that a friend of mine, Eddie, had an older brother, Carl, who was married. Eddie told me that marriage got Carl an exemption. Then, when that was no longer available, you needed to have a child to get an exemption.
>
> I remember thinking, "Hell, why don't I get married?" But no one would marry me. I also remember having a conversation with

myself, putting marriage on one side of the balance and the army on the other. And since I didn't go out and buy a ring, I guess I came up on the right side of the equation there. I knew marriage was not going to be the solution.

My mother definitely did not want me to go into the army. She was frantic about the whole thing. I remember she called our rabbi and asked him about conscientious objectors and what the rules were. That got dismissed pretty quickly.

I told her, "Look, you don't have to worry. I can tell you one thing for sure: I'm not going to Vietnam. I'm not going in the military. I may have to hide in Canada; I may have to hide in America; I may wind up in a jail, but I'm not going in the military. You can worry about all the other things in life, but you can take the army right off the list. That. Will. Not. Happen."

The first year of law school was a free student deferment. I managed to get thrown out of law school at the end of the first year, so I don't know if that deferment would have continued had I stayed in school. My friend Roger had just finished his first year of law school and told me about the National Guard. He was in Indiana, and I started looking into it and found out how burdensome his commitment was—so many years. His father-in-law-to-be was a lawyer in Indiana, knew everybody, and got Roger into the Guard.

What I did find out, though, was that if you were a college grad, you could teach in the inner city of Detroit without a teaching credential, using what they called a provisional credential. That would give you a deferment since it was deemed a critical job. Whatever it was, I didn't have to go back to school for more classes. I may have needed to take a one-week program to obtain the required paperwork. I taught at a junior high on Fort Street. It was what I imagined Attica Prison to be: a war zone. There was no teaching going on. I was a math teacher, but I may as well have worn a hard hat and a flak vest. I did that for one school year, September 1968 to June 1969.

When that deferment expired, I got a doctor I know to write a letter. It took a lot of persuasion, to say the least, because I don't think there was anything wrong with me. I took that to the first physical, along with wearing my pink panties. Yup.

At the physical, there was a lot of defiance on the part of the Black men and a lot of anger and cockiness on the part of the Jewish guys. A lot of them were like, "I'm exempt; my parents belong to Tam O'Shanter or Knollwood [country clubs]; nothing bad's gonna happen to me"—implying that family connections would save them. But despite all the pretense, we were all in the same boat.

You went, you presented the letter, and they rejected you. They said go home, and then you got a notice about your status.

They didn't give me a 4-F, I know that. There was another category: 1-Y. That's what they gave me. It meant you weren't fully exempted, but if and when their threshold was low enough, they'd come and get you.

I never got called back for another physical. I finished my teaching in June 1969, then I moved to Chicago in August and started law school in '70. In between was when they had the lottery. By the time of the lottery, I was more openly opposed to this war. I had been in a few marches in Chicago before I moved there. I came close to getting my head beat in. I was in a march once where there were two columns of cops who just swooped in from both directions on the marchers, and here I am with a big bull cop on either side of me and hundreds of them in line. It was really frightening.

When I was in Chicago, I did a little anti-war counseling. I wasn't a law student there yet, but I had been for a year at Wayne State University. I did counseling in 1969 and 1970.

During the Democratic Convention in 1968, Mayor Daley gave the "shoot to kill" order. I hated that son of a bitch. He was a fascist tyrant. The street battles between the cops and the demonstrators were on worldwide television. A year later, October 1969, the Weathermen faction of Students for Democratic Society held a demonstration called the Days of Rage protesting the war. This was at the time when there was a city attorney who chased some kid. The attorney—who later became a Cook County sheriff and judge—fell, injured himself, and was paralyzed. The guy had no business chasing the kid. The kid was protesting or something; the attorney happened to be there and was particularly offended. Maybe the kid gave him the one-finger salute or something. But he chased after him and fell, and I remember thinking, "Served that fucker right."*

With regard to the march in Chicago with the two lines of cops, many years later I met and represented a Jewish man who had, as a child, been the only survivor of a pogrom in his tiny Polish village because he happened to be climbing a tree at the time and was not seen by the attackers. When he described the experience to me, I immediately flashed back to how I felt that day in Chicago. Sheer luck that he wasn't caught. Sheer luck for me, too.

In the lottery I drew number 181, and that was it. I thought it was high enough that I wouldn't be drafted.

The whole draft experience made me wonder if I am genetically cowardly. I would have gone to Canada or jail or into hiding or somewhere else. I still wanted to be a lawyer, even though I had initially flunked out of law school. I knew I would jeopardize that if I hid out in Canada or got landed immigrant papers there. I thought about those consequences, but I knew I couldn't do two years in foxholes. I knew I was not going in the damn army. Period.

I had a lawyer friend I'd met in California who enlisted in the marines. He had a disadvantaged childhood in Cleveland and looked at this as a stepping stone, as a way out. I guess it was. It ultimately provided college and law school for him. He was shipping out, and the boat was about two hundred feet from the pier when it dawned on him what he had gotten into, that he had screwed up by joining. He went to Vietnam, but he said, "You know, I was all gung ho, gung ho until that boat pulled away from shore, and then I was like 'What the fuck did I do?'" He came back, but he's now a hard-core alcoholic, and I have to wonder how much of that is the result of his Vietnam experience.

---

* Sid is referring to an incident at the Days of Rage protest in which city attorney Richard Elrod was seriously injured while chasing and tackling protester Brian Flanagan. Elrod was partially paralyzed from the neck down after the altercation. Flanagan was charged with attempted murder, aggravated battery, felonious mob action, and resisting arrest. In 1970, after a three-week jury trial and conflicting testimony, Flanagan was acquitted on all counts. (Bryan Smith, "Sudden Impact," *Chicago Magazine*, June 20, 2007.)

Sid Greenbaum (photo by Jackie Greenbaum)

I'd like to believe that my opposition to the war in Vietnam grew out of patriotism. However, I must acknowledge that my politics might have been greatly influenced by my desire to stay out of harm's way. Whichever came first, I can say with certainty that my dovish leaning, which came about when I was draft eligible, continued long after my eligibility ended.

When I look back at my life for the origin of my attitude of distrust and suspicion of government and power, I don't need a PhD in psychology to recognize that these attitudes were born of my parents' experience. They were newcomers to America when I was born in Detroit in 1945, and had narrowly escaped the Nazis when they left Vienna in late 1938. When a law professor told our class to read a case, my natural inclination was not to read the case because I didn't like someone telling me what to do, and I habitually pushed back. That would not have served me well in the military. Eventually I grew up, learned when to push back, and, more important, when not to push back. I have no regrets about the way I avoided military service.

What determines mental fitness—the kind of mental fitness that makes you malleable and suitable for participation in military activities? The Selective Service operates under the presumption that the men it calls up are able to perform their military duties. That one way or another, even if you are resistant, you can be persuaded, convinced, or coerced to take part and carry out orders. Otherwise, you're going to be a problem. They may not always want to, but in the end, soldiers obey or they are in trouble.

If a man isn't willing or able to participate, the burden is on him to make a convincing case that he is unfit to serve. This goes back to the idea that the army doesn't care what it does to you; it cares about what you could do to it. The last thing the army wants is someone who may disrupt the status quo or is just too much trouble to deal with. One pathway to being declared unfit and being rewarded with a 1-Y or 4-F classification was to be found unsuitable for other than physical reasons. That pathway can be very wide—and during the Vietnam War era, it was heavily trafficked.

Carey Binder was most recently involved in the hospitality business, an appropriate field for the outgoing and personable man he is. For more than twenty years, he and his partner, Gig Vernon, were co-owners of a bed-and-breakfast outside Bar Harbor, Maine. Two handsome, articulate, and affable men, their personalities were as much of a draw to the inn as its scenic location on the rugged Atlantic coastline. Carey speaks easily and openly about the Vietnam War. His position on the war as a draft-eligible young man in the late 1960s, and as a retiree today, has been consistent, direct, and succinct: "The war was immoral. There was no reason for us to be there."

Carey earned his degree at Brown University. At his graduation in 1969, the then national security advisor Henry Kissinger was the commencement speaker. Most of the students and many of the parents, including his, opposed the war and turned their backs to Kissinger in protest when he spoke. The draft issue confronted Carey soon after graduation. Once out of school, he lost his 2-S deferment just as Vietnam activity was peaking. Combine that with his low draft lottery number—30—and Carey was exposed.

Carey grew up in the Boston area. His parents were supporters of progressive politician Henry Wallace, the thirty-third vice president of the United States, who served under Franklin D. Roosevelt. His mother was involved with New York's liberal-leaning theater community; his father was a businessman who had served in World War II and was later active in the Business Executives Move for Vietnam Peace, a national organization opposed to the war. Carey's parents weren't comfortable with the prospects of seeing him drafted.

Carey and his father discussed the war frequently. His father was concerned about Carey being called up. "What will you do about the draft?" his father asked. "How will you avoid it?"

Not knowing exactly how to do it, but definitely looking to resist induction, Carey initially considered leaving the country. He thought about establishing residence in Canada and then going on to Denmark, where he had been a high school exchange student for a year. However, Denmark was not receptive to US draft-avoiding immigrants. His father asked him if he would go to a psychiatrist if he found one who was sympathetic. "You must have some issues that could keep you out of the army," he suggested. His father suspected Carey was gay. In fact, he was but had not yet come out about his homosexuality.

His father's comment made sense to Carey. Rather than passively hope for the best, he decided to find a reason to be rejected by the Selective Service. He started looking at various options and realized a psychiatric diagnosis could ultimately be a good out. He decided to seek out a psychiatrist for a letter that would make him an unappealing candidate. "There were several shrinks in my area, Newton, Massachusetts, who were writing such letters for a fee, but the Selective Service knew which local doctors were inclined to do this, and their letters weren't always respected," Carey told me. However, he found a psychiatrist in Newton who was not well known to the Selective Service. The shrink said, "I won't lie, but I will focus on certain traits that might keep you out of the army." After interviewing Carey, the shrink wrote a letter that stated Carey was gay and should not serve in the military.

The psychiatrist's statement was not unusual. Many doctors were sympathetic to the plight of draft-eligible young men, yet honest and accurate in their medical assessments. Doctors who opposed the war could look for conditions or disabilities that would give a man a 1-Y or 4-F classification. Writing a bogus letter could put doctors at risk with their respective medical associations and conceivably lead to a suspension or loss of license. Physicians who wrote too many letters could also be noticed by the Selective Service physicians and lose credibility; their letters could be ignored. Still, there were doctors who would write a disqualifying letter for a fee.

Carey took the letter to his physical, where a panel of three doctors reviewed it. Since so many people were bringing notes from psychiatrists, they were a little suspicious; however, his letter was ultimately honored. Several days later, he got a 4-F classification in the mail.

Carey had a definite impression of the physical process:

> It was a perfect display of classism. We were divided into shirts and skins. The shirts were from Newton—White, middle-class. The skins were from Dorchester—working-class. When we were asked, "Who has letters?," almost everyone from Newton did; only two from Dorchester did. When I got my 4-F, I was relieved and guilt-ridden. I'd seen the dichotomy of socioeconomics: the poor Blacks and Whites were the ones sent to fight. In retrospect, I have no regrets about avoiding the draft, but I would have been more than happy to do some type of universal service if it had been offered as an alternative to the military. I'm not sure I would have done anything differently, though leaving the country might have been a braver alternative than paying for medical attention. But I carry some guilt over getting out of something others could not get out of.

This ultimately became a common refrain among the men I spoke with: pleased to get out, while feeling guilty that someone had to take their place.

Interaction with a local Selective Service board should not have been difficult or confusing, but based on my interviews, confusion and inconsistency were the norm—maybe not so much in terms of the inner workings of the local board but certainly more so regarding communications with the registrants. In addition, at times the local board was determined to handle registrants its way regardless of information it had from its military cousins. I heard several stories from men in different parts of the country about the relationship between the local draft boards and the US Army Reserve. At times, a man had to push back.

For example, Daniel Stede, now retired, was a sales executive at an East Coast plumbing supply company. When he graduated college, he was reclassified 1-A and realized he would soon be facing the draft. His parents were neutral about the war, but when they saw it could have a direct impact on their son, they wanted him to avoid the draft and Vietnam, agreeing that even leaving the country would be acceptable. While he was mulling over various options—enlist and choose his fate, go to Canada or Europe, or just take his chances with the draft—he was called for a physical. The examination itself was superficial. At that time, Daniel didn't know he had a heart murmur, and the army doctors didn't notice anything wrong. He passed the physical. Then, realizing that being drafted into the army might not be the best choice, Daniel's parents were able to connect him with a retired army general who had contacts in the reserve. Daniel met with the man, impressed him favorably, and was able to join a local reserve unit.

Once inducted, Daniel was designated for basic training at Fort Leonard Wood in Missouri; however, before he could go, he began having some medical issues. A doctor diagnosed him with a heart murmur—more specifically, a valve problem that would probably need repair or replacement at some point in the not-too-distant future. He received a medical discharge from the reserves and that terminated his brief military career. End of story. Or so he thought.

The draft board saw it differently. As far as they were concerned, Daniel was still 1-A. They ordered him to report for another physical. He called the board and explained his stint in the reserve and the medical discharge. The board said they were aware of that, but it didn't matter because the reserve is separate from the regular army and he needed to go through the army's process; after all, the board said, the army might see it differently. Daniel suggested the two entities talk to each other. He refused to go to the physical and cut off all further contact with the board. He was upset with the process, his health, and how it would all play out. About six weeks later, he received a 4-F classification. One can surmise that someone at the board finally looked into the situation and reached the sensible conclusion. The lack of communication between the two military entities—whether limited to a few draft boards and reserve units across the country or symptomatic of a bigger issue—shines a light on the inefficiencies of the bureaucracy that existed and how those silos could exacerbate a young man's anxiety and frustration.

Chapter 8

Hiding in Plain Sight

While some individuals resigned themselves to the perceived inevitability of the draft, others were determined to follow whatever path was necessary to beat it. Frequently, this required a compromise with the ethical self. How far would you go to avoid the service? What would you risk? What price were you willing to pay? What laws were you willing to break? For some, bending the law, if not actually breaking it, was fully justified. One solution: make your files disappear.

Al Stern is a friend from high school. A retired biochemist, Al now lives in Washington State. He's a good guy with an idiosyncratic and strong personality. We got to know each other in our senior year when we walked together to school. We also worked together at summer camp. Al is a fit outdoorsman who has always enjoyed canoeing, camping, and hiking and is now an accomplished photographer. He is very much his own person, a man with a distinctive way of seeing the world. He has always been well respected by his peers. And he was not one to let the Selective Service make life decisions for him.

No way was Al going to fight in Vietnam. No way was he going to be drafted. No way was he going to be cannon fodder in a bad war. But if his draft board was going to bust his balls, he would bust theirs. As Al puts it:

> I would have avoided military service under any circumstances. The Vietnam War was particularly awful from any point of view—ethical, philosophical, political, strategic, tactical, legal. This was a war of

Chapter Eight

Al Stern during the Vietnam War era (courtesy of Al Stern)

choice that stupidly replaced the racist French colonial occupiers with Americans and was fought brutally and illegally by the United States.

The number of United States military fighting this war began to increase dramatically as I reached draft age and started college in 1963. By 1965 military manpower requirements depended on a large number of draftees. The draft was universal, but the rules were arbitrary and contained many categories of individuals that could not be drafted (student, head of family, conscientious objector, etc.).

The student deferment was one example of White privilege that could increase the proportion of minorities in the military and reduce opposition to the war at college campuses.

I lost my deferment in May 1967 when I graduated from the University of Michigan. During the last part of that year, I received a letter from my draft board saying I was reclassified to 1-A and had to report for a physical that would determine whether I actually would be drafted. My vague backup plan was to move to Canada, but first I would try to prove I was medically unfit for military service. I knew people who had been classified 4-F after doctors wrote letters documenting various physical problems or psychiatrists said they were nuts. I don't know if it was chutzpah or stupidity, but I decided to convince the military doctors myself.

Going past the military police guardhouse at the entrance to the Fort Wayne army base in Detroit was frightening. I had entered enemy territory. All morning hundreds of scared young men were herded, dressed only in their underwear, to military doctors at stations devoted to one simple test or another—blood pressure, turn your head and cough, etc. Most of the morning was spent waiting in lines. The military certainly knew how to make us feel scared and powerless—impotent. To my dismay, bad feet and an allergy to bee stings didn't impress the doctors.

A medical deferment seemed doubtful, but at least we were able to wear clothes for the remainder of the day. I didn't try to fail the aptitude test, since the questions appeared to require no more than a third-grade education.

The next part of the exam ostensibly was designed to identify recruits who were unsuitable because of subversive tendencies. I thought I was certain to be discovered. Organizations designated subversive by the attorney general were listed, followed by questions about involvement with these organizations—similar to the House Un-American Activities Committee [HUAC] hearings. To some questions, e.g., "Did you ever attend parties or other social gatherings with members of these organizations?" I answered, "I don't know. I was just trying to meet women and didn't ask about politics." My response to several questions was "I refuse to answer based on the First Amendment." I didn't feel guilty about anything so I didn't want to invoke the Fifth Amendment. This was silly, but I was getting angrier and more defiant as the day progressed. My answers pissed off the large sergeant administering the test. He loudly observed that I was the only person in the room of about two hundred people who had answered any of the questions "incorrectly." He stood over me and screamed the "correct" answer for each question. When I refused to change any of my answers, he sent for a lieutenant who did the same thing and then sent for a captain. When the captain walked away, the testing continued as if nothing had happened. Unfortunately, none of this disqualified me from the draft. Apparently the goal was actually to force political correctness rather than screen the pool of recruits.

Lastly, we filled out a medical history, including a series of questions probing psychological fitness for military service. I admitted I took a lot of drugs and checked other categories that might indicate psychological problems. My reward was an appointment to speak to an army psychiatrist a few weeks later. Finally, some progress.

Chapter Eight

I didn't want to appear normal, so I was high on LSD when a friend drove me back to Fort Wayne for my psychiatric appointment. There was a lot of activity on the base this time. Some of the anti-war activists demonstrating at the entrance had snuck onto the base and were trying to disrupt draft physicals. Military police were capturing them, and some were beaten. I was sympathetic to the cause but not suicidal, so I just picked up the forms from my previous visit and waited to see the psychiatrist. After the obligatory long wait, the interview with the psychiatrist probably lasted thirty to forty minutes. As proof of my incompatibility with military life, I took a tablet of LSD out of my pocket, explained what it was, and swallowed it. The psychiatrist said he agreed I would be a bad influence on other soldiers, but that's why the army built brigs. It was clear to both of us who controlled the outcome of this confrontation. I suspect that he may have given me a deferral if my ego had allowed me to act more like I actually felt—a lot less defiant and much more scared.

All that remained was to wait in a long line before turning in the forms that guaranteed I would be drafted. While I was standing at the back of the line, stealing the forms suddenly seemed like a better option. Theft was a conscious option as soon as I received the packet of forms the first time I was on the base. The certainty of being drafted if I didn't steal them made my fear of being caught irrelevant. The bureaucracy had a record that I had kept my appointment. If they couldn't find my physical, they might assume it just was misplaced. In any case, the penalty for getting caught probably would be to be drafted. Catch-22 logic turned on the military itself. I put the forms under my heavy winter coat and walked off the base with my arms folded in front of me so the forms wouldn't fall out.

For a ride home, I called a friend from the pay phone in the bar across the street. I had to get change for a dollar from the bartender. The bar was very warm, but I couldn't remove my jacket because the place was full of MPs getting drunk before dark. The forms were starting to slip out the bottom of my coat, so I had to lean on the bar while getting money out of my wallet.

I didn't hear from the draft board for about six months. Then

I received a letter informing me that I was required to take another physical. No mention of the file I had stolen. I waited a couple of months to tell the draft board that I had moved to San Francisco, waited a couple of months to respond to the next letter, etc. By fall 1969 I had an appointment, this time at a warehouse in Emeryville, California. I used the same general plan as for the first physical, but some of the details changed. This time I didn't sleep for a couple days (Dexedrine) and had a friend who was a former junkie put needle tracks on my arms. I also showed up three hours late. I shouldn't have bothered with such puny attempts to fail. The Selective Service struggled to fill the army manpower requirements for the war. In 1967 it seemed like anyone who could walk was in good enough shape physically to be drafted. By 1969 you didn't even have to be conscious. One inductee was asleep the entire time I was there (several hours). Nobody seemed to think that was odd, and he passed the physical. A doctor checked my heart by touching a stethoscope to my chest for less than a second. There was no undressing. There were no HUAC questions. The documentation was only a couple of pages.

We were supposed to hand the exam form to a security guard as we exited the front door. I rolled mine into my jacket—a thin nylon shell this time—and looked for another way out of the building. All the fire exits were illegally locked. Apparently I wasn't the only potential inductee who stole paperwork. There was no other choice, so I walked out the front door, waving at the guard. He didn't wave back, but he also didn't try to stop me.

The first Vietnam War–era draft lottery was December 1, 1969. The lottery pool included all men born between 1944 and 1950. My birthday was drawn on the 240th pick. The highest number drafted was 195. That was my last interaction with the Selective Service System.

I didn't think about patriotism when I dodged the draft, but if someone had asked, I probably would have claimed it was patriotic to oppose your country's policies if you thought they were wrong. However, that is not how the concept is understood by most Americans. The pervasive requirement that people behave patriotically is just a widely accepted form of political correctness that coerces support for militarism, colonialism, capitalism, and racism. Being labeled unpatriotic is fine with me. Sticks and stones...

Al expressed to me that he is happy that all those years ago it was his belief that the Selective Service did not store registrants' records electronically.

Larry Zeldner, a semiretired financial advisor now living in Seattle, was another one of the guys who registered at Local Board 179 in Detroit, under the auspices of Miss Modelski. I'd known Larry from our neighborhood in Detroit. In 1968, while I was living in Los Angeles, Larry and a couple of mutual friends visited me. They were delivering a large passenger van to San Francisco and invited me to drive up the Pacific Coast Highway with them to the Bay Area. I hopped into the van and we took off. It was a memorable trip. We picked up every hitchhiker we could fit in, told stories along the way, wandered through Big Sur, flashed the peace sign wherever we went, and probably broke a boatload of controlled substance laws en route. Once we got to San Francisco, we went our separate ways. I went to visit friends in Haight-Ashbury. Larry opted to stay in another part of the Bay Area.

In 1969 Larry was still in San Francisco. He was doing odd jobs and just trying to get by at a time when he described himself as being "emotionally off-balance." The Vietnam War was expanding, and he decided to enlist in the army. He thought it might help stabilize him. As he said, "It was an unhappy time in my life, and I was desperate to find myself. I thought the army, the discipline, might help." He filled out all the papers, and the recruiter told him to come back the next day and he would be inducted.

That night he saw his close friend Al Stern (yes, the same Al Stern you just read about who *twice* walked out of a physical exam with his file) and told him about enlisting. Al wouldn't hear of it. He didn't want Larry to go and was emphatic about it. They got drunk, argued, and then got into a physical fight—a wrestling match. Apparently the bout changed Larry's mind: he didn't go back the next day to enlist. Regarding the contest, Al said, "It wasn't much of a fight. I won easily. At least that's how I remember it."

Larry's official residence was Detroit, and in 1969, while still in San Francisco, he received a notice to appear at Fort Wayne for a physical. He flew back to Detroit and went to the physical without any doctor's note or other document designed to qualify him for an exemption. At every medical station, his papers were stamped "passed." Nearing the end of the exam process and no longer remotely interested in serving in the military, he realized he could soon become a prime candidate for induction. "Walking in a line to the last station, I spotted the hall where we had started that morning," Larry said. "I snuck out of line and went to my locker. I got my stuff, took my file, and walked out. I went home and burned it all in the fireplace." Ironic, considering this tactic was similar to the one employed by his friend Al and completely unbeknownst at the time to Larry, because Al wasn't publicizing his actions to anyone.

Larry heard nothing from the Selective Service for two years. He was living in Seattle when, in 1971, the Selective Service apparently reconstructed his file and caught up with him. The board ordered him to show up for another physical, this time in Seattle. He was living in a commune at the time. The night before the physical, his housemates painted his body and covered his crotch and hair with peanut butter. He planned on going to the physical that way, but he dozed off and slept through his appointment. There was no immediate reaction from the Selective Service.

Larry decided the time might be right to tour the world. He made his way to New York City, boarded an Icelandic Airlines flight without incident, stopped in Reykjavík, and flew on to Europe. While traveling around the continent, he was hired to drive a car from Istanbul to Tehran. Once Larry delivered the car in Iran, he decided to continue on to Afghanistan and went to the US Embassy in Tehran to get the appropriate visa. In the process, an embassy clerk recognized his name from an alert list and told Larry that the FBI was looking for him. The clerk advised Larry that it would be better for him to turn himself in. Larry was torn between going home or continuing his journey. He opted to go home, went to the FBI, and was promptly arrested for draft evasion. He was interviewed by two agents who

Chapter Eight

Larry Zeldner (photo by Ivana Rozekova)

offered to drop the charges if he went for the physical. He agreed and submitted to the physical. He later found out that the FBI had gone to his parents' house looking for him while he was traveling in Europe. His mother wouldn't let them in or talk to them. He told me she shooed them away.

By then, Larry was vehemently opposed to the war. He had written on his physical questionnaire that he reacted violently to any authority (a lie). At the physical he was interviewed by a psychiatrist. The psychiatrist had a heavy glass snow globe on his desk. Nonchalantly, Larry picked it up and started walking around the office with it, intending to make the shrink a little nervous. He succeeded. The psychiatrist became uncomfortable, apprehensive about what Larry might be capable of doing. Larry never put down the snow globe. Very quickly, the jumpy psychiatrist rejected him with a 4-F classification.

Was it really that easy to be rejected? Maybe. But Larry believed the army also didn't want him because he was older and not quite so easy to mold. "When you're eighteen or nineteen, you're more malleable. Once we become anti-war *and* older, they don't want us so much," he said.

In 1974 Larry returned to Seattle. "It was like a last chance to think things through and straighten myself out," he said. It worked. He eventually opted to go home and earned a bachelor's degree in English from Michigan State University.

"I did not let the draft run or ruin my life," Larry said. "I paid zero attention to it until I was confronted by it. I was very fucked up and concerned about life in general, not the draft."

Larry said he has no shame or regret for the past but he does retain some mixed feelings. "I don't want to gloat that I avoided the draft. I have respect for those who went. It was sad to see returning vets treated with scorn. So many came back all fucked up." Then he clarified his comment: "I actually do have one minor regret: I'm sorry I didn't finish my trip around the world. It's not so easy to go to Afghanistan today."

Chapter 9

Questions of Conscience

Conscientious objector status could sometimes keep you out of the military, sometimes not. A CO is generally regarded as someone who is opposed to serving in the armed forces or bearing arms on the grounds of moral or religious principles. During the Vietnam War, a great many men suddenly discovered they were COs. Before the war, it had never occurred to many of them that their beliefs might disqualify them for service. Men subject to the Vietnam War draft sometimes saw conscientious objection less of an ethical or moral stand than as a legal way out of service. As they came closer to being inducted, they believed that their religious or personal principles could keep them off the battlefield and out of danger—but that was not always true.

It was up to the local board to decide, depending on the evidence a man presented, whether to grant CO status. However, even if unsuccessful, the process of applying for CO status and the accompanying paperwork, hearings, and appeals could, at the very least, delay conscription. Draft lawyers could be extremely effective in prolonging those delays.

The current Selective Service definition of a conscientious objector is someone who is

> opposed to serving in the armed forces and/or bearing arms on the grounds of moral or religious principles.... Beliefs which qualify a registrant for CO status may be religious in nature, but don't have to be. Beliefs may be moral or ethical; however, a man's reasons for not wanting to participate in a war must not be based on politics,

expediency, or self-interest. In general, the man's lifestyle prior to making his claim must reflect his current claims.*

Men who applied for CO status were in notable company. Over the years, well-known American figures, including essayist Henry David Thoreau, actor Lew Ayres, and boxer Muhammad Ali, were all COs. However, to be granted CO classification, it wasn't enough to simply declare your opposition to war or state that you were a pacifist. A man had to be ready to prove to his draft board that his convictions were sincere, and the board had plenty of skeptics and a lot of leeway in granting CO status, especially when they thought that too many young men were suddenly getting religion or formulating new personal moral philosophies. In addition, during a time of intense manpower demands, such as the Vietnam War era, there can be increased pressure on local boards to be less receptive to CO claims.

Once a man registered for the Selective Service, he could apply for CO status. A man making such a claim would be required to appear before the local board to explain his beliefs. He could support his case with documents, personal writings, and appearances or testimony by people who could vouch for his claims—members of the clergy or credible associates, for example. He would have to explain his beliefs, how he acquired them, and the impact those beliefs had on his life, not only as they related to war. It was then up to the board to decide whether to issue a CO classification. If CO status was denied, the man could ask for a review by a Selective Service Appeal Board and, following procedural rules, take his case all the way to the National Appeal Board and even the courts.

According to Selective Service records, between 1965 and 1970 more than 170,000 men received CO status. Unconfirmed reports assert that in 1972, there were more CO applicants than actual draftees.

Men granted CO status generally served two-year terms in a noncombatant military role or some form of alternative civilian service, generally far from home. A man with a 1–0 classification

---

* Selective Service System, "Conscientious Objectors," accessed August 3, 2023, https://www.sss.gov/conscientious-objectors/.

(conscientious objector available for civilian work contributing to the national health, safety, or interest) might fall under the Selective Service's Alternative Service Program and find himself doing a job, often menial, that somehow contributed to the maintenance of national health care, safety, or other vital interests, which could involve working in education, social services, or conservation. Someone with 1-A-0 (conscientious objector available only for noncombatant service) status could serve in the army as a medic, clerk, or some other role that did not require using a weapon. But immunity from danger was not guaranteed. Many CO medics found themselves where there was the greatest demand for their services: in combat zones. Clearly there wasn't quite as much need for medics away from the battlefield. Corporal Thomas William Bennet and Specialist Fourth Class Joseph G. LaPoint Jr. were two stand-out COs who served as medics, saw heavy combat, and were recognized for their courage. Both died in Vietnam in 1969. Bennet was killed in action after repeatedly exposing himself to danger to treat the wounded. LaPoint was also killed in action while treating the wounded. Both men received Congressional Medals of Honor posthumously. LaPoint was also honored with a Silver Star.

As the war escalated, more men began to ask about attaining CO status. They wanted to know what made a person a CO. Was it religious conviction, personal moral tenets, or—that unspoken bugaboo—cowardice? For CO status, a man's beliefs could be based on religion, but this wasn't always a prerequisite. The CO definition evolved. Whereas at one time an atheist could not claim CO status, that requirement, as Alix Kates Shulman pointed out, eventually fell by the wayside. Timing was almost everything. Depending on when one applied for CO status, an individual's personal morals or ethics could be sufficient grounds for CO classification. An individual's lifestyle before being called up was generally the basis for the decision regarding a CO classification. In other words, sincerity of belief was critical.

Plenty of young men had good reason to apply for CO status. Bert Torino tussled with the possibility of doing so, as the reader may recall from chapter 6. I met Bert around 1995 when I was working in advertising. There were about a dozen of us freelancers—writers, art directors, designers—all working independently and then teaming up when we needed each other's help on a project. Bert was a master of the digital world. If something involved computer graphics or digital technology of any sort, we turned to Bert. When the VoIP phone system went down, a computer went on the fritz, or new software puzzled us, for example, Bert always had a solution. Besides that, he was a nice guy—quiet and unassuming, easygoing, and one heck of a musical talent. Behind that reserved demeanor was a gifted guitarist and composer who spent many of his nonworking hours creating and playing his music. It was a treat to listen to him play and an honor when he chose to gift you with one of his personally recorded CDs. When I approached him about the Vietnam War era, I didn't know what I would get. I found out Bert had chosen a difficult path.

> When the draft lottery was announced, it really caused a disruption in my life. My number was 27, which meant I would be drafted for sure. My brother's number was 2; so he and a buddy ran down to the recruitment office and signed up for the navy the very next day. I took a different approach. A number of years before this draft lottery was announced, I was seriously considering filing for conscientious objector status. I had a long time to think about it. I thought as long as I could get a student deferment, I would not have to worry about filing.
>
> The draft lottery eliminated student deferments, so I would either have to flee the country or file as a CO. It was time to file. I wanted to face up to my convictions and take whatever consequences my beliefs would bring. Being brought up Catholic played an important role in forming my conscience: I really developed a respect for life and could not be trained to kill. I could not purposely take someone's life. My feeling was since most wars are not just wars, it was not a matter of self-defense to be an instrument of war. I was acutely aware of all the political and historical events that led up to the US involvement in Vietnam, which I strongly objected to. I was willing to be assigned to noncombat duty, such as a medic, or spend time in jail for my convictions if that was my fate.

The process of filing for conscientious objector was very time-consuming. On top of school and work, I had to get letters from my pastor, family, and close relatives by going to them one by one and having a face-to-face discussion about my beliefs. Only then could they write a letter. I had to go to counseling sessions on how to file and how to conduct an interview with the Selective Service if and when they finally called me to come before them. Then when my application was submitted, I had to wait anxiously for the Selective Service to grant me that status or not. I had finally acted on my convictions. I wasn't standing on the sidelines anymore. I made my stand.

For some reason, I never heard from the Selective Service after filing the application. I waited for months and months with no response from the government. My wife knew the consequences of a summons that could arrive in the mail on any day in the form of a simple letter. This letter could completely change my life. I could end up as a medic in the military or end up in jail for a couple years. She married me knowing that this was a near-future event that was hanging over our heads. I felt a sense of paralysis until this was resolved. It really created an uncertainty and tension in our marriage. Discussing it frequently and reassuring each other that I did the right thing helped us to pull through.

Finally, the war in Vietnam ended. Around the same time the draft also ended. I finally dropped a number of classes—from full-time down to two—just to handle going to work and going to school at the same time. This whole unpleasant episode in my life slowly faded away, even though it still plagued my conscience.

The Selective Service's draft policy really affected my life. I had to work through school with a partial grant and loan the first two years. I was working my way into my chosen profession—medical illustration—through the back door while going to college. This meant I had to work full time and go to school full time. Overtime in my job caused me to miss classes, and it threatened my full-time student deferment for the draft because of conflict of schedules. I even took a couple of classes to keep my full-time student status, sometimes getting a D and barely passing the course because I missed so many class periods. I even got incompletes that had to be made up by taking, and paying for, the class all over again.

This was dragging my grade average down at a rapid rate. I was usually a solid B+ student. My health was rapidly declining too. I was putting in so many hours between work and school that I was not eating very well. I would get home about eleven thirty at night after taking a bus for forty-five minutes from the Wayne State campus to St. Clair Shores where my parents lived. I had to find cold leftovers from dinner; sometimes there wasn't any food left over. I come from a family of ten kids, me being the second oldest. My family was struggling economically at that time. I had to work to pay my way through college. I didn't really make enough money to eat out at restaurants very often and went many times without meals. If the Selective Service was not putting these kinds of pressures on me to maintain my student deferment, then I would have proceeded at a more logical pace with smarter choices about how to use my time, and how to make it through school. However, I had to keep from being drafted. The student deferment and a CO were my only choices at the time.

Despite the fact that the Selective Service eliminated the marriage deferment, my steady girlfriend of four and a half years and I decided to get married. It was short notice. We only had a few months to plan. We wanted a small wedding. We didn't want to impose a financial burden on our families. My parents agreed to have a potluck wedding at our house. A date was set. Everything was planned. The announcement went out to family and friends. Then about a month before the wedding, I received a letter from the Selective Service saying that I had to show up for a physical the day of my wedding. We had to postpone our wedding date by two days and send new invitations hoping the delay would not cause too many problems for our guests who already committed to the earlier date. Luckily most of them showed up.

After the age of twenty-six, I convinced myself not to worry as much because the age of draftees was between eighteen and twenty-six. Even though the draft had ended years before, my mind could not shake off these insecurities. By the age of thirty, I decided to stop worrying about it and get on with my life. However, until recently I carried my Selective Service card in my wallet. Just a few weeks ago, I decided to make room in my wallet by shredding the card.

The underlying fear, all these years, is that the government has more control over my life in ways that run contrary to my own desires and destiny. This feeling has stayed with me for a very long time.

Bert is semiretired now. He still brings his computer skills to the office from time to time, but music, family, and peace of mind are his priorities.

When pursuing CO status, a man facing his draft board had to be prepared for anything, from friendly questioning to intense interrogation. It all depended on the mood of the board members, the personalities involved, and the pressure on the board to produce draftable bodies. Questions focused on the man's personal attitudes and values and the application of those beliefs regarding lifestyle, the use of force, views on military service, and more. From conversations I had with interviewees, draft counselors, and attorneys at the time I was susceptible to the draft, I learned that typical questions could include

- Why can't you serve in the military?
- What are your beliefs that qualify you for CO status?
- When did you develop your beliefs?
- When did you begin living by them?
- How do they affect your life?
- Do you live by your principles? How?
- Are you afraid to fight?
- Are you a pacifist?
- Is this the only war you object to?
- What do you think are your obligations to your country?
- What would you do if you were physically attacked? If your family were attacked?
- Does your family share your values?
- Do you have friends who share your values?
- Does your spouse adhere to the same beliefs?
- Does your spouse support you?
- What makes you believe your thinking is right?

- Who has influenced your thinking?
- Do you have friends or relatives who are conscientious objectors?
- Are you willing to go to jail for your beliefs?
- What could change your beliefs?
- Which jobs are you willing to do in the military?
- Which alternative civilian jobs can you take on?
- What will you do if your request is rejected?

The questions could sometimes wander far afield. The same question could be asked in several ways. It all depended on your local draft board members and how receptive or hostile they were to you. While the CO examination could be interpreted as an effort to test the sincerity of a man's beliefs, it could also be a genuine test of endurance: How much were you willing to put up with to demonstrate the earnestness of your convictions? That was, in essence, what the draft board was trying to determine. Are your beliefs a matter of convenience or conviction? And if conviction, how firm?

While some men never went through the entire CO application and interrogation process, many others doggedly took it all the way. One was Erick Ryberg.

Erick and I met several years ago at a dinner party. In casual conversation that drifted to attitudes about the Vietnam War, I gathered Erick had pursued a CO exemption. I wanted to learn more about his thinking and asked him if he would speak with me about it.

We got together on a warm and sunny May afternoon at his comfortable home in suburban Detroit. The beautifully adorned house is set back from a busy highway, protected by a surround of trees, shrubs, and well-tended gardens that keep traffic and road noise at a distance. The environment seemed to match Erick's temperament: composed, relaxed, thoughtful.

In our conversation, I learned Erick was raised in Grosse Pointe, Michigan, and attended the University of Michigan in Ann Arbor. He graduated in 1969 with a bachelor's degree in psychology. Today he is a semiretired psychotherapist.

When Erick graduated high school in 1965, he wanted to tour

Europe, as I did, but was reminded that he was required to register for the draft. He did so at Local Board 87. Erick didn't get to Europe that summer, but that fall he did begin attending the University of Michigan and received a 2-S student classification and deferment. While in Ann Arbor, he took part in protests against the war and was sympathetic to, but not a member of, the campus chapter of Students for a Democratic Society.

After graduating from Michigan, Erick applied to the Peace Corps. He was accepted and initially sent to Malaysia. He requested reassignment to Western Africa and returned home pending the relocation. Not hearing anything in a timely manner from the Peace Corps, Erick contacted them repeatedly regarding his relocation and finally learned that the Peace Corps had lost his file (he found out later it had fallen between two cabinets). While this was going on, and because he had graduated, the Selective Service reclassified him as 1-A, making him immediately susceptible to military induction. But then Erick's situation changed. Given the Peace Corps' delays, he had moved on with his life. He was now married, enrolled in graduate school at the University of Michigan, and had regained his 2-S student deferment. Since he was pursuing his studies, Erick declined the Peace Corps' belated offer of an assignment in Senegal. Then, as graduate student deferments evaporated, Erick's draft classification returned to 1-A. He was now in school with no Peace Corps option to possibly keep him out of the army, and again in peril of being drafted.

All along, Erick thought the Vietnam War was immoral and illegal. He decided to apply for CO status. Erick had been raised Catholic and spent three years in a seminary, but he did not use religion as the basis for his application. Instead, he staked his claim on his personal belief system. He represented himself to his draft board as agnostic and laid out his beliefs in a logical, clear, and well-written presentation. In his brief, he concluded with, "I may be an agnostic, but I have a personal moral belief system that is rooted in my religious foundation but no longer justified by an institutional creed." Erick unequivocally asserted he could not participate in the war.

Erick's family had exposure to the military during World War II.

Erick Ryberg (photo by Amy Ryberg)

His father was in the army. Two uncles served in the navy; one was a diver. Another uncle was a decorated marine who served in the South Pacific. However, no family members were involved in the Vietnam War, and his family was not opposed to his efforts to avoid the draft.

A CO hearing at his local board was set for March 6, 1970. It was postponed because Erick had an induction physical scheduled the same day at Fort Wayne. He went to his physical and passed. Induction into the service was held in abeyance until his CO request could be resolved. The hearing was rescheduled for April, then changed to May. He went to the hearing accompanied by his father-in-law, a lawyer, and stated his case. He was denied CO status and retained his 1-A classification. Erick then appealed the decision and a hearing was scheduled for June. Again there were postponements and finally the hearing was held in August 1970.

At the hearing, Erick again made his case and reaffirmed his position. In essence, the *CliffsNotes* version of his appeal was "I cannot in good conscience serve in the military or hurt my fellow man." He then went home to wait for the board's decision.

A few weeks later, he received a letter notifying him that by a 3-0 vote, he had been awarded CO (1-O) status. In retrospect, Erick said, "I was confident I would qualify as a conscientious objector, but it was still quite a surprise."

He attributes his success to the logical and obviously persuasive argument he presented to the board. He never heard from them again. If he had not received CO status, Erick says he would have gone to England, where his sister had been living since 1963. Fortunately, he admits, it didn't come to that.

When I met with Erick, I was impressed with how much thought he gave to each of my questions. No quick, glib replies. He was very deliberate with his responses, thinking them through, weighing his words to make sure they conveyed exactly what he wanted to communicate. I also got the distinct notion that long-dormant issues were coming to the forefront. Erick mentioned that as a psychotherapist he'd counseled many Vietnam War veterans who continue to be emotionally tied to those days. "The guys I saw in my practice never took issue with my stand on the war, all they asked was if I had served, and I told them my story. I realize that many of us from that time have never totally left that era behind us. It left its mark, sometimes with scars and sometimes with a never-ending belief that we can choose a better course."

We traded several emails after our initial meeting. In one of our exchanges, Erick forwarded to me an excerpt from *On Killing: The Psychological Cost of Learning to Kill in War and Society* by former US Army Ranger and paratrooper Lieutenant Colonel Dave Grossman. The book discusses war studies by Brigadier General S. L. A. Marshall that include the debatable thought that most soldiers are reluctant to fire their weapons when confronted by the enemy. Grossman relied on Marshall's studies from several wars to address the issue that most men harbor a resistance to killing their fellow man. (In response, the military has developed techniques to break down a soldier's reluctance to kill.) Assuming this is true and that killing isn't easy for many men, is it so surprising that a man would request CO status and base it on his personal value system and an inability to kill? Proper justification for the CO request, perhaps? One could say that the more impersonal a war is—bombs dropped from great heights, missiles and rockets launched from vast distances, armed drones dispatched from ships or control centers miles away from the battlefield on faceless enemies—the easier it is to distance yourself from actual killing and perhaps be able to sleep at night. But come face-to-face with the enemy and the situational equation could change.

The Selective Service Act, passed in 1948 and amended in 1951, required conscientious objection to be based on a religious belief that included faith in a Supreme Being. Supreme Court cases have since modified the basis for conscientious objection. In 1965 the court ruled in *United States v. Seeger* that formal religious training was no longer a CO requisite.* Being a member of a traditional pacifist religious group, for instance Quakers or Jehovah's Witnesses, would not be required for CO status. The court accepted and upheld the argument that individual religious beliefs must be considered in determining a man's CO situation. The court also accepted for the first time pacifist variations of common religious expression such as Judaism, Islam, and Buddhism. However, the local boards still had the power and option to interpret the ruling as they believed appropriate. And atheists were still out of luck.

Atheists were brought into the fold when the entire religious condition was removed in *Welsh v. United States.*† In that case, the court ruled that an objection to military service based on a deeply held personal ethical system—with no reference to a Supreme Being—was acceptable; "depth and fervency" of personal belief was sufficient. However, in 1971 in *Gillette v. United States*, the court narrowed the CO window by stating that an individual—whether religious or atheist—could not gain CO status by objecting to a particular war, a decision that affected thousands of objectors to the Vietnam War.‡

One of the best known CO cases involved three-time World Heavyweight Champion Muhammad Ali. Known as Cassius Clay at the time, Ali was classified 1-A in 1966 and applied for CO status because of his Black Muslim faith and his commitment to the teachings of the Holy Koran. He embellished his position with a now-famous statement, "I ain't got no quarrel with the Vietcong. No Vietcong ever called me nigger." His local draft board viewed his beliefs as insincere and denied the CO application. After refusing to be inducted, Ali was indicted by a federal grand jury and subsequently convicted by an all-White trial jury of violating Selective Service laws by refusing to be drafted. He was sentenced to

---

* United States v. Seeger, 380 U.S. 163 (1965).
† Welsh v. United States, 398 U.S. 333 (1970).
‡ Gillette v. United States, 401 U.S. 437 (1971).

five years in prison and fined $10,000. He was also stripped of his heavyweight title. Ever the fighter, Ali refused to give up. He took his case to the Court of Appeals, lost there too, but again refused to give up and appealed his conviction to the Supreme Court. In 1971, in *Clay v. United States*, his conviction was overturned by a vote of 8–0, with Justice Thurgood Marshall abstaining due to his previous involvement in the case as an official in the US Department of Justice.* It should be noted that the court's decision was not based on the merits of the case and Ali never actually attained CO status. The court determined that the government had failed to properly indicate why Ali's application for CO status had been denied. This misstep required the conviction to be overturned. Although I've reduced Ali's situation to fewer than three hundred words, his case is a significant example of the legal machinations, religious and racial prejudice, and Selective Service bumbling that sincere conscientious objectors had to endure.†

---

* Clay v. United States, 403 U.S. 698 (1971).

† For a review of the Muhammad Ali case, see Dave Anderson, "How a Clerk Spared Ali from Prison," *New York Times*, December 17, 1979, and reprinted June 11, 2016, shortly after Ali died.

Chapter 10

Choice versus Chance

Sometimes beating the draft meant simply getting ahead of the local board: making your own military choice before it was made for you. Aside from the US Army, Navy, Air Force, Marines, and Coast Guard, the cafeteria of service selections included military reserve units and the National Guard. There were also special programs, including the Berry Plan—the so-called doctor draft, which allowed physicians and dentists to defer obligatory military service until they had completed medical school and residency training—and JAG, the legal branch of the military for lawyers. The plans allowed men to finish their education or coordinate it with their military service before being inducted. A military band was also an attractive option for musicians, although a very high level of musicianship was required.

Joining any of those units, however, didn't ensure that you'd be away from combat zones: Think of the TV show *M*A*S*H*, or of combat medics under fire, of military lawyers carrying out legal duties in war zones, of reserve and guard units being called up. Still, getting into one of these units might reduce your chances of ending up in Vietnam in combat or in a body bag. But it wasn't always easy getting into a unit; it was quite a challenge, with lots of guys applying for a limited number of spaces. It was like a game of musical chairs—if a space opened up, you had to be there at that minute to get in. Alan Hitsky was one of those who was at the right place at the right time.

Alan spent six years in the army reserve, from September 1967 to September 1973. After completing six months of active duty

Chapter Ten

Alan Hitsky, then and now (courtesy of Alan Hitsky)

training in 1968, he worked for a suburban Detroit daily newspaper and then for Wayne State University in public relations. He started working at the *Detroit Jewish News* in 1974 and rose to the position of associate editor before retiring.

I met Alan in high school and regarded him as a no-nonsense straight arrow who dotted his *i*'s and crossed his *t*'s. He wasn't one of the flashy kids, just a smart, solid guy who, in his words, "knew his ass from his elbow" and wasn't afraid to express his opinions. He got good grades and opted for high school ROTC for its discipline. I liked him because he was trustworthy, possessed a dry sense of humor, and had an insightful sense of self. Here is Alan's story as he told it to me.

> I had been out of college for three months in 1967 when the little white envelope appeared. My student deferment had been changed to classification 1-A, prime bait for Vietnam.
>
> It was the end of August, and I had already made up my mind

to quit my first job in journalism as a business reporter for the *Muskegon Chronicle*. Writing free advertisements for businesses in western Michigan was not how I had pictured my newspaper career.

I returned home to Detroit to mull over my future. An observer of—not necessarily a child of—the 1960s, I was opposed to the war because I didn't see the sense of it. But I wasn't strident or passionate enough to do anything about it. So that little envelope from my draft board came as a shock. All of a sudden, I was just a few months away from the war becoming personal. Suddenly, it was going to affect me!

Remember, this was near the height of the fighting. Things were heating up in a hurry, and the casualties were mounting on both sides. There weren't too many options for males my age.

One option was Canada. But I didn't think that joining thousands of expatriates on the other side of the Detroit River, with the possibility of never being able to return, was an appealing solution. Another was trusting my flat feet. Young men were being excused from military service for lesser medical reasons, but I just didn't have enough faith in my arches to trust that they would get me out. Yet, another was enlisting: joining the military and letting them train me in something useful. Of course, whatever that was might put me in the middle of a firefight. And the military wasn't known at the time for keeping its promises to enlistees.

In hindsight, I was young, naive, and hadn't experienced enough of the world to know my own mind, trust myself in new situations, or know what to expect. And I was scared.

So after several dark days, I came up with a fourth proposition. As a ROTC cadet in high school (it was either that or gym class), I had risen to the rank of lieutenant, was on the rifle team, and was commander of the drill team. I didn't think that would necessarily impress the National Guard, but it was worth a try.

The Detroit Artillery Armory, which had been a staging ground for federal troops during the Detroit riots just months before, was only a few miles from my house. One morning, I worked up the courage to try my luck. Entering the armory, I found that five National Guard units were headquartered in the building. Making my way from one to the next, I quickly ran up against a common theme: at the tender age of twenty-one, I was too old for the National Guard! With the war on and a vast choice of young men to choose from, the guard was only taking eighteen-year-olds.

I got the same message from the last sergeant I spoke to, the personnel noncom for a communications unit. But after reading my résumé (he was the only one who bothered to)—and noting my ROTC experience—he gave me a tip: an army reserve unit across town was looking for recruits. "You'd better go over there today," he said.

I went and was selected. I was the last of twenty-one young men who enlisted. We were the first recruits in this suburban Detroit training division to actually go to drill sergeant school. I later learned that I was the only one in the group who did not have a friend or relative in the division, and I was the only one who knew in advance how to march. My ROTC experience was my ticket in.

Weeks later, when we went to old Fort Wayne on the Detroit River for our preinduction physicals, I pointed out my flat feet to the examining physician. "Yes, they are very flat," he told me as he passed me with flying colors.

In late December 1967, at one of the most intense moments of the Vietnam War, we were shipped off to basic training at Fort Leonard Wood, Missouri. Our group was mixed in with other young men—draftees, enlistees, army reservists and National Guard, mostly from the Midwest. We spent Christmas Eve with unloaded rifles in our hands, standing outside in ten-degree weather, steadfastly guarding abandoned, derelict, empty barracks.

As we got to know our bunkmates, squad members, and others in our 250-man company during eight weeks together, we would talk. On rare occasions, it could get highly personal. And as older recruits—mostly college grads—among a majority of younger trainees, it was enlightening.

I remember two conversations. One draftee, from Chicago's South Side, seemed older than even us. He carried the swagger of the 'hood with him, but he had his serious side. I asked him why he was in the army. Turned out that a judge had given him a choice: military service or a prison term for drug dealing.

Then there was a quiet eighteen-year-old I greatly admired.

He was intelligent, an athlete, and easily passed the classes and the physical training. A Kansas farm boy, my friend left his high school sweetheart at home to enlist in the army. That was a three-year commitment, compared to the two years that draftees served.

While we were polishing our boots one night, I asked him why he enlisted. He replied, "I wanted to do something important for my country."

After those eight weeks of basic training, we were assigned job specialties in February 1969 and shipped all over the country. We twenty-one preassigned reservists from Detroit stayed together—eight weeks of advanced infantry training at Fort Dix, New Jersey, then back to Leonard Wood for six weeks of drill sergeant school.

We never saw our basic training buddies again or learned how they made out during the last three years of the war. I'm sure my Kansas friend served our country well. But I was never confident that I did.

Over the next six years, I spent one weekend a month at an army reserve center near home and two weeks each year at a regular army fort out of state. Our group caused a lot of grief—and complained mightily (goldbricked, some said)—whenever we were asked to "play the game" during the year, but we became very serious during the summers when we were teaching trainees who could soon be going off to war.

Did I serve my country or just avoid the war? I ask myself that question every time I attend a Fourth of July concert or Memorial Day or Veteran's Day event. I proudly fly the flag on those holidays to honor those who truly served. But I always hesitate when anyone tries to include me as one of those honorees.

Special talents and skills could get you a jump-start in the service. Doctors were naturals for enlisting voluntarily, going through basic training, coming out as officers, and then being sent to the front. But a proclivity for music could also help. George Riordan fell into this category. He graduated from Michigan State University in 1971 with a bachelor's degree in music. Now retired, George was the director of the School of Music at Middle Tennessee State University in Murfreesboro. During the Vietnam War era he was conflicted between duty to country and the fear in the back of his mind of being sent to Vietnam. As George remembers it,

> I really didn't see the point of serving in Vietnam. In fact, along with most of my male contemporaries, I was horrified at the idea of being sent there, both from the standpoint of the pointlessness of the whole endeavor, and because I was focused on building my career. A detour to Vietnam would not have helped me move my future forward (it might also end my future). But most of the fellows that I grew up with who had low lottery numbers were able to find a friendly physician who would write a letter on their behalf for a medical deferment.
>
> My father told me that "the men in our family are expected to serve" and related that he and his brother had both served in World War II. But I could never quite tell if he was just giving me a line—since almost everyone in his generation had to serve in World War II (a fundamentally different war than Vietnam)—or if he really believed what he said. He volunteered for Navy Officer Candidate School, and I always assumed it was because he wanted to stay out of the draft and not end up as a rifleman; we never discussed that point. Neither of my grandfathers served during World War I; one of them had a heart murmur; I'm not sure why the other didn't serve.
>
> The Vietnam War lottery began while I was attending Michigan State University. I must have been a junior when it was held on December 1, 1969. The guys in my dorm created a pot. Everyone threw a dollar in the pot, and the loser—the guy who drew the lowest lottery number—got the pot. My number was 153. The joke was that "the winner was the loser" or "the loser was the winner"— little solace for a low draft number. I was not at all the lowest and didn't come close to winning. As a side note, the first number called was September 14, my brother's birthday. Fortunately, his medical deferment had already been granted, yet one never knew for certain when deferments could be taken away.
>
> In my case, the lottery number came into play a year later, when I was ready to graduate. Prior to the lottery it was pretty easy to get deferments for undergraduate school, then for graduate school,

having a child, or teaching in the schools. For a time, simply being married warranted a deferment. I remember that the graduate school deferment was done away with after the lottery, and some of the other deferments disappeared at various points. In my senior year, I checked with my draft board, and administrator Mary Kelly—our nemesis—advised me they were on track to reach number 153 that year—my number.

By this time, of course, most of my fellow college students and a large percentage of Americans realized that the Vietnam War was a terrible mistake, and that we shouldn't have been there. Thanks to 20/20 hindsight, this belief has been borne out, but at the time, I was less interested in the morality of the war and more focused on staying out of it.

Because I knew that my deferment was set to expire, I hoped that my injured right knee would keep me out of the draft. At an annual physical with my physician, he checked me out, and said, "Yes, it is injured and will probably need to be operated on someday, but it won't keep you out of the army."

Now I was anticipating being drafted. Several of my friends from Michigan State had joined the West Point Band (formally named the United States Military Academy Band or USMA) to stay out of Vietnam, and, as a bonus, to gig and continue their studies in New York. I found out that there was an opening for an oboist, arranged for an audition, drove to New York, played, and won the position! The military bands are one of the few breaks that musicians get in life.

Sure enough, my expected draft physical exam notice arrived shortly after my audition. The physical was surreal. It was like being at my high school reunion (except there were no women). I saw so many of my friends who had all gone off to various colleges and were getting ready to graduate. I wasn't worried though, as I already had my West Point Band letter—my ace in the hole, although I would have much preferred to stay out altogether and go on to graduate school. I told the draft doctor about the knee. He examined it and said, "Yes, it is injured and will probably need to be operated on someday, but it won't keep you out of the army."—The same assessment as my personal doctor, verbatim! I passed the physical.

At this point, late spring 1971, I went ahead and enlisted in the

US Army for three years to join the USMA Band and avoided being drafted and sent God-knows-where for two years. It also meant that I had to go through basic training. Fortunately, my friends advised me to not to tell anyone during boot camp of my special assignment, so as not to risk special scrutiny from the other recruits—and especially from drill sergeants.

My basic training at Fort Knox, Kentucky, took place during the opening days of the "all-volunteer army," and our platoon was drawn up entirely of volunteers—no draftees. Only two guys in my platoon had any kind of college education; in fact, the education level of the recruits was depressingly low at that time, as guys were still being sent to Vietnam, and the army was looked down upon by most educated young men. But once I was sent to West Point, I was secure in staying in the United States.

Upon completing basic training, USMA bandsmen were given the rank of Specialist Five after their fourth month of service. This is a very fast promotion—I went from E-1 (recruit) to E-2 (private) to E-5 in just a few months. About a year after I went to basic training, I was promoted to Specialist Six (E-6, the same pay grade as a staff sergeant). Since Special Bandsmen are highly trained, they were promoted very quickly. E-5 was the lowest rank in the USMA Band at the time.

Once I was at West Point and in the band, I found out that many of my bandmates, like me, had signed up to avoid the draft. There was a big divide between short-timers and long-timers in the band. Short-timers, like me and other draft avoiders, often looked down at long-timers (called lifers), career men, and other uncoerced enlistees regarding musicianship. We wanted to do more with our musical talent than just play in an army band. We were only there to avoid Vietnam. Lifers, in our opinion—an unfair opinion, in retrospect—were satisfied with just being in the band.

There were more than one hundred men in the band. I played oboe in concert settings and cymbals when the band marched. Because of my musical ability and the opportunities it gave me, I didn't have to think about the war the way other guys did. But without the band, if I had been drafted, I would have been compelled to serve—or would've had to find another way out.

A friend of mine from elementary school, Cub Scouts, and high school committed suicide after college to avoid the draft. That was extreme. He was the sweetest guy. His friends and I think that the draft was one of the major issues that pushed him over the edge. He was having problems with his dad, so there were some issues there, but he killed himself just prior to reporting for shipping off to Fort Knox for basic training. It appears that the draft—with induction looming—was the major trigger.

Looking back, I probably should've complained less and practiced more. I was very glad to get lots of good experience, to study with a great teacher, to make good professional contacts, to read a great deal, to go to lots of concerts and explore New York City, and to live in a beautiful part of the country, the Hudson Highlands. Perhaps most valuable of all, those three years helped me to grow professionally—and to grow up a bit emotionally.

Aside from allowing him to avoid Vietnam, George's enlistment gave him some attractive benefits. Based in West Point and close to New York City, George was able to study in his free time with the acting principal oboist of the New York Philharmonic and take classes at the Manhattan School of Music. He could go to concerts at the Metropolitan Opera and Carnegie Hall and play professionally in the city and outlying areas. For his service, he was able to get a VA mortgage and GI Bill benefits to help pay for his graduate degrees. He is nonjudgmental about others and whatever they did to avoid the draft or, as he says "their decision to serve." Then he adds, "My dad died right after my junior year of college. I'm sure that he would not have wanted his sons to go to Vietnam."

Some of the staunchest opponents of the Vietnam War wound up with critical government jobs. Working for the government didn't mean being a hypocrite. Being anti-war didn't necessarily mean being anti-American or anti-government. Working for the government could also give a person a chance to do some good in the world. New Yorker Lance Haroldsen avoided the war and built his career in the Veterans Administration helping war veterans. This is his experience.

I was in school when I turned eighteen and registered for the draft. I was pretty apolitical and my father and grandfather were both combat veterans, so it was not military service that I was necessarily against. My grandfather served in World War I; my father served in World War II, my uncle too, but he wasn't in combat.

When I started college we had mandatory two-year ROTC training, and after a year of that, I was pretty disgusted by the experience: the stupidity and some of the people who ran the show. While I met some very fine military officers, NCOs, and enlisted personnel, at the time I was in ROTC the army apparently put the dregs in there. Many of these guys were awful—to the point of selling the answers to the final exams. It was not inspiring. After a year, I had injured my left knee, and I went to the doctor. He wrote a note for me, and I was out of ROTC for the second year.

I didn't want to go to Vietnam for a number of reasons: I didn't want to put my life in the hands of morons. I was also not eager to kill people I had nothing against or even kill people I might have something against. Aside from the possibility of combat, it's two years of your life spent polishing things and taking out garbage. And that's the best of it. It's two years wasted. My dad was telling me there are only so many thousand casualties in Vietnam—that's nothing compared to World War II. But what if I'm one of them? Dying or wounded—for what? And my mother was just worried about me in general. She knew I was 1-A, and she knew there was a war going on. She was upset.

I wasn't called up for a draft physical until I transferred colleges. I left my first school and went to another one, and in the interim—I was nineteen years old—the old school notified my draft board. I was slated for induction and went down for my physical. I had it at Whitehall Street, the main induction center in lower Manhattan. I didn't submit anything—no documents or doctor letters—to try to get out of it. I just went through it, no tricks, claims of psychiatric illness, or anything like that.

It was kind of an interesting experience. There were a whole bunch of people there, some of whom I recognized from my neighborhood. Some of them had been in trouble with the law and had gotten into this diversion program—go to jail or go into the military, so they were being treated separately. They were all laughing and goofing around. Military service seemed a good alternative to them.

I went through the physical and passed. Then in the fall my mom got a call from an army recruiter who said I was going to be inducted in a week or two. So I went down and talked to the guy. He was very straight with me. He said that I should stay in school. He said that if I wanted to join the military afterward, I could, but I really wasn't doing anybody any good by not getting my degree. His recommendation would be that I not enlist at this time, at least not until I got my degree, and he said he would call the draft board and tell them I was actually in school—which I was. I don't know what his motivation was for telling me all that and not pushing me to enlist, but that's what he said. They classified me 2-S, and I continued with that until I graduated about a year later and went to graduate school. My deferment lasted for another year, and then I went into the Peace Corps.

When I joined the Peace Corps, we—my then girlfriend, now my wife of many years—were told we were going to Korea. We were also told that we'd be teaching university-level English in Seoul, which was okay; that was what I was planning to do—teach English. But when we got into the Peace Corps training program in the States, we learned that we wouldn't be training university students in Korea as we were first told, but rather Korean military personnel. We also found out that only women volunteers would be stationed in Seoul and the men would be in remote areas of the country including Pusan. At that time it wouldn't be safe for women to be in the countryside—men were sent to the countryside. The whole thing sounded like a crock, and then I learned that Peace Corps volunteers returning to the States, including some of our instructors, were being drafted. I figured I'd rather take my chances with the draft than go to Korea. When we learned all this, we deselected ourselves from the Peace Corps and decided to seek teaching opportunities in the States instead.

I quit the Peace Corps and was 1-A for a while. I got a teaching job in a junior high school, and then my girlfriend and I got jobs at Northern Illinois University where we taught for two years. I got a teaching deferment. I did a little draft counseling in that first year and then gave up my deferment and took my chances with the new lottery. That was the only thing I ever won. My number was 326. It was a really good number.

The knee thing that cropped up in ROTC was still there, but I never used it to get out of the draft. It was ironic. Back when I had to take a physical again to get into the Peace Corps, the doctor who was examining me, apparently sympathetic to prospective draft dodgers, thought I was being drafted and said, "Is there anything wrong with you? I can get you out." I said, "No, I actually want to get in—to the Peace Corps."

This whole draft thing started in 1966 for me. I was nineteen then. It lasted through the early '70s. I have mixed feelings about it all. I'm more tempered in my view now. Because I didn't get drafted, somebody else got picked. Somebody else was sent to Vietnam, somebody else bears the scars or was destroyed in that process, or not. I feel guilty about it sometimes. On the other hand, would I have wanted to be there? No. Absolutely not. And I was lucky not to. I have more understanding and a lot more compassion for the people who went. I wasn't one that was going around spitting on GIs. I certainly didn't feel that way at all.

Once I got the lottery number, it didn't alter my thoughts at all, but from '66 to '71, the war and the draft were very much on my mind. You just had this thing hanging over your head. If you had a job you didn't like, but it got you a deferment, you weren't going to quit because then you'd have another job you really wouldn't like. And I know I wouldn't have done anything differently.

I once had an interview for a job I wanted but didn't get: I was accused of evading the draft. I said no, I didn't evade the draft. I said that my country felt that what I was doing was more valuable for the country than carrying a gun. It was a great and truthful response, but it killed getting the job, a law job with the Department of Labor, which is where I wanted to be. But I found another one, with the Department of Veterans Affairs. I spent the next thirty-two years serving veterans and their families with the VA, retiring as the acting chairman and vice chairman of the Board of Veterans' Appeals. I was the first non-vet to hold that position. It's a pretty high job. I worked with a lot of disabled veterans, and veterans in general, and it seemed more of a handicap not being a veteran myself. But nobody was like, "You're a draft dodger." Most people understand that you want people who want to do well by veterans, who are going to take care of veterans, give them the best possible treatment, rather than just have somebody who's a vet. I really liked my job. On the other hand, sometimes it felt like I was paying a debt I owed.

And so a draft avoider ends up working with and for the people who served. There's something poetic in that.

These days the guy I once knew as Mitch Kleba calls himself Budd Haya; tomorrow it could be something else. But ever since I've known Budd—he went to my high school, in college was my fraternity brother—one thing has been constant: he is quirky. He is his own drummer, a good guy who thinks for himself, and has a way of looking at things that is at once amusing, enlightening, and thought-provoking, all of which at times belies his serious and perceptive nature.

Budd lives with his wife in an uptown neighborhood of Chicago. He taught social science and economics as a full professor at DePaul University. He's now formally retired but still teaches one class each semester because he likes teaching and thinks students help keep him mentally sharper. During the Vietnam War, Budd was a student at Wayne State University and held a 2-S deferment. He didn't particularly enjoy school, but the draft was out there, so he planned on attending graduate school to retain his deferment.

"I wanted to do other things, such as travel, but I'm a creature of inertia," he says. "I didn't want to lose my 2-S."

To ensure that he could stay in school, Budd found professors who were sympathetic to the anti-war movement and were liberal graders even when a student didn't do well scholastically. The mutual objective was to keep students in school and out of the draft. It was also to a school's benefit to keep collecting tuition.

While a senior, Budd got a girlfriend pregnant. ("I should've paid more attention in biology class," he said.) They considered and decided against an abortion. Instead, they had a shotgun wedding and became parents: a daughter was born in 1968. Budd was twenty-two. He found it tremendously stressful to be a husband, father, and student. There were constant demands—financial, academic, marital, and emotional. Budd is a sensitive soul and all these burdens at once were a difficult load. Nevertheless, he was determined to fulfill his domestic obligations and advance his education and started graduate studies in economics at the university. Some financial relief appeared thanks to thoughtful professors who arranged a position for him as a teaching assistant. The job paid for graduate school.

While teaching and studying, Budd lived on campus. He focused on caring for his wife and child, and his own survival. Going into the army didn't fit with his life plan. Being a parent changed his draft status from 2-S to 3-A, a hardship classification that included registrants with a child or children and provided a deferment. It was likely he would never face induction, and he didn't. When asked what he would have done if he had no deferment, Budd reviewed his options. "Going to Canada? In retrospect, that might've been a good idea," he said. "Maybe self-medicating to fail the physical, or trying to get CO status. A friend did that. But there was a stigma attached to it. Public opinion could equate a CO with being a draft dodger. I didn't want to be labeled that way or have the stain of a nonpatriot."

While life was difficult for Budd, knowing that he had a deferment took away one worry, but it didn't alter his anti-war position. He met progressive, like-minded people and spent hours in anti-war discussions with them over coffee at MacKenzie Hall, a campus gathering place, and nearby Johnny's Restaurant, where Greek salads and gyro sandwiches made for cheap meals. His pro-peace leanings were strong, and he acted on them. He and his wife had a friend who joined the army thinking he could adjust to the military life. The friend realized he'd made an error, didn't agree with the army's policies, and deserted. Budd and his wife, risking arrest, let the friend stay with them until he was able to make the easy hop from Detroit to Canada.

As a young boy Budd enjoyed playing with his toy soldiers. He thought it would be fun to shoot guns, fire cannons, be in a submarine, or fly a jet. "It was all a boyhood fantasy," he said. "As an adult

I realized I could get hurt and hurt other people. I didn't like that. I wasn't going to go to Vietnam."

Budd delivered that last statement in an even, firm tone. There was no anger in his voice. None of the rage I'd heard in the '60s or '70s from guys opposed to the war. None of the passionate rhetoric I hear even today. Yet, I knew exactly what Budd meant. His opinion was very strong and similar to what I'd heard from other men. There was no nuance to it. It was a solid declaration reflecting an inflexible position. There was no need to yell or scream. If called, Budd would not go. It was that simple. He would've followed his friend across the Ambassador Bridge or through the Detroit-Windsor Tunnel to Canada.

Over fifty years later, his feelings about the war are unchanged. Looking back, Budd says, "I wish I had been more active in the antiwar movement. I marched in some local protests but not many. I wore buttons—I still have a collection. I'm a little ashamed of one I have that reads 'Sterilize LBJ. No More Ugly Children.' I regret I didn't do more to protest the war. The war was wrong, I should've done more."

Today, Budd is an activist involved with many progressive causes. "I am trying to make up for the peace and civil rights marches I should have attended as a young man but didn't." He worked on Bernie Sanders's 2016 primary campaign for president, attended many of the Occupy Wall Street rallies, is a nuisance to the City of Chicago (writing op-eds when the city tries to tear down old neighborhoods), and goes to protests to raise awareness on behalf of powerless people harmed by more powerful groups or countries.

Though he was not a frequent public protestor in his twenties, Budd did occasionally attend peace lectures and related events. He told me of one eye-opening experience he had.

> An exciting thing happened to me. I went to hear anti-war activist and SDS co-founder [and later a California assemblyman, state senator, and author] Tom Hayden speak at Wayne. I think he was dating or married to actress Jane Fonda at the time. He was just off the plane from Hanoi. After the lecture, I went up front with some other people to hear more. Hayden said he needed a ride to Ann

Arbor, could anyone take him? I volunteered—I hate to drive, but this was a once-in-a-lifetime event—and drove him, along with another guy. I thought Hayden would tell Jane Fonda stories, but instead he slept most of the way. There was just a little discussion. I spoke against the draft, but Hayden disagreed. He said that with an all-volunteer army, no one would protest; the draft was needed to make sure political people and rich people's sons were subject to the draft like everyone else. He believed that would motivate the powerful to avoid wars. I dropped Hayden off at a big house in Ann Arbor. A party was going on and Hayden invited me in. My mind was blown: I'd never seen such sexy women in one place at a political event. Being anti-war wasn't just for schleppers, there were beautiful women involved.

Laugh about it or shrug off Budd's comments as you wish, but the man may have a point about sexy women. Consider the Vietnam War–era poster showing the folk singer and political activist Joan Baez sitting on a couch with her sisters Pauline and Mimi. The headline above them reads "Girls Say Yes to Boys Who Say No." (An image of this poster appears on page 151.) Was there some truth to that or just a provocative offer? The message seems to be that taking an anti-draft stance could have rewards. I'm sure some guys said no in hopes of hearing a yes.

Religion could make an impression on a draft board. While the most obvious use of one's religious beliefs might be in pursuing a CO deferment, for those who couldn't elude the Selective Service that way, there was the possibility of becoming a member of the clergy or a student of divinity. Clergymen were often granted a 4-D exemption, a classification reserved at the time for a minister of religion or student of divinity.

During the Vietnam War era, hundreds of men turned to the nondenominational Universal Life Church as the basis for the 4-D deferment. The church had been founded in 1962 by Kirby Hensley and was known in the resister community for ordaining ministers for a fee via mail order. The buzz was that the mail-order ordination

"Girls Say Yes to Boys Who Say No" poster (courtesy of Division of Political and Military History, National Museum of American History, Smithsonian Institution, gift of William Mears, photo by Jim Marshall, poster by Larry Gates)

would qualify a man as a minister and exempt him from the draft. I, of course, jumped at the possibility and acquired my ordination in 1967 (in the form of a card-size certificate) by paying a ten-dollar fee. I never presented the certificate to my local board because I quickly learned that the Selective Service was not buying it. Universal Life Church ordination was rejected by local boards and would not keep a man out of the army, but it was recognized by many states as legitimate for other purposes: it empowered a man to perform marriages and other clerical-like functions. A friend in California was also "ordained" at the same time and in the years since has performed fifty-one marriages.

While a Universal Life Church ordination was questionable, studying for the clergy was worthy of a draft board's consideration and held the possibility of a 2-D deferment.* For some men, the thought of becoming a minister or rabbi had its appeal based on their sincere personal beliefs and religious commitment. For others, it was something they might never have thought of as a means to avoid the draft, but it was there, and if a man knew where to look for it, how to acquire it, and how to manage it, it could keep you out of the army.

In 1971 Paul Siegel, a "nice Jewish boy" from Queens, New York, was fresh out of school. He'd just graduated from the State University of New York at Buffalo (SUNY Buffalo), with a bachelor's degree in behavioral psychology. He'd held a 2-S deferment throughout his undergraduate years and was facing reclassification to 1-A. To top it off, he'd received number 57 in the draft lottery. It was a sure bet he would be called up.

Paul was not a good fit for the military. He was very much a part of the counterculture of the day. "I was hippie-like," he said. "I was heavily committed to the national change of consciousness of the 1960s. I was very opposed to the war. I marched at demonstrations

---

* Draft classifications evolved over time. In 1963, when I registered, the 4-D exemption covered ministers of religion and divinity students. Later, the 2-D classification addressed students while the 4-D category retained its focus on established clergy.

in Washington and Albany. I had my values, and the Vietnam War was something I could not accept. It was wrong."

But Paul was a bright, healthy, mentally stable kid. He played the piano at Catskills resorts and was in a wedding band during high school and college. He had a social life. As far as the Selective Service was concerned, he was a normal guy, and there was no way he would fail to pass a physical; nor would he qualify as a CO. Paul knew this and did not believe he had a legitimate basis for an exemption or deferment. "I wasn't going to take drugs, wear a dress, or do something like that to get out of the army. That just wasn't me," he said. "But I wasn't going to Vietnam either. I would not be part of that war. I had cousins in Toronto, and if I had to, I would go live with them."

Hoping to get some kind of break, Paul applied to VISTA (Volunteers in Service to America), the anti-poverty program created by President Johnson's Economic Opportunity Act of 1964. VISTA was often referred to as the domestic version of the Peace Corps. Its volunteers served in communities throughout the United States, providing educational programs and vocational training for the nation's disadvantaged classes. Paul was accepted and assigned a teaching position in Atlanta. "I wanted to go," he said. "The opportunity to teach in VISTA appealed to my social justice values. This was something in which I could do some good, something positive."

It's important to back up and consider Paul's home life. He was raised in a conservative, comfortable environment. His father, the general manager of a car dealership in Brooklyn and the dominant voice in the family, was a Nixon Republican. His mother was more of a moderate Democrat. As Paul described them, they were both pro-government and not opposed to the war. "The reality is they were more conformist than right-wing," he said. "They thought Vietnam was necessary because the government said so." His father had served in World War II. He was stationed in Alamogordo Air Base in New Mexico and never went into combat, never went overseas. Paul's maternal grandfather was a veteran of World War I and was awarded a Purple Heart after surviving a mustard gas attack in France. Military service was not out of the question in the Siegel family.

There was more. Paul's upbringing was Jewish. The family

observed the Sabbath, went to synagogue on the holidays, attended to most of the rituals, and enjoyed Jewish culture, which included a focus on education and doing right in the world. Paul was part of it. He went to Hebrew school, had a bar mitzvah, and overall, liked the commitment to Judaism. However, the family's religious lifestyle was not strict. It was somewhere between Conservative and Orthodox Judaism, or as Paul called it, "Orthodox Lite." But being Jewish didn't mean being unsuitable for the Selective Service. There were plenty of Jewish men routinely being drafted and serving honorably without a qualm.

Now Paul was 1-A and facing the Selective Service draft process. Soon he would be called for a physical. Suddenly, with his son vulnerable, Paul's father had a change of heart, the war was getting too close. He wanted Paul off the Selective Service's radar and told Paul not to commit to VISTA—it wasn't enough of a guarantee for deferment. There had to be another path. Paul's mother concurred.

Paul's father began looking around for an escape hatch for his son. He began making inquiries and through some relatives learned about a charismatic Hassidic rabbi who had gotten out of Europe with some of his flock at the start of World War II, before the Nazis invaded. He had started a yeshiva (a Jewish educational institution that focuses on the study of traditional religious texts) a short hop—just fifteen minutes away—from Paul's home. The rabbi had a large following and had founded the yeshiva primarily to help keep Jewish boys out of the army and secondarily to bring them closer to Judaism. The yeshiva itself was legitimate, properly established with all the right accreditations in place. The cost to enter and study there was considerable. However, students enrolling in the yeshiva received a highly sought-after perk: a 2-D classification and the accompanying draft deferment. Local gossip also said it was not the only yeshiva in the area to offer this appealing benefit; apparently these schools popped up as the war grew.

At his father's insistence, Paul reluctantly declined his VISTA assignment and entered the yeshiva. There, the black-coated senior rabbi and his son properly conducted classes and discussions for a couple of hours each day. There were approximately ten other boys attending. Paul described them as "young longhairs." If their studies led them to becoming rabbis, so be it, but the shared priority was avoiding the draft.

Paul was a hard worker. He took his yeshiva studies seriously and remained enrolled for more than a year. While there, he earned money as a clerk at a Budget Car Rental office and as a New York cabbie. Once the draft threat receded, again at his father's insistence, Paul went on to SUNY College of Optometry in New York City, resulting in a career he did not initially embrace but one that has served him well.

The Vietnam War and the draft are still major topics of conversation with his friends and family. Paul remains opposed to America's involvement in Vietnam at that time. Looking back, he displays an anger and frustration with his generation. "The 1960s were a tremendous opportunity," he said. "We had so much promise. My generation was given so much and we did so little with it. Look at the world now. We had every opportunity to see the light, and instead we let the incentives of capitalism prevail."

As a retired optometrist now living in Florida, Paul considers himself a traditional ritual-focused Jew. "I love letting go of the world and embracing the Sabbath," he says, fully at peace with his life.

Chapter 11

Go North, Young Man

If you passed your physical, if you couldn't acquire CO status, if you weren't enthusiastic about the idea of going to jail, and had no plan B, C, or D to avoid the draft, what tactic was left? Look north.

Faced with the very real possibility of being conscripted into military service, thousands of men made their way to Canada. It started as a trickle in 1965; by 1966 there was a steady flow of young men crossing our northern border. At first, the influx of US draft resisters into Canada caused some controversy there, but in due course the Canadian government chose to accommodate and even welcome them.

As a refuge or sanctuary, Canada wasn't an unattractive option. The climate might be a little chillier, but English was the national language (along with French), the beer was good, and many Canadians were receptive to the stream of American talent. Best of all, there was no extradition treaty between the United States and Canada addressing the issue of draft evaders. As far as Canada was concerned, the arrival of American men—for any reason—was an immigration matter. However, that didn't mean getting into Canada was always an easy process; there were restrictions and there was some early discrimination against draft resisters. Canadian authorities initially attempted to discourage evaders from entering the country by suggesting they could be prosecuted or deported. In fact, until Canada ended its discrimination against US draft resisters, American men had a dodgy time getting into the country and acquiring landed immigrant status that would qualify them as residents, not merely visitors. The process was inconsistent: some attained it easily, some had difficulty. In many cases the decision was simply up to the first border guard a draft resister met; some customs and immigration officials at the international crossing points were sympathetic and didn't ask too many questions, others were less accommodating. It was also that way with the public. Some Canadians resented the flood of Americans. But those who did not agree with US actions in Vietnam felt that the men were justified in crossing the border and welcomed them. Many evaders received assistance from locally based anti-war groups. Consequently, many men who were able to get into Canada stayed underground until resentment eased up and they could surface. Once that happened, thousands of Americans decided that resettling across the border, wearing sweaters more often, learning all about hockey and curling, and eating poutine (french fries and cheese curds topped with gravy) would be just fine, much better than training for combat and being sent off to hot and humid Southeast Asia.

Depending on whose estimate you accept (and the numbers are disputed)—the Canadian government's immigration statistics, the Canadian Broadcasting Corporation's estimates, or any other credible source—anywhere from twenty thousand to one hundred thousand or more draft-age Americans opposing the war (not all of them subject to the draft) moved to Canada beginning in 1965, either as a last resort or as a form of protest. The surge of educated men, often accompanied by wives or girlfriends, continued through 1975 and presented Canada with a steady stream of young talent that was, for the most part, a welcome addition to the labor force. Some Canadians even say it was the most remarkable migration of talent—bright young educated people—ever to come into the country. Montreal, Toronto, and Vancouver were the most popular destinations.

Many of the American men ultimately made contributions to the arts, sciences, and education, went into politics, established businesses, or became involved in social justice activities. Some of them had subsequent brushes with American authorities even though they were living outside the United States. Some eventually returned to the United States once amnesties and pardons were in place in 1974 and 1977; others decided that Canada made a lot of sense as their new permanent home.

Canada seemed to be a reasonable option the closer you were to it geographically. For Americans living in the northern part of the United States, Canada was a familiar and comfortable place, often the destination for family vacations or weekend breaks. Before 9/11, crossing the border into Canada required only a US driver's license or birth certificate. For Michiganders, Windsor, Ontario, was just another Detroit suburb that happened to be in another country across the Detroit River. Plenty of Windsorites commuted daily to jobs in Detroit. There were additional crossing points in Port Huron at the Blue Water Bridge and in the Upper Peninsula at the Sault Ste. Marie International Bridge. Canada was where we went to party (because of the lower drinking age), camp, and check out the nudie bars. Access was easy. We could easily live there, the transition wouldn't be difficult. However, if you were living farther south in a state not bordering Canada, Canada was another world—a foreign country, a distant land, unknown, and maybe even exotic, yet nowhere near as unknown as Vietnam.

Regardless of where you came from in the United States, camaraderie and assistance were there for you in Canada. In 1968 *The Manual for Draft-Age Immigrants to Canada* was released. Written by Mark Satin—an American counselor at the Toronto Anti-Draft Programme—and published by House of Anansi Press in Toronto, the book reportedly sold close to one hundred thousand copies. The book gave draft dodgers practical information and guidance about living in Canada and included tips on immigration, expenses, culture, history, and more. It was sold in Canada and in the United States, although it was sometimes confiscated from college campus bookstores by US Customs agents. The book was reprinted several times and was reissued in 2017 as a fiftieth anniversary edition with a new foreword and afterword. Also available was a Toronto-based newsletter titled the *American Exile in Canada*. Initially launched in 1968 as a two-page mimeographed newsletter, it evolved two years later into a magazine known as *AMEX: The American Expatriate in Canada*. In 1971 it became *AMEX-Canada: Published by Americans Exiled in Canada*, a well-produced war resister newspaper that was read throughout North America and around the globe. The publication's circulation went from twelve hundred in its first year to more than four thousand by 1975.*

While Canada served as a sought-after haven for some resisters, moving there still required a degree of courage. Leaving family and friends behind, perhaps permanently, could be life-changing, scary, and needed forethought.

David Anderson, a Californian (and not to be confused with journalist Dave Anderson mentioned on page 134), was one of the many who looked to the north for his future. Originally from San Jose, David chose to leave the United States and settle in Canada, but, oddly enough, not before trying Vietnam first.

In the mid-1960s, while a student at the University of California, Davis, he became radicalized as the war was ramping up and a national draft resistance network was forming. David participated in numerous anti-war protests and demonstrations, mostly in Davis and at the Berkeley campus of the University of California. He was involved with a group called Alternatives, which provided information about CO strategies to draft prospects.

David's draft board was in San Mateo, a White, middle-class city. His board was starved for bodies and most of the eligible targets were college students. At the time, David had a 2-S student deferment he believed he would soon lose. He had decided not to participate in the war and wanted a way out.

While attending Davis, David saw a sign on campus with the headline "Come to Vietnam," promoting the International Voluntary Services (IVS) organization. The IVS, a Peace Corps–type group, was a private American nonprofit organization that placed students in villages around the world, including Vietnam, to help with educational, agricultural, community development and other humanitarian projects. It was assisted in part by the US Agency for International Development (USAID). David applied and picked community development.

---

* Daniel Ross, "'Unknown Territory': Canada and American War Resister Identity in the Pages of AMEX, 1968–1971," in *Canada-US Borderlands Colloquium* (Toronto: York University Library, 2010), 8–9.

In 1967 the IVS accepted twenty college students. David was one of them. He was twenty years old and had dropped out of Davis in 1966, giving up his 2-S as a political act.

He was selected for a three-month summer program in Vietnam. He learned the Vietnamese language and was placed in a small refugee village in Binh Duong province just north of Saigon with other American civilian volunteers along with other individuals who were on a two-year contract with the organization. David lived with a Vietnamese family in a village comprising three hundred Catholic North Vietnamese who had traveled south seeking safety because the refugee camps in which they were living had been accidentally bombed by South Vietnamese forces.

The US military regarded IVS volunteers as Viet Cong sympathizers. Whether they were or not didn't matter; that's how they were perceived. David didn't know that half the villagers were, in fact, Viet Cong guerrillas; by day they were quiet villagers, by night they were active fighters. The army recommended that the civilian American volunteers carry guns, but the volunteers refused. They did not want to be thought of as armed fighters and, consequently, subject to combat.

Seeking economic stability and hoping to generate income, the village decided to build an eel farm. David was given an extension beyond his three-month stint to stay until February 1968 to help develop the farm. David negotiated with the US military on behalf of the villagers to bring in material support including water barrels, food, and clothing. However, David did not get the chance to see his efforts come to fruition. In late '67, all US citizens were ordered to leave Vietnam immediately. The IVS program was terminated. Military intelligence said the Tet Offensive was coming, and it did. The village was overrun by North Vietnamese fighters. Any Americans found in the area would've been killed or captured. According to David, WHAM (an acronym for "winning hearts and minds" and referring to a slew of programs, including IVS, that the United States and South Vietnam employed to win the support of the Vietnamese people and help defeat the Viet Cong) never had a chance. He believed that Americans didn't really understand the Vietnamese culture. "Americans were oafish, clumsy, and classless—and the Vietnamese saw this," he said.

David stated that he loved his Vietnam experience: "Vietnam is paradise, beautiful, but it was incredibly dangerous." He said he wouldn't have gone if he had known how unsafe it was to be an American anywhere in Vietnam. Yet, it was a remarkable transition for him: he went from student radical to a volunteer "in country"—a term defined as being in or taking place in a country that is the focus of activity, in this case, military activity.

When he returned from Vietnam, David gave talks at Davis as a pacifist. It was then that David's fling with the Selective Service began. Once home, the local draft board sniffed him out. He tried for CO status and went with his father to the hearing but was rebuffed because he was not a Quaker; being a pacifist was not sufficient at the time. He was also against the Vietnam War specifically, and that did not qualify as grounds for exemption. He was reclassified 1-A. Only a few months later, the Supreme Court ruled that personal beliefs and pacifism merited CO status, but David had already been denied—confirmation that timing is everything—and his objection to a specific war did not help.

The CO rejection did not diminish David's objection to the war. He tried to persuade others to avoid the draft and would sit near the army recruiting table at Davis holding a sign stating "There are alternatives to military service." The local paper, the *Sacramento Bee*, ran a photograph of David holding the sign. In due course, David soon found his own alternative.

David tried to leverage his Vietnam experience and language skills with the draft board. He offered to go back in a noncombat role, but the board rejected that suggestion. In David's words, the draft board gave him a choice: "Shoot people or go to jail." Neither option appealed to him. David had another idea.

At the time, David's father was working in Newfoundland, Canada, and offered him a plane ticket to Canada from San Mateo. David took him up on his offer, and in 1968 he arrived in Montreal on the way to meet his father. When David landed at the Montreal airport, Canadian immigration officials were surprised at his Newfoundland destination—most Americans coming to Canada were heading for the metropolitan areas of Toronto, Montreal, or Vancouver—and gave him landed immigrant status on the spot.

David found a job in Stephenville, Newfoundland, as a teacher in an adult education school. While there he received a draft notice ordering him to report for duty. In response, he renounced his US citizenship and sent his draft card and a no-thank-you letter to his board. Surprisingly, there was no reaction and no further contact.

After teaching for a year in Stephenville, David moved to Vancouver. He found a couple who helped American draft avoiders; they assisted him in settling into life in Vancouver. His social circle, a mix of Americans and Canadians, included people who shared his political thinking. David went to university and got a teaching degree. He taught for thirty years in the Vancouver area and retired in 2006. Along the way, David married a Canadian woman and became a Canadian citizen in 1975.

Since his return from Vietnam in the late 1960s, David visited California many times once pardons and amnesties were in place and he was allowed to enter the country without risk of arrest. He maintained his anti-war beliefs throughout his life. He continued to be an activist for social justice supporting anti-war and anti-racist movements through his union involvement as a teacher and into his retirement as a musician playing for benefits and fundraisers for social causes.

David died in 2020, but when we last spoke he told me that he regarded himself as a Buddhist-type pacifist. Looking back, he said, "I learned a lot about the courage and determination of the people of Vietnam, and given the outcome of the war, I stand in awe of the love these people have for their country, their freedom, and their culture. I would like to visit Vietnam again."

When asked if he would've done anything differently, David said, "When amnesty came it was too late for me, I was established in Canada. I hated the ugliness of war and never saw myself as an American again. I have no regrets about not being in California. My whole life is here. No regrets whatsoever. Basically I would not change anything I did. I do not regret giving up my US citizenship."

A few days after that last conversation, I received an email from David in which he elaborated on his experience and admitted that there were, in fact, some regrets:

Thinking about the story I told the other day, I left out an important idea that only came to me after our phone conversation. The reason I sought a volunteer civilian position with IVS was not clear as I recounted the history.

As a pacifist-activist, I believe I thought going to Vietnam would give me the actual story about US actions so that I could come back and testify about the truth as I saw it. I never really took this up when I got back, because at that point my life was too chaotic. I also drank the USAID Kool-Aid, and I thought I could make a difference in the lives of the Vietnamese people by volunteering with their [IVS] organization. So I went with the hope of doing good, and with the desire to see and tell about the war up close. I had no idea how close I would be. I also couldn't know how futile my community development efforts would be in the long run.

I would also like to say that I realize I did not get injured physically, I didn't lose a family member, so I put my anguish in perspective. I landed relatively on my feet. Many people lost far more than I did.

In terms of what I lost, however, I should add to my regrets pile. I lost the chance to live with my family and to see and care for my parents as they lived out their lives. I removed myself from the traditions and holidays my family would celebrate in San Francisco, and that was a real and palpable thing to give up. I ended my many friendships with high school friends, cousins, and aunts and uncles. I would have kept all those things if I could have figured out a way to avoid the war. In the end, I took the chance to build a new life in a new country, one that did not force military duty on its people. I gained some and I lost some. But I would have been happy to stay if it had been an option.

David Anderson certainly wasn't alone in crossing over to Canada. Plenty of soon-to-be expatriates found their way to that country by way of numerous crossing points across the northern US border that served as convenient exits for draft dissidents.

Bob Delgado chose Montreal for his entry into Canada. Bob had an attitude similar to David's: he wanted nothing to do with the war.

Considering that Bob was born in warm and sunny Havana, Cuba, moving to a colder climate made his anti-war statement an even more emphatic gesture.

Bob was used to moving around. When he was thirteen, his family came to New York City and became permanent US residents. Just a few years later, they relocated to San Juan, Puerto Rico, where Bob began attending high school. At eighteen, and required to register for the draft, Bob was back in New York where he signed in at his local board in Queens. After high school, Bob furthered his education at the Cooper Union for the Advancement of Science and Art in Manhattan, a unique institution dedicated to the proposition that education is the key to civic virtue and harmony as well as personal prosperity. Bob studied and enjoyed fine arts and architecture. While in college, he received a 2-S classification and student deferment.

As the Vietnam conflict expanded, Bob got involved with the anti-war movement. He was a follower of the teachings of Mahatma Gandhi and was strongly against the war. He was anti-nuke as well. In 1967, while still a student in New York, he mailed his draft card in protest to U Thant, secretary-general of the United Nations. The result of this action was unexpected and similar to my experience when I wrote my protest letter to President Johnson: somehow, his draft board learned of his protest and changed his draft status. As he said, "My 2-S was suddenly yanked, and I was given a 1-A classification. I was vulnerable."

Bob applied for CO status but was denied. The board said he was not a follower of any of the government-recognized pacifist religions and, therefore, was not eligible. Bob had deeply entrenched personal beliefs and values that would not allow him to participate in the war. But, as with so many other draft resisters pursuing CO status, timing was Bob's enemy: he made his claim prior to the Supreme Court ruling that adhering to a traditional religion wasn't necessary for CO status.

Intending to slow down the Selective Service process, Bob moved back to Puerto Rico and declared it his official residence, allowing him to have his draft file transferred to the island. He continued his studies and earned a BA degree from the University of

Puerto Rico. Then, in April 1968, Bob received a notice for a physical. He panicked. "I had fifteen days to act, to do something."

At the time, it was easy to enter Canada and apply for immigrant status. Bob decided it was his moment to go. His family had mixed feelings about him leaving but understood that Bob had to stay true to his convictions. Within the Cuban expatriate community, however, there was strong pro-war support—the community was anti-Communist and the Vietnam War was seen as a legitimate fight to halt the spread of Communism. He went to Montreal on his own. Within four months he acquired Canadian landed immigrant status.

Bob's move to Canada was a major change psychologically, culturally, and spiritually for him. There was also the practical reality of moving from a familiar tropical climate to a new and significantly colder environment. Bob explained why he selected Montreal.

> I chose Montreal because it was beautiful, prosperous, avant-garde, French, and open-minded. It changed my life completely. Before I moved to Canada, I was a middle-class mama's boy, timid and shy. I was quite unprepared for the sudden culture shock that greeted me. I had to confront a new world. Going from New York to Puerto Rico to Montreal was like landing on the moon. I entered a new world. It was different from any place I'd ever known.

Bob's first year in Canada was challenging, but 1968 was Montreal's Summer of Love, which made it easier to adjust. At the time, the city was still basking in the glow of Expo '67, the international fair that had drawn millions of visitors to the city the year before. "That year changed my life," he says. "It was truly a movable feast." Bob was like a kid in a candy store finding an appealing lifestyle he'd had no exposure to while in Puerto Rico. He looked for work, went to school, and got involved in the local underground press. He made new friends—people on the fringe of the counterculture—and hung out with a bohemian community of American draft dodgers and deserters who naturally fused with the English-speaking minority youth segment. (The English-speaking population of Quebec province in 1968 was about 12 percent and the French about 88 percent.)

Within a short time, Bob got his first job in Canada, teaching Spanish as a second language at the YMCA. He was settling in.

While Bob was adapting to Montreal, there was a wave of new arrivals to Canada from around the world. Bob is an artist, a poet, a person who cares about others. He found his calling working as a community organizer advocating for the well-being of ethnic and racial minorities, primarily immigrants. He has a strong belief in human rights and social justice. He is also an entrepreneur and a self-taught closet intellectual. He believes the entrenched capitalistic economic system is rotten and wants to change the world through community activism. He was one of the founders of ACCÉSSS (Alliance des communautés culturelles pour l'égalité dans la santé et les services sociaux, Alliance of Cultural Communities for Equality in Health and Social Services), an organization created in 1984 to facilitate better health care for underserved people. ACCÉSSS is now one of the largest national organizations serving immigrants in Canada. Bob is retired but still helps out and has an office at the organization's headquarters in Montreal.

Bob maintains a Buddhist perspective on life. Looking back, he doesn't think he'd do anything differently and doesn't regret his decision to go to Canada, nor does he regret the changes in his life brought about by moving there. He thought of himself as a refugee. He was used to being uprooted and was already a nomad when he saw Canada as his only option. Though he says "being a refugee has colored my life," Bob ultimately found the challenge was not insurmountable.

Bob believes the twentieth century was a depressing and scary time: "Genocides abounded—the Holocaust, Armenia, Rwanda, Pol Pot's transition of Cambodia, and let's not forget the threat of nuclear war. New waves of violence against entire populations continue today."

Although he has come close, Bob has never married. Reminiscing, he mentioned that when he was younger, he had a "free love" lifestyle and a few important relationships. He has no children. "Why should I bring children into this world?" he asked rhetorically.

While Bob was in Canada, and because he failed to show up for his physical, a delinquency notice was placed in his Selective

Service file. At the time, general sentiment in Canada was anti-war and anti-violence. Canada was not part of the US coalition fighting in Vietnam, so it had no extradition treaty for deserters or draft dodgers. (Years later Canada was involved as a peacekeeping force after diplomatic negotiations had quelled the fighting.) However, the FBI could have picked up Bob in Montreal prior to his attaining immigrant status. After President Ford's conditional amnesty in 1974, Bob returned to the United States a few times—to New York, Florida, and Puerto Rico—to see family and friends. There were no hassles, no tense moments with US Customs and Border Protection authorities.

Bob's view of the Vietnam War has not changed. "The war was a crime. But we, the draft dodgers and deserters, the ones who said 'no,' we made a stand. I'm proud of my life. No regrets."

For some men, crossing into Canada was an impulsive or spontaneous move. For others, like Tim Ames, it was a more deliberate maneuver. He was born in New York and currently resides in Vancouver. He spent the bulk of his working years in the area as a primary- and middle-school teacher. He is now retired, but hardly inactive. Civic-minded, he serves on the board of the local community center and stays in excellent shape by participating in the region's senior athletics badminton competition in the fifty-five plus division. He is a skilled player, a champion with gold singles, bronze doubles, and silver mixed doubles wins and awards to his credit. He's raced cars, now rides a bicycle almost everywhere, and is happily addicted to pickleball.

Tim was living in Brooklyn when he turned eighteen and registered at his local draft board. In 1962 he was called in for a physical in New York and received a psychiatric deferment. He didn't have a letter from his psychiatrist when he went to the physical; he got his deferment the old-fashioned way, the hard way. This is how it happened: At his physical, Tim talked back to someone who was ordering him around. Rather than being reprimanded, he was sent to see a psychiatrist. The psychiatrist said something now long forgotten that provoked and infuriated Tim even more. He instantly

Tim Ames during the Vietnam War era (courtesy of Tim Ames)

leaped over the desk and physically attacked the shrink. He was restrained by military personnel, but his actions were not appreciated or disregarded. Tim did not indicate to me whether he had staged the confrontation or if it was a genuine spontaneous action. Regardless, the altercation cast a behavioral shadow and earned him a deferment—a 1-Y, a temporary stay, subject to review at a later date.

Men with the 1-Y classification were often lost in the shuffle, forgotten, or simply dismissed; many never heard from their draft board again. Not so for Tim. Two years later, in 1964, while, ironically, a psychology major at the University of Tennessee in Knoxville, he was ordered to submit to a physical in Tennessee. As with the first physical, he went without a doctor's letter. The physical was routine, however, he took the vision test without his glasses (he had 20/400 and 20/200 eyesight) and was very late raising his hand during the hearing test. Essentially blind and deaf—compromised in two critical senses—he was still acceptable by military standards; he passed the tests. While ordinarily this would classify him as 1-A, he was given a student deferment. He also received an acknowledgement that he was doing work that was benefiting the US government as a research assistant on a project using rats to test the effects of radiation on behavior.

In 1966, after two years of graduate school and on his way to a PhD, Tim took a leave of absence and drove with his wife to California. They stayed several months in a commune in New Mexico before making their way to San Francisco. While in the Bay Area, he worked the graveyard shift for Canco (a packing company), taught at a free school during the day, and was active in the anti-war movement. In 1968 Tim received a notice from his draft board saying he had been reclassified 1-A.

In San Francisco, Tim had been going to anti-war demonstrations. He decided that if he was called, he wouldn't accede to the draft or go to Vietnam and would fight to stay out. In his words:

> It's a matter of personal values, the principles I choose to live by. The United States was wrong, and I wasn't about to advance the nation's efforts in Vietnam. My philosophy was simple: don't invade other countries. Vietnam was invaded by the French and now by the Americans. The US government thought it was a good idea to invade other countries. I didn't agree, and I refused to participate in the war.

But then, how does one avoid the possibility of being dragged into service in an unpopular war? Tim didn't want to go to jail, and he didn't trust the justice system to give him a fair hearing if it came down to being charged with draft evasion. Eventually, he received his induction notice and realized it was time to act on something he had been considering as an alternative to the draft: leave the country. His wife was not opposed to him going and within a week of his notice, he was in Canada. In fact, he went to Canada twice. He took an earlier, pre-notice "just in case" trip to scout and a second, more serious exploration to see if Canada would be a good choice. On his first visit, he spent about a month in Vancouver surveying the city and assessing the possibilities of relocating. He had already taken steps to apply for immigrant status, but nothing had been finalized.

The next trip to Vancouver, in August 1968, was a bit weird, as Tim described it. He delivered a police car to Bellingham, Washington, near the Canadian border, for a California auto dealer. Once the car was turned over to the local police department, Tim crossed into nearby Vancouver as a tourist. He could have been stopped at the border by US agents, but no one questioned him or asked to see his draft card—a common practice back then to prevent "escapes" to Canada. Once in British Columbia, Tim got a job picking strawberries. He then presented a letter to the authorities showing that he was accepted to the University of British Columbia (UBC). The letter allowed him to get Canadian landed immigrant status and gave him the freedom to settle in Canada. He pursued his education, attended UBC for a year, and received certification to teach in British

Columbia's primary and secondary schools. Shortly afterward, his wife joined him, and the two of them and their dog shared a house with several like-minded people.

Tim's parents and family were anti-war and very understanding of his position. His step-brother was a CO. As a result, he had his parents' support throughout his draft-avoidance process. His father, born in New York, was a union organizer and believed that people had to unite for strength—exactly what the anti-war forces were doing. Family and friends visited Tim in Vancouver and even alerted him that because he had not shown up for his induction, the FBI was looking for him.

Tim told me that in Vancouver in 1968, there were rumors of FBI agents entering Canada to kidnap alleged draft dodgers, take them back to United States, and arrest them on draft evasion charges. Urban myths? Paranoia? Maybe, maybe not. Sometimes there are good reasons to be paranoid. But Tim went on to say that back then two men had come to his front door and told him they were "selling insurance." Putting them off for a moment, he went out the back door, snuck around, and looked inside their car. He saw items that identified them as FBI. Tim called the Royal Canadian Mounted Police (RCMP) for assistance, but they initially dismissed his concerns and did nothing. He called again and told the RCMP, "I have a shotgun, and I'll shoot them if they come into my house." The RCMP came out immediately, sent the FBI away, and thanked him for letting them know. After that episode Tim was no longer harassed.

When asked if he gave up anything by moving north, Tim pointed out that he is treated with more respect in Canada than he had been in the United States. "The RCMP call me 'Sir,'" he says. "Life in Canada is just fine. People are friendlier here." He has no desire to return to the United States and no regrets about what he did to avoid military service.

Tom Sandborn is a freelance writer who has been involved in community activism since the 1960s. "Community activism" in his case means social justice and a keen eye on civil rights, environmental concerns, issues concerning racism, equal rights for women and

First Nations (indigenous) people, and the peace/anti-war movement of the 1960s. While Tom is definitely on the left side of the political spectrum, it wasn't always that way. As Vietnam was making its way to the front pages of the newspapers, Tom was straddling the fence.

Tom was born in Cordova, Alaska. After stays in Bremerton, Washington, and San Francisco, his family moved to Oroville, California, where he attended high school and registered for the draft. He was a junior in high school when the Gulf of Tonkin incident took place in the summer of 1964.

With President Johnson positioning the incident as an unprovoked attack by North Vietnam on American forces, Tom's reaction was a red-blooded, gung-ho "I'm gonna join the marines and get the Commies!" He may well have been suffering from John Wayne syndrome, he acknowledges, but his older brother, who had served as a marine and understood what military service was about, wouldn't let him enlist. "He threatened to break my arm and keep it broken until I went to university," said Tom.

Tom took his brother's threat seriously and went for the academic option: he accepted a scholarship to the University of San Francisco (USF). As the war cranked up while he was attending the Jesuit school, he was being pressured and cajoled by both pro- and anti-war elements to see the Vietnam issue their way. Despite both sides' attempts at persuading Tom to align him with their thinking, he remained undecided. He was classified 2-S at the time and was working as a reporter with the USF college newspaper, the *Foghorn*. The decisive "aha" moment came when he went to cover a speaker, a former US Marine and anti-war activist in the Catholic Worker Movement, who was lecturing about the war. Those involved with the movement make informal vows of poverty and absolute pacifism. Tom listened closely to the man's presentation, mulled it over during a sleepless night spent tramping about the San Francisco streets, and by the following morning, he saw his vacillation as a genuine spiritual crisis. Regarding himself as a "vulgar atheist," he found a young priest, discussed his personal views, and joined the Catholic Church. He also decided to stop attending the university's mandatory ROTC classes and turned in his ROTC rifle. As a result of his act of protest, he was expelled from school. He appealed the administration's decision, sympathetic professors lobbied for him, and he was readmitted. The incident did not change his views or behavior. Still working on the university newspaper and becoming more firmly committed to his anti-war beliefs, he wrote and published a satirical article "Kill a Commie for Christ" in the school newspaper. The article was not well received by the administration and did nothing to enhance Tom's standing with the school's power structure. However, at least one of his Jesuit professors took the satire as it was intended and recommended the column to his students as "the best defense of the Christian soldier I have read in years!"

Reviewing his now fully formed attitudes about the war, Tom wondered if he could qualify to be a CO. In the end he decided not to apply for the CO exemption from the draft.

In 1967 Tom married. He and his bride had a big wedding. Without consulting his wife, Tom wrote to his draft board, declaring that he "wanted no part of war." He said, "I intended to do anti-war work until they took me away." Tom acknowledged that he should have discussed this decision with his wife before making that move. "Something like that could have consequences for her."

At the time, he was also tutoring young Black kids in the community, and in his view it was clear that their older brothers would be drafted. "Blacks and hillbillies were making up a large part of the draft board's quota," Tom said.

Tom's anti-war stand was firm, and he was prepared to go to jail if that's what it came to. A friend sat him down and described what would happen in prison. Family pressure also came into play: his younger brother believed that Tom going to jail would kill his mother and asked him to stay away from that option. Tom realized jail was not a good choice. Tom also knew that he wouldn't qualify for a physical deferment or exemption. So what escape routes were left? Canada was the immediate possibility, but where in Canada? He had a conversation with a drug dealer acquaintance who recommended Vancouver, a liberal progressive city. This time, Tom discussed the prospective move with his wife and with her okay took their wedding money and flew to Vancouver in December 1967.

In due course, Tom's wife joined him and they applied for

landed immigrant status. Tom told me that part was easy because "draft dodgers were not yet on the radar." His family had no idea of Tom's move to Canada until after he arrived there. His mother was relieved that he would not be drafted or go to jail, yet mortified and embarrassed that her son had run away. She received hate mail, and a cousin was so upset he said to Tom, "You're as much of an asshole as your father." Tom believed that the cousin said that out of spite because Tom's father, "a feckless alcoholic," was not popular with his mother's family. Once he was safe in Canada, Tom's mother visited him every summer. His brother also visited, fell in love with Vancouver, and moved there as well.

While Tom's move to Canada was positive and he was well received by other American expatriates, there was a disheartening experience. Arriving in Canada, he looked for work as a truck driver at a dairy. When the interviewer found out that Tom was a draft dodger, he abruptly concluded the interview. The man wanted nothing to do with draft dodgers. Coldly rejected, disappointed but not discouraged, Tom simply looked harder and was ultimately able to find work. He took jobs in group homes for teenagers, doing whatever was needed. He drove cabs and trucks and shuttled disabled people in vans. He also attended the University of British Columbia, earned a bachelor's degree in English literature, and did some writing on the side. In addition, he trained as a gestalt therapist and conducted a private practice, leading groups and providing individual therapy. After he stopped his therapy practice, he became a truck and bus driver. In 2001 he shifted from driving to fulltime freelance journalism. He has since written for Canadian publications including the *Globe and Mail*, the *Vancouver Sun*, the *Tyee*, and the *Georgia Straight*, on a range of social policy subjects and as a book reviewer.

Long before Tom left for Canada, he returned his draft card to his local board. The board turned the matter over to the FBI, and the agency eventually tracked him down in Vancouver. He received a disciplinary induction order: show up at the Oakland induction center or be subject to arrest. Whether the FBI would have sent agents to Vancouver to apprehend him is unknown but probably unlikely. What is known, however, is that the RCMP told Tom that the FBI had asked them if he was planning on returning to the United

Tom Sandborn (photo by Louise Alden)

States. How the FBI expected the RCMP to know is a matter for speculation. Tom's legal advisor in Canada told him not to go back: "Don't worry; you won't be extradited from Canada." Tom ignored the draft board notice and the FBI. He did not hear from either agency again.

Toward the end of the Vietnam War, the US government became aware of the backlog of Selective Service draft avoidance cases and winnowed out the ones that would be difficult or inefficient to win. By that time, Tom was a Canadian citizen but had not given the board formal notice of his change of status. He did not know where his case fit in terms of prosecution priority. In 1974 he returned to the United States for the first time for a family visit. He was concerned and anxious about what could happen when he tried to cross the border: Was there an outstanding warrant for his arrest? Would he be detained? As it turned out, nothing happened. "There was plenty of flop sweat," he said, "but no problems." When I asked Tom if he considered applying for amnesty, he said,

> No, I didn't apply for amnesty and would not have been willing to do so. When the Selective Service conducted my case review after I was a permanent resident of Canada, I was reclassified. I can't remember the exact classification, but I do recall that I was considered politically unreliable. I would only be called up if Ho Chi Minh got to Sacramento. But, by my own making, I was a Canadian and no longer subject to the draft.
>
> I've had it very easy, I eluded the draft. This was less possible for men of color and men from the working class. Race and class bore on everything. I have no regrets. None. I'd do it again, but with

more research and preparation. No Vietnam. Jail first. Resisting your country when it is waging immoral wars is a high form of patriotism. Today I am the happiest man in Canada.

Tom added that Vietnam War–era reunions are still held in Nelson, British Columbia, where a Vietnam draft dodger memorial was proposed but then halted by a group representing the US Veterans of Foreign Wars.

It has been almost fifty years since Alan Zisman moved to Canada. He spent the first ten years in Montreal before relocating to Vancouver, where he now resides. His introduction to Canada began when he was about to turn eighteen.

Alan grew up in Hillside, New Jersey, as he describes it, "a White-flight city." When he was seventeen and in the twelfth grade, he started asking what many teenagers on the brink of adulthood ask: What do I do with my life?

That's when Alan began thinking about college and the draft. He would be turning eighteen in December 1968 and knew that he had to register with the Selective Service. He also knew that college would give him a 2-S deferment, so the draft, for the moment, was not a concern. But the Vietnam War was exploding, and he knew that it would probably have an impact on his life at some point.

Alan applied for college and was accepted to his top three choices: Columbia, Rutgers, and McGill, in Montreal. McGill, Canada's worthy equivalent of an Ivy League school, was one third to one half the cost of the other two schools, making it an attractive financial option and putting it at the top of Alan's university preferences. Perhaps a bigger factor in its appeal to Alan was that if he chose Rutgers or Columbia, he would still be living at home; at McGill he would be on his own in foreign, exciting, and cosmopolitan Montreal.

In the spring of 1968, in the midst of the proliferation of anti–Vietnam War protests, Alan made the short trip to Manhattan to meet with a draft counselor at Columbia University to find out how susceptible he might be to the draft and what his options were.

When Alan mentioned his opportunity to attend McGill, the counselor's eyes lit up: he remembered something important. The counselor jumped up, went to a bookshelf, and pulled out a copy of the Selective Service regulations (Title 32 of the *Code of Federal Regulations*, Chapter XVI). The counselor leafed through a few pages and found the section he wanted. The regulations said that upon turning eighteen and registering for the draft, any man registering outside the United States and not having a US address as his residence is automatically assigned to Local Board 100 in Washington, DC. This rule applied to men living outside the country—generally the children of foreign-based diplomats, military personnel, and business executives. To Alan's delight, the regulation also applied to men attending school outside the United States at the time of registration.

According to the draft counselor, being assigned to Local Board 100 meant that the chance of being drafted was almost nonexistent because the board's quota was zero; the board had rarely, if ever, drafted anyone. As Alan described it, there were two theories for this:

1. The board population makeup consisted largely of the children of overseas military personnel. They were likely to enlist voluntarily, thereby reducing the draft quota.

2. Enforceability was an issue. The ability to enforce the draft induction process abroad was questionable. As long as someone stayed outside the United States, it was doubtful he would be drafted or persecuted.

Given the situation, Alan's mother suggested he opt for McGill. She did not want her son in the army. She was anti-war and encouraged him to move to Canada. Alan's uncle was a lifelong left-wing radical and also opposed to the war. Neither of them objected to Alan opposing the war. Alan's father, on the other hand, was a Nixon Republican and hesitant about openly opposing the war. But Alan's father could easily rationalize his son going to McGill. In his view it wasn't about the war, it was about an education, and McGill was a great school. And cheaper than the American options. If going to McGill meant avoiding the draft, that was a bonus.

Alan happily chose McGill. For the first few months there, almost everyone he met was American. This was not surprising. Canada was culturally similar to the United States and popular because its government had taken a hands-off approach to American draft evaders and their issues. More specifically, McGill seemed to be a magnet for the counterculture. In his freshman year, when he actually turned eighteen, Alan was involved in the student occupation of the school's political science department. The students were demanding participation in and democratization of the department's committees. The occupation held Alan's attention, but the next morning he had to focus on something else: a visit to the US Consulate to register for the draft (he was still obligated to do so).

When Alan walked into the consulate, the coat he was wearing had "Fuck US Imperialism" written on the back—not the smartest fashion statement to make in front of US diplomatic personnel; it was almost like a Kick Me sign. Someone had inscribed it on his coat and Alan didn't realize the statement was there until later in the day when he had already left the consulate. That evening he removed the statement from the coat. While at the consulate, Alan filled out the required forms, registered, and gave only his Montreal address. He was told to return the next day to speak to the consulate general about why he wasn't providing a US address. On his return visit, Alan explained he was attending school in Montreal, and, therefore, lived in Canada. The address he gave them was his residence, and he had no other. The consulate general then asked about the writing on his now-clean coat. Alan feigned wide-eyed innocence—"What statement?" The consulate general wasn't happy with Alan's response, but there was nothing anyone could do about it.

Alan eventually received a 1-A classification while outside the country, but there was no threat of being drafted because he was, as expected, assigned to Local Board 100. "I never knew whether their 'quota of zero' was official or just anecdotal," he says. "Except for a letter I received from them implying that I wouldn't be drafted as long as I lived outside the United States or in territories like American Samoa, I never heard anything else from them." He could not return home to live in the United States, but he had a Canadian student visa and could come home to visit—and did. Montreal was also close enough for his family to visit him over holidays.

While in school, Alan had a part-time job at a hostel that catered to American war resisters. After two years in Canada, he applied

178   Chapter Eleven

Alan Zisman (courtesy of Alan Zisman)

for and was granted landed immigrant status. He graduated from McGill with a degree in psychology and stayed on to attend graduate school.

All told, Alan lived in Montreal from 1968 to 1977. He did whatever was necessary to make ends meet. He became a daycare worker, then bought a van and moved people and their goods. Eventually, he moved himself, his girlfriend, and their dog to Vancouver. It was time for a change. In Vancouver, Alan became a teacher and something of a tech wizard writing articles and blogs about computers and peripheral issues. He is now retired, and much of his time is taken up with music. He is an accomplished pianist and accordionist playing with several musical groups including the Vancouver Squeezebox Circle. He's also an impresario bringing together musicians and audiences at various sites around Vancouver.

Alan told me his attitude about the war was fuzzy at first. He was sympathetic to pacifists but scuffled with police at protests in which windows were broken. Even so, his opinions weren't fully formed yet; some of his actions might have been attributed to the excitement of being part of the anti-war wave. But eventually, his thinking evolved and he saw America's actions as imperialism.

> I couldn't support the building of an empire. I believed that America looked at Vietnam as a start on the road to empire and was already marching to conquest. Vietnam was not a just war that went bad.

Vietnam was just a bad war. If I stayed in the States I would get, at worst, a 2-S. My working-class pals didn't get deferments. If there was no draft loophole for me, I'd like to think that I would've fought against the war. I would like to believe that I would've taken a principled stand if drafted, but who knows what that might have been.

In retrospect, Alan states he would not have done anything differently. His wife is Canadian. They married in 1980 and have two children and two grandchildren. While he has regrets regarding individual slights and at times being a "stupid young man," he has no regrets regarding his life path. He was left-leaning and socially connected to anti-war people. "I had no thought of returning to the United States. My life was so much better in Canada. It began when I got off the plane in Montreal."

When Leonidas Paris ("Leo" to his friends) registered with the Selective Service, Canada was not top of mind. Far from it. As with several of the other US expatriates whom I met, Leo was born and raised in California. He was living in San Francisco in the 1960s at the height of the counterculture. Marijuana highs were making people smile and flashing the peace sign was as good as a handshake. The Monterey Pop Festival that he attended with friends had put music in the air and set the stage for the epic Woodstock event that was yet to come. In Berkeley, embryonic free speech and anti-war protests were hinting at greater demonstrations on the horizon.

That's what it was like in 1967 when, at the age of eighteen, in college, and classified 1-A, Leo enlisted in the US Marine Corps Reserve. This was an odd move for a young man who really wasn't keen on possibly going off to Vietnam to fight a war he was opposed to.

"Since I was a full-time university student, I should not have been given a 1-A draft status," Leo said. "When I saw that, being just eighteen, it never occurred to me that I could challenge the misclassification. The only option to avoid killing innocent people seemed to be to become a reservist and stay stateside."

Leo acknowledges that enlisting in the reserve when he was very young was his way of avoiding the draft. He thought he would be able to dodge Vietnam by volunteering and remaining in the United States. As he explains it,

> I did not support the war and did not want to take part. I believed that evading the draft was the only way for me to avoid killing people, something I did not want to do. At no time did I, or most of my friends in the reserve, worry about what would happen to us. We felt we were right. We had that sense of righteous immortality that most young people have.

While seeing the Marine Corps Reserve as a way to stay out of Vietnam, another key reason Leo had for signing up was that the recruiter told him that after serving for six months, he would be eligible for the GI Bill to pay for college. That was an attractive perk for someone who could use some help to cover school expenses. As Leo quickly found out, however, recruiters would say whatever they needed to get a trusting teenager to enlist. The recruiter's promise was a lie; reservists were not eligible to receive GI Bill benefits. Regardless, in 1968–69, Leo was locked in and stationed in San Bruno, California.

Leo admits that he was naive at the time he joined the reserves, but he swiftly learned the politics from other reservists. Exposure to the alternative lifestyles of the San Francisco Bay Area, he states, helped broaden his thinking. In addition, underground anti-war newsletters such as *Marine Blues* and a similar bulletin for air force reservists were passed around among the troops. Leo paid attention.

> While serving, I got the sense of how the military hyped things to reinforce pro-war impressions on the young reservists. Activism was coming alive in the reserves, and the brass was starting to get nervous. Little incidents were taking place. When grapes were served during the California grape boycott, the men in the unit refused to eat them; when attending a lecture positing that chemical warfare was great because it killed people without destroying property, half the men stormed out of the room in protest.

Many of the men in Leo's unit were thinking for themselves, looking at what was going on around them, uncomfortable with the stands the military was taking. Further unsettling Leo and his buddies were rumors circulating that their unit would be ordered to go to Berkeley to keep the peace during a People's Park protest near the University of California campus. On Thursday, May 15, 1969—a day that became known as "Bloody Thursday"—students and sympathetic area residents marched to the park in protest against the university's plans to turn the site into an athletic field. The march was becoming an energized demonstration, some referred to it as an uprising, and Governor Ronald Reagan sent in police to quash it and rid the area of protestors. But the march turned into a bloody riot, and the clash between the police and demonstrators left dozens injured and one dead. Acting as a police force in Berkeley was not something the marine reservists had signed up for. They weren't opposed to the protest and having to take orders to turn on people they sympathized with was making the men more than uneasy. Several reservists voiced their opinions, and the men in Leo's unit decided that if they were sent to subdue the People's Park resistance, they would wait until they were in front of the TV cameras, throw down their weapons, and declare solidarity with the community. Their officers were not pleased. In the summer of 1969, two men in Leo's unit were singled out to go to Vietnam as punishment for their activism and to serve as a deterrent—and an example—to other activist marines. Leo was one of them. That was his breaking point.

On the day he was to ship out, Leo failed to report. He simply disappeared and went underground. He stayed away from the base, stayed away from home, and stayed away from friends and relatives. For several weeks, he lived in his car in Berkeley. He was no longer simply an activist or an anti-war protester: Leo was AWOL, soon to be a deserter, and on the run. The military police began looking for him. They came to his family's house and surrounded it. The FBI got involved and convinced some neighbors to spy on the family home in case Leo showed up. He didn't. Years later, Leo used the Freedom of Information Act to look into his FBI file and received a highly redacted memorandum in which the names of witnesses and investigators had been blacked out.

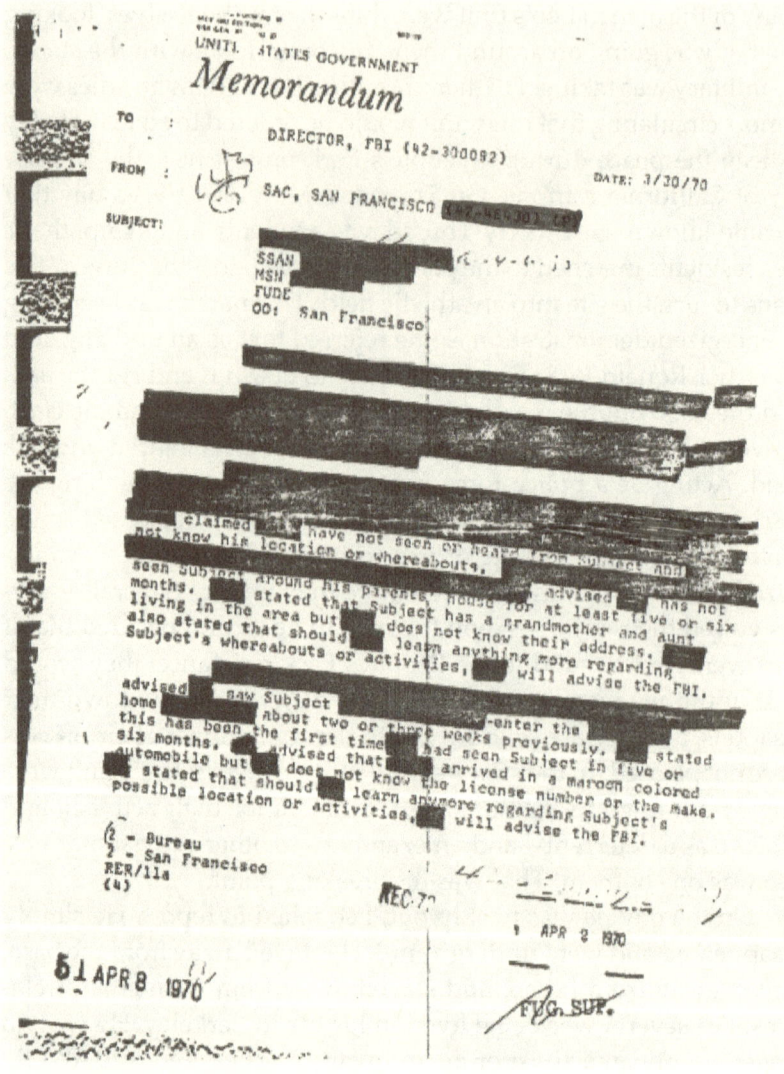

Redacted FBI memo regarding search for Leo Paris obtained through FOIA request (courtesy of Leo Paris)

His father, mother, and sister supported him and his decision even though his father and about a half dozen of his uncles were all in the military in World War II. They did not disclose any information to the MPs regarding his whereabouts. At one point, while still underground and having minimal contact with family, Leo was secretly driving with his father when he spotted a police car behind them. "Don't worry," his father said. "If they're after you, I'll lose them."

Leo didn't hang around for long. Canada was now on his radar. He first went to Seattle with the assistance of the draft resistance "underground railway" and its network of anti-war sympathizers who moved him northward. In Seattle, he contacted the Quakers, reliable pacifists, who protected him. He had a scary moment when a cop randomly stopped him in Bellingham, Washington, close to the US-Canadian border, and asked for his draft card number but not, strangely, his draft card. That was a stroke of luck for Leo because he didn't have the card—which registrants were supposed to carry on their person at all times—but he had written down his number and read it aloud to the cop. The cop never asked for the card itself, probably assuming that Leo had it, so any issues about violating applicable card-possession laws or regulations were avoided. The next day, Leo crossed without trouble into British Columbia and contacted a Canadian war resistance group.

The Vietnam War–era underground railway Leo used was similar in concept to the one that carried US slaves from the southern states to Canada in pre–Civil War days. Through word-of-mouth contact, anti-war organizations and individual sympathizers would help draft resisters to avoid the authorities by providing shelter, food, transportation, and moral support while moving them surreptitiously from one house to another on their journey north.

When Leo was safely in Canada, any doubts his family had about whether he had done the right thing were quickly dismissed by a letter they received from one of his uncles, a professor of history and a World War II veteran. The image of this letter appears on page 184.

In Canada, Leo quickly found work. He, like other immigrants, did whatever he could to bring in money: he sold papers on the street, worked in the shipyards, took odd jobs, anything to earn a buck. Eventually he applied for and received landed immigrant status. His thought was if he had to make a new life, "Canada's not so bad."

At the time, Canada had government grants to help young

> Dear ▆▆▆ and ▆▆▆:
>
> The other day I had a thank you note from ▆▆▆ and learned for the first time that he was in Canada. I take it for granted that both of you are concerned about him and his future. For whatever my opinion may be worth you need not be. Any young man that has the couragee of his convictions to the extent that ▆▆▆ has demonstrated will stand pretty tall in the end.
>
> He is to be highly commended for refusing to engage in an immoral and unconstitutional war that has absolutely no meaning. If I were in his shoes I would have chosen the same path. In fact that I tell my students to do this if their draft number comes up. When sanity returns to this country, it is those who refused to participate that will emerge as the real heroes not those who went 10,000 miles from home to kill a helpless people that have never done anything to us.
>
> Cheer up and mark my words,
>
> ▆▆▆

Letter from Leo Paris's uncle (courtesy of Leo Paris)

people do community work. Leo qualified for a grant, went back to school, and continued his university studies. He led a quiet life in the Vancouver area. His family visited him a few times. In 1974 President Ford issued a conditional amnesty for Vietnam deserters, and Leo was able to return to the United States.

Once cleared to re-enter the country, Leo attended classes at the University of Colorado and earned a bachelor's degree in psychology. But he didn't stay in the United States. He had acclimated to Canada and in 1981 he opted to become a Canadian citizen. He eventually earned a master's degree at the University of British Columbia. In 1990 he began teaching courses on political ideologies and philosophy, the human condition, and international political economics at the university level. He still teaches today and has written topical articles for the *Globe & Mail*, the *Vancouver Sun*, *Scientific American*, and other noteworthy publications. He also works as an extra in Vancouver's television and movie industry. Leo currently retains his socially progressive leanings. He volunteers with Oxfam and was a candidate for provincial and federal office on the left-wing New Democratic

Party ticket. When asked how his Vietnam experience had affected his teaching, he forthrightly said, "It definitely colors my teaching. It makes me passionate about what I teach, especially about critical thinking."

Looking back, Leo regrets only the loss of time with his family. "We were very close. My entire extended family was supportive—cousins, aunts, uncles, and my beloved grandmother."

Leo added that he would not have done anything differently and viewed opposing the war as a true act of patriotism. "Trying to stop one's country from committing war crimes and killing innocent people, while its own sons and daughters are sent into combat, is very patriotic, especially in contrast to those who did nothing to stop the war or those who supported the war but only as long as others did the fighting—Johnson, Nixon, then Bush, Cheney, et al., in the Iraq War."

When the men I interviewed spoke of amnesty and pardons, they were referring to programs Presidents Ford and Carter implemented after the Vietnam peace agreement was signed. President Ford, on September 16, 1974, issued Presidential Proclamation 4313 that established a conditional clemency program for men who evaded the draft during the war and those in the military who deserted while serving. The program, as noted, had some conditions attached: men who applied for such amnesty had to reaffirm their allegiance to the United States and serve two years working in a public service job. In his proclamation, as reported by the *New York Times* and other media, Ford termed desertion and draft evasion in time of war as serious offenses but said, "Reconciliation calls for an act of mercy to bind the nation's wounds and to heal the scars of divisiveness."*

On January 21, 1977, the day after he was inaugurated, President Carter kept a controversial campaign promise he had made and issued Presidential Proclamation 4483 in which he granted "a

---

* Margaret Hunter, "Ford Offers Amnesty Program Requiring Two Years Public Work; Defends His Pardon of Nixon," *New York Times*, September 17, 1974.

full, complete and unconditional pardon" for draft evaders who fled the country, did not register, or otherwise eluded military service.* Unlike Ford, Carter set no conditions for accepting the pardon, but the offer was not extended to deserters or convicted civilian protestors who had engaged in acts of violence. Not everyone eligible accepted the amnesty or the pardon.

---

* "Proclamation 4483—Granting Pardon for Violations of the Selective Service Act, August 4, 1964, to March 28, 1973," National Archives, Office of the Federal Register, https://www.archives.gov/federal-register/codification/proclamations/04483.html.

Chapter 12

We Could Complicate Things

While the Selective Service appeared ready to try and draft anyone and everyone, who did the army really want? Certainly not the rabble-rousers, hard-core activists-pacifists, idiosyncratic nonconformists, or troublemakers. And probably not the men with iffy medical conditions that might require attention at some point down the road. Or did they?

RJ Gibson is a native Detroiter and devoted, lifelong baseball fan who has lectured in the California State University system and now teaches American history at a community college in San Diego near Camp Pendleton Naval Base. Many of his students are military veterans or current enlistees. He attended Cranbrook School, an elite private prep school in Bloomfield Hills, Michigan. No snooty, spoiled rich boy, RJ was there on scholarship. Combining an exceptional education, a strong personality, and lots of native smarts, RJ Gibson has never been one to hide his opinions—or his priorities. He is a dyed-in-the-wool egalitarian unafraid of speaking his mind or throwing a fist when necessary. Had he been a citizen of France during the July Revolution of 1830, he would be represented in Eugène Delacroix's allegorical painting *Liberty Leading the People*. When I visited him in his spacious home in San Diego, I found that he had mellowed somewhat, but *somewhat* is relative and refers only to his voice being a little softer, the fire in the eyes just slightly less fierce, and—because we're all a little creakier as we've aged—he displayed a bit less fury in his demeanor. As our conversation wandered across the Vietnam War era and into the modern inequities of the world, a baseball game aired on the big screen TV across the room and RJ cheered for the underdog. I saw that the conflagration still simmers deep inside him, and I could sense that all the people who have been shortchanged in life still have a friend in RJ Gibson.

RJ attended Wayne State University. In 1967–68, he was active with SDS and took on the self-appointed role of "traveler," or regional representative and recruiter for the organization. In school, while other students were concerned about grades, RJ told his professors, "Just give me a B, a C would be fine too, and leave me alone, SDS is more important." The professors often complied, even though some students not subject to the draft were not happy with the apparent favoritism.

RJ became well known in local activist circles. He was arrested on several occasions and spent time in jail for disruptive SDS activities, including participating in anti-war demonstrations and handing out leaflets. He was often regarded as a labor instigator—intentionally recruiting into unions those workers who were not always sympathetic to management.

Aside from being thrown *into* jail, RJ was also thrown *out of* places, schools in particular. As a student, he was expelled from Cranbrook, and when it was time for higher education, he was asked to leave Western Michigan University, Central Michigan University, the University of Michigan, and Wayne State University—all because of his tendencies to break the rules. At Western Michigan, for example, RJ set up an MC5 rock concert with permits properly applied for and issued and all details addressed. At the last minute, the school suddenly realized who the MC5 were (a controversial and provocative hard rock band with the big hit album *Kick Out the Jams* featuring lyrics with the unacceptable word *motherfuckers*), tried to cancel the concert, and locked the doors of the arena concert site. The students took issue with the school's decision. With RJ's help they broke down the arena doors and had the music going for ten minutes before state police came in to break it up. When the police stopped the concert, a riot ensued with RJ right in the middle. One might call RJ's bane "authority issues"; however, the consequences were never severe enough to deter him. He always managed to enroll in school somewhere and ultimately earned a doctorate in education and history.

Members of SDS and the regional collective of anti-war organizations, the Detroit Committee to End the War, had long discussions about who should, or should not, allow themselves to be drafted or enlist. The intention was to have designated undercover people comply with the draft, be inducted, and work from the inside to "screw up the military." The collective said definitely *not* RJ Gibson. He was considered too hot-headed. SDS also had a discussion about who should go to Chicago in 1968 for the Democratic National Convention. As RJ recalls,

> I cannot remember where all the student meetings—SDS and others—were, but there were quite a few meetings about going to Chicago, good idea or not. We all felt it would be a police trap. People would probably get hurt, maybe killed, but we wanted to connect with the "Get Clean for Gene"* kids. I was in Detroit in '67, during the rebellion [referring to the city's race riots that year]. I saw how the cops, then the state troopers, and then the National Guard, operated. It looked like a police riot as much as a rioters' riot. I worked at [Detroit] Receiving Hospital downtown as a volunteer for a while. I saw how cops beat up people and saw people who had been shot. I was at the march on the Pentagon that October. The cops and troops were more restrained and organized, but the beatings were still pretty rough.
>
> I knew a lot of stories about the Chicago police and the Daley machine. Since I was then in Kalamazoo, at Western Michigan, and Chicago was close, the group figured I knew Chicago pretty well and thought I'd be pretty good there. I really didn't know anything about Chicago, but I went, we demonstrated, and like everyone else, I got the shit kicked out of me. I was not arrested.

Around this time, RJ received a notice that he was about to be drafted into the marines. He went to Fort Wayne for a physical, where he was given a routine IQ test. He scored a zero on it. The army NCOs monitoring the exam said, "But you went to Cranbrook. You're smart." It took a few minutes for it to finally dawn on him

---

* This refers to US Senator Eugene McCarthy of Minnesota, a candidate for the 1968 Democratic presidential nomination.

that RJ intentionally failed. "You did this on purpose," he yelled, but still let RJ leave the exam center.

RJ was later called back for a second physical and immediate induction. While he and other draftees were in a room waiting for whatever would come next, he made a speech urging the men not to comply and not to go to Vietnam. Army officers came into the room and told the men that they were being inducted. They were further told that as soon as they crossed a line on the floor, they were in the army. RJ refused to cross the line. They dragged him out of the room but again inexplicably let him leave.

At home and not knowing what would happen next, RJ did a little research and sent a personal, pointed letter to each member of his draft board. It read simply *This is who you are and this is where you live*. He never heard from his draft board again. Did the army consider him too much trouble? Was his arrest record daunting? Did he unwittingly flunk his physical? RJ doesn't know. RJ believed some of his draft problems were caused by his involvement with SDS. But his real problems, the ones that poison our society in his view, rose up from the war and racism or, more broadly, capitalism and imperialism. It was his condemnation of these concepts that molded his character and staunch opposition to the war. RJ continues:

> While the main things on my mind, say in '65, were the civil rights movement and the anti-war movement, I guess the draft actually changed my life. Of course, that was a product of the war.
>
> I was terribly afraid, but less afraid of jail than the draft. I was frequently arrested, but other inmates didn't bother me because I was political. The draft itself was not my biggest fear—what it could lead to was even more frightening. Always hanging over my head, more on point, I was afraid of being in the military because I thought *they*—the military—would find a way to kill me, and I didn't want to die at their hands for something that I opposed in every way.
>
> I hoped to be an English major, to become a writer and write short stories. Then, the war and the draft woke me, not so gently, from that fond dream and I spent my life fighting what I suppose could be summed up as empire and racism. Most of it has been a

kick, but I do wonder what might've come of all those short stories that became political leaflets instead.

I spent years and years writing leaflets and I found that writing a political or academic essay longer than two sides of a flyer is almost presumptuous. If you can't say it in that space—WTF? However, I am proud to have been an infamous SDSer.

Eventually, time just ran out on the draft. Committed to his ideals, RJ joined VISTA in 1970 and was sent with other students to Greeley, Colorado. They were supposed to be reading specialists, but he was really training the locals to be community organizers. "The students were nice, young, earnest people from all over the country," he said. "I don't know if VISTA ever found out what I was doing."

Given the aggressive nature of his opposition to the war and the company he kept, RJ was exposed to a great number of rumors about events around the war and the draft: like the story about a friend who went to his physical chained to priests who accompanied him and declared, "If you take me you have to take them." Military police simply cut the chains and sent them all on their way.

RJ also believes his name was on a "bad guys" list that President Nixon inherited from Lyndon Johnson. He said, "I think it was called the ADEX list. There might be a file on that in the Reuther Library or the Michigan-Detroit Red Squads."* RJ knows his stuff. The ADEX, or Administrative Index, was a list the FBI kept from 1967 to 1971 of people who might be considered a threat to the security of the country.

RJ regrets not studying more in school, but he's not sorry about what he's done. He says, "I was tremendously lucky. I had a scholarship at Cranbrook where I saw the ruling class. Grades seven, eight, and nine at Cranbrook. It was amazing, and I stayed in touch with the boys, and the place, ever since. What would I do different? Study the classics. Write short stories."

---

* RJ is referring to the Walter P. Reuther Library, Archives of Labor and Urban Affairs, located on the Wayne State University campus.

Chapter Twelve

Regarding patriotism, RJ didn't hold back. "I was never patriotic. I even hated school spirit, flags, etc. By the time I was eighteen, I figured this was 'their' country, not mine."

Therein lies the rub for him: If you're not respected as part of the nation, why fight for it? RJ wanted to write stories. He wound up writing and teaching about capitalism and war. And watching baseball.

At the time of the Vietnam War, Richard Busey was a senior at Michigan State University majoring in packaging, part of the business school marketing curriculum. He was going to classes, enjoying beer and pizza with his buddies, sitting in on dormitory poker games, in short, he was a fairly typical college student. Because of his 2-S student deferment he wasn't about to be drafted, but others were. He took notice.

Richard graduated in 1967, at the age of twenty-two, just as draft pressure was mounting. He was worried about what would happen to him. There were desirable jobs in his field that he wanted and probably would have gotten, but he was concerned about being called up. If he accepted a job, he would lose his deferment and be exposed. As much as he wanted to start his career, he decided to wait, go to graduate school, and hold on to his student deferment.

Richard had reasonable grades, but not necessarily high enough to guarantee admission to a well-regarded graduate program. On the other hand, he was a good test-taker, did very well on his GMATs, and was able to find two good schools that focused more on test scores than on grades; one was the University of Georgia. He applied, was accepted, and enrolled at the Athens, Georgia, campus that fall, allowing him to maintain his treasured 2-S deferment.

While at Georgia, Richard was on friendly terms with one of his professors, also a man of draft age. He asked the professor why he wasn't in the army. The professor said he had a teaching deferment that was keeping him out of the military. That got Richard's attention. He didn't know this was possible—that a university teaching position could deliver a legitimate deferment. Aware that his student deferment would evaporate as soon as he finished his graduate studies and the war showing no hint that it would end before his deferment disappeared, Richard began to investigate teaching possibilities for himself. He found that Central Missouri State University (CMSU, since renamed the University of Central Missouri and coincidentally the same school where a close friend of his had landed), in Warrensburg, was looking for a marketing professor. He applied for the position, went to the university for an interview with the department chairman, was offered the job, and accepted it the same day. After signing his employment contract, he notified his draft board, Local Board 182 in Northwest Detroit, and was given the appropriate deferment—2-A (registrant deferred because of civilian occupation).

Richard taught at CMSU for two and a half years. While there, teaching deferments were eliminated. With the draft still in place, Richard needed to find another solution. He had bad knees, maybe this would be enough to keep him out of the army, but were his knees bad enough?

Richard weighed his options. He would soon be out of deferments. As much as he did not want to be drafted, he considered enlisting in order to have some choice in how and where he served. That idea was quickly dashed when he spoke with military recruiters who told him they didn't want him as an officer—the knees—but also warned him that he could be drafted since the Selective Service and the army weren't as choosey about general draftees. Fearing he was going to be pulled into the service, he contacted the Draft Resistance League of Kansas City. When Richard mentioned his bad knees, draft counselors directed him to a local physician. The doctor evaluated Richard's symptoms without ever touching his knees and wrote a two-and-a-half-page letter that would advise the Selective Service that, for medical reasons, Richard was not qualified for military service. Richard sent the letter to the draft board. He was told he would still need a physical.

Then in early 1970, back in Detroit, a fiery reprieve: someone burned down Richard's draft board. An unknown individual had broken into the board office, pulled files out of drawers, poured accelerant on them, and started a fire. The blaze destroyed the building. All records were gone. According to Richard, the arson was never made public. He knew about the incident through a contact in the Detroit Fire Department. However, Richard pointed out that there were notices in the local paper, the *Redford Record*, advising everyone in Local Board 182 to contact the board immediately. Richard never did. He didn't think that many other guys did or would. Why would they? He never heard from his draft board again. At some point along the way he burned his draft card. A fitting metaphor.

Throughout this period, Richard's father had told him that if he wanted to go to Canada, he would arrange it. Richard never seriously considered that as an option. As it turned out, he never really had to. He always believed he'd find a way around the Selective Service. In his words,

> I think I played the system as well as I possibly could, and I have no regrets. I struggled to get into grad school after reviewing every university catalog in the MSU library, and I found a good school. I had to find a university teaching job, as I had no teaching certificate qualifying me to teach K through twelve, and I found one. I had to find a doctor who was sympathetic enough to write a letter, as many doctors who supported the war would not help me. Again, I found one. I was resourceful, determined, and lucky at each stage, and I worked at it day and night.

Richard's attitude about the war was not flattering to the decision-makers who inhabited the White House and congressional offices. "Vietnam was a bunch of political nonsense between world leaders, with questionable relevance to the true security of the United States," he said. "It was as though the leaders were playing a video game, and I wasn't going to be part of it."

The draft experience did have some value for Richard, however. "In the end," he says, "this period created a level of resourcefulness that's lasted with me to this day, an ability to do whatever is necessary to achieve an end. The draft, and my aversion to it, had something to do with it."

Richard was, and still is, a highly motivated individual. Once past the draft, Richard continued teaching and, appropriately, became a tenured professor of entrepreneurship at a Southern university. He is now enjoying retirement.

I've known John R. Rodan since the early 1980s when he hired me as an adjunct professor at the Wayne State University School of Business Administration in Detroit. I was a lawyer, but I was also an advertising agency creative director and copywriter. John was a marketing professor by career and the department chairman at the school at the time. He needed someone to stand in front of the class and lecture about copywriting. Somehow I was referred to him or he was referred to me, in any case, we made the connection, and I was hired. Now retired, John—known as "Smokey" to his friends—was born and raised in Metropolitan Detroit. He graduated from Michigan State University, where he earned a bachelor's degree in hotel and club management, worked in marketing research in St. Louis, and received an MBA in marketing from the University of Missouri. He continued in that field, earning a PhD from the University of Kentucky.

John was teaching at CMSU in Warrensburg, Missouri—where his friend Richard Busey was also lecturing—as the Vietnam War was cranking up. He was attempting to get a 2-A classification, based on his teaching at the college level. According to John, his local draft board administrator, Mary Kelly—the same woman who oversaw many of his friends' fates—was hostile to deferments and took them away at the slightest opportunity. The board had to meet a quota, and in 1968, without warning, the 2-A deferment vanished and he was reclassified 1-A.

John was well aware of the Vietnam War and its background. He was a military buff and knew the history of Southeast Asia. To him, it was obvious that the Vietnam conflict was a civil war and outsiders should not be involved. As he told me,

> Eventually, colonial powers are always kicked out by locals, witness the French experience. We knew they were stupid—I'm referring to our government—now we knew they were crazy. The presidential advisors lied our way into the war. The fictional Gulf

of Tonkin episode was an example of those lies. The domino theory was bullshit. Vietnam was a civil war: Viet Minh versus the South Vietnam puppet government. The Vietnam run-up was American imperialism at its best. Iraq and Afghanistan are the more recent parallels.

In the summer of 1969, John was ordered to go for a physical at an induction center in Kansas City. Faced with the possibility of being drafted, John thought, *No way am I going into the army. No way am I becoming cannon fodder.* John had grown up with a father who was a navy veteran, the captain of two different ships in both World War II theaters, but his family was sympathetic to his views and understood why he was opposed to the war.

At the time, the Draft Resistance League of Kansas City provided young men with anti-war counseling and referrals to lawyers and doctors who would help with draft resistance. John went to the league for assistance. The group suggested a physical checkup to try for a medical deferment. John accepted their counsel and decided to go for a 1-Y.

> I'm blind as a bat—20/800, but not blind enough to flunk a draft physical. So I went to a local doctor for an overly acidic stomach that I'd had for at least three years. An X-ray showed that I had a duodenal ulcer. On a home visit, I went to the library and looked up the Selective Service classifications and specific number codes for different types of medical rejection and sent the information to the draft board. It worked.

John received his 1-Y letter—"a great cause for great celebration"—and never heard from the draft board again. Adding to John's drama at the time was that in the first draft lottery his birthday drew the number one slot. John has no regrets about his anti-war position, then or now. If the 1-Y hadn't worked out, he said he would have gone to Canada—"a real option at that time."

It was a simple enough story for someone with a legitimate medical condition. But given the number of times medical conditions were ignored, misinterpreted, or their importance minimized by army doctors, there was no assurance a particular condition would keep a guy out, and if he was drafted, no assurance the condition would be properly attended to in the service. If Richard or John had not pointed out their medical conditions, would those conditions have come to light in their respective army physicals? If they had been drafted and their conditions were diagnosed after they were inducted, would the army have gotten its return on investment in them? Perhaps all the guys with the doctors' letters were really doing the army a favor.

Would the US Army welcome a lifelong activist? Steve Daniels wasn't sure, but he hoped not. Steve is a schoolboy friend. We've known each other since we met at a summer day camp when we were eight years old. Steve is quite bright—highly intelligent and book smart. After following a variety of academic paths at the University of Michigan, he settled on medical school and became a trauma specialist, an emergency room doctor. While at U of M, Steve was an activist. He was a member of SDS, participated in numerous protests and sit-ins, and later in life continued to apply much of his protest energy to social issues of the day.

Today Steve is retired and lives in a California coastal city where he is able to enjoy his passion—music, in particular, the blues. He hosts a weekly blues music radio show and serves as emcee on blues-themed ocean cruises. Occasionally, he'll pick up a harmonica and make his own musical contribution. The Vietnam War is far behind him, but the memories are clearly still there. As he saw it,

> While a student at the University of Michigan from 1963 to 1967, I received two draft notices. Both times I replied that I was an undergraduate in college, and duly received a 2-S student deferment. In 1969 I cut short a stint in graduate school and moved to San Francisco. I lived in the devolving Haight-Ashbury district and worked as a psychiatric technician, followed by a year of odd jobs in the Santa Cruz area, then embarked on medical school and my subsequent thirty-year career in the medical field.
>
> In 1969 President Nixon (may he rest without peace) instituted

Steve Daniels, then and now (courtesy of Steve Daniels)

the draft lottery system. I had moved to San Francisco by the time the first random lottery numbers were chosen on December 1, 1969. We draft registrants who were previously exempted prayed that our birthdates would draw a high number; it was predicted that nobody with a number higher than 200 would be drafted or even called up for a physical, and that even a number over 100 was relatively safe. (As it happened, 215 was the highest number called for preinduction exams in the ensuing years; in 1970, my lottery year, 195 was the highest unlucky number.)

Of course it wasn't fair that many of us would avoid the draft by a stroke of luck, while many underprivileged men chose to enlist because military service, even in wartime, was the best of otherwise bleak occupational alternatives. The system was unfair, and we knew it. We didn't want them to go, but we sure didn't want to go ourselves.

The day arrived when a letter appeared in my mailbox with the Selective Service return address. I had received similar letters in the past, twice calling me for draft exams and then twice getting a student deferment. The arrival of the letter was not a surprise, but it was a shock. This time the envelope held a number.

My fantasy was to burn the unopened letter, and claim, if ever confronted, that it had never arrived. What if I had drawn a high number, though? I would be home free, still plagued by guilt at my good fortune while others suffered, but relieved nonetheless unless the war continued going poorly for US forces, in which case more troops might be needed and no number would be safe.

Yet if I burned the letter, might I not be subject to jail, or even be drafted punitively if my act were discovered?

I opened the letter: unlucky number 13. More fear. Agitation. Indecision.

I faced an agonizing personal dilemma. There was no way that I would report for the draft exam, pass it, and be inducted into the army. That was as unlikely as my enlisting. Even had the US not been engaged in a war which I opposed vehemently, I could not envision myself as being part of the military. The regimentation, unquestioned obedience to authority, and training in the exercise of lethal violence were inimical to my personal values and incompatible with my personality. I had been in only one or two fights as a child, never as an adult, and couldn't conceive of harming another person deliberately except in an extreme situation of self-defense, or in a blatantly (although still arguably) "just war," such as World War II. Or was I rationalizing to protect myself? No matter, in this particular case I was not going to be inducted to assist the continued prosecution of the Vietnam debacle.

What were my options—conscientious objector status? I had considered applying for that exemption in the past, but had not done so partly because of procrastination born of denial (I wouldn't be called), and primarily because it was well known that religious grounds were the only basis on which the Selective Service would grant CO status. I didn't have a religious background or the means to concoct a fake history of religious devotion. Flight to Canada? I was still in the midst of an academic career. I knew nobody in Canada, had no friends planning to flee there, and knew that leaving the US would sever treasured relationships with many friends and devastate my parents. Commit a felony or significant misdemeanor to become exempt on moral grounds? Jail or prison seemed like a dismal alternative to the army, and a criminal record was not something I wanted. Maim myself—maybe not a disabling injury, just something sufficient to render me unattractive or ineligible to the Selective Service—I was desperate enough to contemplate it, but couldn't think of a viable plan or a safe and relatively painless way to do it.

What remained was taking the draft physical exam and either hoping I would be rejected for some reason not yet obvious to me, or rendering myself temporarily unfit. The latter seemed the more promising option. I knew that high blood pressure was deemed unacceptable by the services, so I determined to have hypertension on the day of the exam.

Other than a rare beer and the occasional smoking of marijuana, I had never been a drug user. However, I knew that speed—amphetamines—would raise my blood pressure, probably to an unacceptable level. It would also raise my heart rate. Would that be a tip-off that I was faking hypertension? Wasn't a rapid pulse an expected consequence of the anxiety that comes with undergoing a draft physical? Well, then, wasn't elevated blood pressure also a natural occurrence to be discounted in such a situation of high anxiety? Would I be caught? Would I be kept overnight and reexamined? Would I have to return the next day or the next month for a repeat exam? Would my blood or urine be tested? How many pills would I need to take? How long before the exam should I take them? How dangerous was it? Would the drug give me a heart attack or stroke? Thinking about all the variables must have already raised my blood pressure!

I acquired some Dexedrine or Benzedrine pills and took them before reporting for the draft exam on the day I had dreaded.

The actual exam was held in a large army facility in Oakland. I remember being fearful, sweaty, and agitated, the concomitants of any stressful situation, but also the side effects of amphetamine use. I remember my group of docile, frightened young men marching from exam station to station. I remember bending over with pants down as a doctor (I hope) went down the line, giving each of us an anal finger probe. I remember checking "homosexual tendencies" on my questionnaire, and confirming said tendencies in a brief interview with an official. I remember someone taking my blood pressure and me sneaking a peek at the (high!) result recorded in my file. I remember feeling like I was going to explode or faint at any moment. I remember leaving and the profound relief of getting out of that building and that military environment.

During the ensuing weeks and months of heightened anxiety I awaited the next letter from the draft board. 1-A? 4-F? Had I fooled them?

I will never know. I never heard from the Selective Service again, and I definitely was not about to contact them and ask whether they had forgotten me.

Or maybe I was rejected by the Selective Service. Friends speculate that the Selective Service knew what I (and certainly not I alone) had done in taking amphetamines and decided that I and similar misfits trying to elude the draft in sundry ways would just create problems in the military and were not worth pursuing. Alternatively, the Selective Service may have had access to an FBI file on me and decided my anti-war activities were unwelcome in the army. I was a longtime activist, although never arrested and never involved in illegal actions.

Years later, through the Freedom of Information Act, I inquired about any FBI file on me. To my surprise, there was one, and I sent for it. The several pages had many phrases and paragraphs blacked out, probably to conceal the names of undercover informants. The remaining exposition listed my participation in a few demonstrations—and the make and model of my father's car that I drove to one rally—but detailed nothing either exciting or incriminating.

The Vietnam War dragged on until 1975, with its horrible effects on that country and ours. I continued to protest, angry about US foreign policy and its inertia, despite public opposition; guilty about my personal safety and comfort; and hopeful for a better future. Looking back, I wouldn't have done anything differently and have no regrets about what I did.

Were those of us who were so resistant to the draft rejected because we were viewed as potential pains? Who needs a noncom grunt asking questions or stirring up things? Maybe the Selective Service was smarter than we thought—smart enough to know the army had enough problems without us in there.

Chapter 13

Connections

At some point in our lives, most of us have heard the old adage, "It's not what you know, it's who you know." Whether it's a family member, a business associate, a friend or neighbor, or an old schoolmate, the idea that a personal connection can help an individual achieve a goal—land a job, gain admission to a college or club, close a business deal, even swing a bargain price on a car—is one of life's realities. Knowing someone that can pull the right strings can make a difference. For some people during the Vietnam War, it made all the difference.

Ernest Garrison is a year or two younger than me. We would occasionally run into each other in the neighborhood. He is smart, perceptive, logical, and a talented artist.

Ernest was in college at the time of the Vietnam War and had considerable anxiety about being drafted. He had a definite, widely held, and often stated position about the war: "It was stupid and immoral." With his strong opposition to the war, he felt that somehow, some way, he would get a deferment or exemption; induction was simply impossible. When the draft lottery was held, it was a rude awakening: his number was 34, low enough to ensure being called up. The low number moved the possibility of being drafted from hypothetical to "uh-oh."

As Ernest puts it, "At that point, I wasn't certain that I wouldn't be inducted. So I made a decision to do a number of things, whatever it took, to avoid the draft because I was convinced I wouldn't go to Vietnam, no matter what. It just wasn't going to happen. I said I'd go to Canada before I went to Vietnam, but that may have been bravado."

Bravado or not, Ernest was not a good match for the military. He grew up in upper-middle-class surroundings with a family that emphasized art and culture. He has too much respect for life and too much consideration for other people. The thought of Ernest as an aggressive soldier out to wage war is a nonstarter for those who know him. He is physically fit, a dedicated cyclist, loves nature and the outdoors, and will crawl all night through the woods on a mission to count frogs for an environmental survey, but he is spiritually unsuited to take up arms against his fellow man. Given an order to go into battle or take punitive action against Vietnamese villagers, Ernest would ask, *Why*? and not budge until he got an acceptable answer (and in his eyes that would be a near-impossible challenge to meet), or he would refuse outright. He was a perfect candidate for stockade time.

Ernest's parents were on his side about the draft and said they would help him avoid it. They suggested a medical deferment. They knew that certain medical conditions could keep him out, and they would help him get the documented confirmation that he had one. His father, a doctor, had confidence in his professional connections and told Ernest, "You're going to a doctor who will get you out." Ernest knew his parents' plan would work. And so, his father arranged for him to be examined by a compliant doctor. "The doctor knew how to phrase a letter for deferment in a certain way," Ernest said. "It was the same thing doctors do with Blue Cross or Medicare to make sure a patient's costs are covered: they don't lie, they just code it favorably."

At his physical, Ernest presented the carefully worded letter describing and enhancing a particular medical condition. The army doctor recognized Ernest's surname and casually asked if he was related to the doctor of the same name. Ernest responded with "Yes, that's my father." The army doctor knew Ernest's father. He also knew the letter-writing doctor by name and reputation. With a glance at the letter, a slight pause, and without further conversation, the doctor signed a form and gave Ernest a 1-Y deferment. He never had to go back.

His father's influence among medical colleagues pulled Ernest from the gray area of maybe being drafted to the security of the "you're definitely out" category. He was able to avoid the draft purely because of his father's connections, an advantage—fair or not—that many other men did not have. Without those connections, he would have had to make some hard choices about his next steps. Ernest explained:

> I felt relieved. But I felt it wasn't entirely fair. I had an edge. And it made me safer than the others—those who didn't have the right connections. If I was some poor guy without influence, the result would be different. I did, and do, feel aware that my social position and family connections made it possible for me not to have to risk my life or possibly kill another person. That has always seemed incredibly unfair, probably the most extreme example in my personal experience of how unfair the world is.
>
> Clearly I did, and still do, have a sense of guilt over the advantages that my accident of birth afforded me. I always felt guilty because I never got to the point where I had to make a decision. It was all taken care of.
>
> If it was a different situation, not a decision about a war I considered to be immoral, I would call it [referring to his father's intervention] unethical. But the war itself was stupid and immoral.
>
> Would I have been willing to shoot somebody? For a cause I thought was wrong? No. It was an immoral war, and killing someone in an immoral war is immoral. And I don't think that I ever worried about cowardice. I may not be remembering correctly, but I don't believe that the fear of getting killed or injured was a major factor in my thinking. My decision had nothing to do with patriotism or lack of it. I never thought of myself as a patriot. In my family, nationalism, tribalism—any kind of us-versus-them thinking—was discouraged.
>
> Viewed from the point of whether the government has the power—not the right—to make me do what I don't want to do, from a position of morality or justice, at what point do you say no? When is enough, enough? Our social compact gives the government some power over our choices in life, but sometimes the government abuses that power. Forcing young men to kill or be killed is just one example of that abuse.

> I regret that other people did not have the same chance to resist the draft that I did, and it would be unfair for me to judge those who fought and those who killed.

Sometimes it's not who you know, it's who someone you know knows.

Paul Tessler retired in 2007 from his post as a US Navajo Hopi Indian Relocation Commission attorney in Flagstaff, Arizona, and now lives in the San Francisco Bay area. In 1969 he failed his preinduction physical. He was a junior high school social studies teacher in Madison Heights, Michigan, married, and holding a 2-A occupational deferment at the time, but that didn't excuse him from a physical. His draft board wanted him prepped and ready to go for induction just in case that deferment was withdrawn. As more bodies were needed for Vietnam, draft boards were looking for ways to reclassify men. But Paul really had no concerns. He had a long history of severe allergies, plenty of legitimate documentation from his doctors, and, best of all, a backup letter attesting to his medical condition from Martin Friedenberg, an osteopathic physician who happened to be his father-in-law at the time. Dr. Friedenberg held an anti-war view and he and Paul had a close relationship. In other words, Paul was well protected.

However, Paul was also a recent law school graduate and knew, through friends who had gone through draft physicals, of the mercurial nature of Selective Service physicians. It was a long shot that he could be found acceptable regardless of the number of doctor letters he presented. Still, that was enough to raise some anxiety, so Paul had a plan B: escape to Toronto, an arrangement he hoped he wouldn't need to implement.

"I became aware of the Vietnam War in the mid-1960s," Paul said. "Wayne State University was a hotbed of activism. You couldn't not know about the war, but I did know that I wouldn't be part of it. I never talked to a draft counselor; I just knew I'd find a way to get out."

Paul went through the physical, presented his letters, and fortunately, they were accepted. The Tessler household released a collective sigh of relief. A few weeks later, Paul received an official notice advising him of his 4-F status. Toronto was off the table. Life, as Paul knew it, continued.

But Paul's close friend, Lou Shoemaker, in the same draft board as Paul, had similar critical allergies and encountered a different anxiety-provoking experience. Lou was a young, bright attorney well on his way up the legal ladder when his notice for a physical arrived. No problem, thought Lou. Just like Paul, he had been receiving regular anti-allergy injections for years from his allergist. When it came time for the physical, Lou asked his doctor for a letter confirming the medical history. His doctor refused. "I don't write letters," the doctor said, giving no further explanation. Lou was flummoxed. The medical history was there, yet the doctor was uncooperative. A flat *no* was all Lou got. Frightened and confused, Lou turned to Paul, who suggested that he see Paul's father-in-law.

Dr. Friedenberg examined Lou and legitimately diagnosed hypertension and anxiety. He had no problem writing a letter attesting to these conditions, no need to get into Lou's allergies. Lou took the letter with him to his physical. At the induction center, Lou was so nervous he was unable to urinate to provide a sample. A man standing at the urinal next to him noticed the problem and offered to fill Lou's bottle. Lou took him up on the offer. It turned out to be a needless gesture: Lou was ultimately rejected on the basis of Dr. Friedenberg's letter.

"My father-in-law would've written a letter for anyone. He was happy to help Lou. He wasn't a fan of that war," said Paul, and added, "After I went through all this and I was beginning to practice law, if anyone asked me about the draft, I warned them not to ignore it. I referred them to counselors and alerted them to stay on top of their situation if they wanted to avoid service."

Lou was lucky to know Paul and, through him, Dr. Friedenberg. For Lou, it might've been a connection he didn't even know he had . . . until he needed it.

When I interviewed Paul, he had long been divorced from his first wife and was married to Philadelphia native Psylvia Gurk. I spoke with her as well. Psylvia, a computer repairperson, told me that the war was a major issue in her family's home. "My parents

Psylvia Gurk and Paul Tessler (photo by Barbara Bloom)

were pro-war hawks and I wasn't," she said. "We couldn't even have a calm family dinner together."

Psylvia left home as soon as she graduated high school in 1968. A year later Psylvia and friends attended Woodstock, which she described as life-changing. She was one of the people who actually was there and has her pictures from *Life* magazine to prove it. The Woodstock Festival was billed as "Three days of peace and music," a tagline Psylvia confirmed. "Woodstock was peace, love, and music, all with a strong anti-war vibe," she said. "There was lots of anti-war sentiment. The crowds were talking about it; musicians on stage were singing about it. The war was underlying everything that was going on around us." Psylvia said that she remembers Country Joe and the Fish singing the "Vietnam Song" with its uncompromisingly strong anti-war lyrics and getting the crowd to enthusiastically join in. Psylvia also mentioned that there were plenty of draft dodgers in attendance. She sympathized with them and told me about a war protest at New York's Columbia University in which she participated.

> There was a group of us—maybe a hundred, hundred and fifty people—and a couple of the guys burned their draft cards. Obviously, we women didn't have draft cards, but we stood up and gave our names in solidarity with the men. I felt as if I was a draft dodger too, we were putting ourselves on the line with the guys. Then we formed a circle around the men to protect them from the New York police who wanted to stop the demonstration, creating a makeshift sanctuary for them. But the police came in and arrested us all. I was charged with trespassing. I don't know what

the guys were charged with—probably trespassing and burning their draft cards. It was the only time in my life I've been arrested. All the women were put into one or two cells with no room to sit or lie down. They treated us the way people treat zoo animals: they were scared of us but knew we were locked up. They insisted on fingerprinting us. We spent the night in jail and were arraigned the next day. The group that organized the protest supported us and paid our fines, twenty-five dollars each. I'm proud to have been arrested for that."

To this day, Psylvia considers Woodstock a point of reference of a changing society. "I'm still a hippie. I have an open mind. I try to be accepting of people."

Like many other men, Barry Sinclair never believed he would be drafted. There was too much wrong with him. He was completely deaf in one ear, colorblind, and suffered numerous debilitating allergies that had compromised him ever since he was a kid—a seeming cocktail of health flaws that could lead to a failed physical and a 4-F classification.

When Barry went in for his physical in 1966 armed with detailed letters from his doctors, he thought that at the end of the day he would simply walk out of the induction center, go back to his family's Detroit-area home, and continue his life as he had. The army didn't quite see it his way. Instead, the army saw a legitimate candidate for military service, a young man whose medical issues would not stand in the way of a possible trip to Vietnam. Barry passed the physical and was shocked to find that he received a 1-A classification.

Barry's status was upsetting to him and his mother. His father, a manufacturer's rep, however, found no fault with it. In his eyes, military service was not to be avoided. It was something you had to do. His position was understandable. He was a World War II veteran who had served in General George S. Patton's army in Europe. He had fought in the Battle of the Bulge and was the sole survivor of a vicious German tank attack on his platoon. He came out of the army with a

Bronze Star and a Purple Heart. He had proudly served his country and believed it was now Barry's turn to do the same. Barry disagreed vehemently. He did not support US involvement in Vietnam.

Barry had unwittingly placed himself in this awkward situation. Although a full-time student at Wayne State University, he had dropped a class not realizing he would lose his full-time student status and his 2-S deferment; receiving a notice for a physical and a 1-A reclassification was, to say the least, a surprise. Still, he was confident that his health issues would result in rejection. When things didn't quite go as planned, he appealed and was granted a second physical. Army doctors again reviewed his letters but the results were the same: acceptable for service. Barry was disappointed but undeterred. Figuring the third time would be a charm, he appealed again and was granted a third physical. Once more, he was found acceptable.

Instead of weakening his resolve, the growing odds of induction into the military were reinforcing Barry's strong opposition to the war. A confrontation with his local draft board's secretary didn't help matters. He objected to the results of his physicals and was thrown out of the board office after giving the secretary a middle-finger salute, but he did get the opportunity to be granted one more physical examination with an ENT (ear, nose, and throat) specialist. "I was deaf. I had a disability. I would not make a good soldier. I wanted the army to understand that."

While his appeals for additional physicals were proceeding well into 1967, Barry received a notice from his draft board to report for induction on September 17, 1967, at Fort Benning, Georgia. His mother was distraught. His father was not. But his mother let his father know she was angry. She, like so many other mothers, did not want her son in the army, especially not anywhere near Vietnam.

The fourth physical, with the ENT doctor, took place just a few blocks away from the Fort Wayne induction center. Barry appeared as required and was led into an examination room. As Barry looked around, he caught sight of a plaque on the wall. The doctor was a lieutenant colonel in the US Army Reserves. As Barry tells it, "I knew right then and there I was screwed."

When the doctor examined Barry and ultimately declared him fit for service, Barry objected, pointing out that since he was deaf in one ear he could not carry out the duties expected of a soldier. The doctor assured him that he would be assigned an appropriate role—a clerk-typist for example. "But I can't type," Barry said. "We'll teach you," the doctor replied. At that point Barry declared he would refuse to be drafted. The doctor informed him that he would be arrested, to which Barry stated, "You'll have to come to Canada to get me." Barry had a job waiting for him there if he chose: two high school buddies had just started a successful company in Toronto and were ready to hire him. Unmoved, the doctor said, "You're fit. You'll serve. Or you'll be in jail."

Dismayed, Barry went home. The order to report to Fort Benning was still operative. He had three days till the induction date. It was at this time that Barry's mother flew into action. According to Barry, she laid into his father and made it clear that if he didn't do something to keep Barry out of the service, he would live to regret it.

Throughout this process, Barry's opposition to the war had crystallized. "The draft caused me a great deal of anxiety. There was no threat to this country. If there was a threat, I'd go. I'd join up, no question, but that wasn't the situation. I'm not gonna go to Vietnam and kill guys just because they don't believe what we believe. No way."

With Barry's opposition firm and his mother threatening her husband, Barry's father was forced to act. According to Barry, his father called a close friend, Lawrence Gubow, United States district judge for the Eastern District of Michigan. Judge Gubow, in turn, then called his close friend, Michigan senator Philip Hart, known as the "Conscience of the Senate" and an opponent of the Vietnam War. Senator Hart's wife, Jane, was an outspoken critic of the war. She had visited North Vietnam to meet with American prisoners and was arrested with dozens of other protestors at the Pentagon during a peace demonstration. It was reported that she also stopped paying her federal income taxes to protest the US role in the Vietnam War. It is uncertain exactly what Judge Gubow or Senator Hart did, if anything, but the day before he was to report to Fort Benning, Barry received a special delivery letter from his draft board. When he opened it he found that his status had suddenly changed. He was reclassified as 2-S. It was baffling. The peril of being drafted had evaporated overnight. It was never confirmed, but it would appear that Barry's father knew the right people to make the draft disappear. After Barry received the student deferment, he returned to school, eventually earning a bachelor's degree and launching a successful career in sales.

Barry and his father had always had a good relationship, but the issue of the war caused significant friction between them. Eventually, his father came around to Barry's way of thinking, saw that the war was wrong, and realized that to preserve his marriage and family he needed to protect his son. He knew the people who might have helped him do just that: a federal judge and a US senator. And he made the call.

The Selective Service was designed to collect as many able-bodied men as possible and deliver them to the armed forces. There was no exemption for noncitizens, as Jürgen Dankwort found out.

Jürgen is a retired university professor. He has taught at the University of Quebec, the University of Houston, and Kwantlen Polytechnic University in British Columbia. He knows his way around academia. He is also knowledgeable about history and politics. Even as a young man he had an understanding of world affairs and diplomacy. He was born in Sweden to a German father and Swiss mother. His father—a German national with German citizenship—was a diplomat in the German Foreign Office. When his father was appointed as the West German representative to Canada in 1951, the family, including Jürgen and his brother, moved to Ottawa. A few years later, his father was transferred to Rio de Janeiro as the German ambassador to Brazil, and then in 1958, to the United States, where he served as the West German observer to the United Nations. The family moved with him. All this gave Jürgen a pointed interest in world affairs. As he acknowledged, the travel was a great benefit allowing him to immerse himself in a variety of cultures. But the time spent in the United States might have made the greatest impression on him. During their stay in the country, Jürgen's family lived in New York City, where his father spent most of his time at the UN. Jürgen attended a private high school and continued to grow up as a

Jürgen Dankwort during the Vietnam War era (courtesy of Jürgen Dankwort)

"diplomat brat"—much like an army brat, always changing countries and cultures, albeit doing so in a rather privileged and exclusive way. Life was easy, things were going well. In 1960 Jürgen's father retired. Opting to remain in the United States, Jürgen's parents were offered permanent resident status as a gesture of gratitude for Jürgen's father's diplomatic service. The entire family received green cards. His parents bought a house on Cape Cod and began a quiet retirement lifestyle. Jürgen soon graduated from high school and entered Bard College in Annandale-on-Hudson, New York. While he was not a citizen, he was still required—as a US resident and holder of a green card—to register with the Selective Service. He did so at his local draft board in nearby Poughkeepsie.

While at Bard, Jürgen was given a 2-S classification. After a year he transferred to Boston University and held on to his student deferment. Much to his chagrin, the Vietnam War was stoking up. Jürgen decided to get involved. He had become a human rights activist in high school and was even reprimanded by the principal for participating in a Fair Play for Cuba demonstration in front of the UN. In college, he continued his activism and found himself spending more time at anti-war protests and teach-ins than he did in class. He dropped classes at Boston University and lost his full-time student status and with it his 2-S deferment. He was now 1-A and susceptible to the draft.

Jürgen wondered, What next? He was wholly against the war and decided to apply for CO status. Jürgen based his claim on the fact that the United States did not follow the UN charter before responding to the Gulf of Tonkin Bay ship attack. While the charter recognizes a country's right to defend itself, Jürgen argued that the United States omitted a key procedural step in the process by failing to first bring the attack to the attention of the Security Council. Jürgen stated that he objected to the US refusal to comply with the charter and explained he was not opposed to war per se; he was opposed to illegal US involvement in the Vietnam War and, therefore, could not and would not take part. However, at the time, religion was a key factor for a board in determining CO status. Since no such factor had been raised by Jürgen, his CO application was denied.

By this time, Jürgen had passed a draft physical and received an induction order to report to the South Boston Army Base. He was now faced with limited options: (1) enlist and hopefully avoid Vietnam, (2) leave the United States, or (3) defy the induction order and face arrest, trial, prison, and possible deportation to Germany (where he had never lived).

Enlisting was not out of the question for Jürgen if he could be assured that he would not be sent to Vietnam. But he eliminated that option when he learned that promises made to enlistees about where they would serve could still be changed once the men were under military authority. Nor did he want to leave the United States. He consulted with well-known human rights and anti-war attorney William Kunstler. Kunstler wanted to represent him, fully appreciating the political significance of protecting the son of a German ambassador from being drafted by the United States to fight in what he considered to be an immoral and illegal war. But Kunstler didn't come cheap. Jürgen didn't have the funds, and while his father was sympathetic, he would not cover the legal fees. Instead, his father quietly inquired in diplomatic circles about alternatives Jürgen might have, hoping that his standing in the diplomatic community might yield possible ways to funnel Jürgen into some form of alternative civilian service such as the Peace Corps. "My father was a realist," said Jürgen. "He was trying to find a practical and acceptable way to help me stay out of the military and likely to be sent to Vietnam." But there were no special favors available. (So much for who you know. Sometimes it just doesn't matter.) At this point, Jürgen was thinking about confronting the Selective Service over his status.

> I was willing to go to trial, and I accepted the possibility of going to prison. My parents realized this and became increasingly alarmed. There were shouting episodes over this issue in our home as my dad tried to talk me out of it. Once my father realized that I was seriously willing to face prison, he calmed down and then thought that I should consider returning to Canada, where we once lived. Canada, as you might expect, with the government knowing the family name because of my dad's diplomatic tour there years before, posed no obstacles to letting me return.

After anguishing over his options, Jürgen realized that leaving the country was his best solution. He could continue his anti-war activity across the border. His parents were supportive of his effort to avoid service, and Jürgen's father, upset and accepting that his son could face military service or prison, urged him to continue his university education full time and offered him a ticket to Montreal. Jürgen accepted it and then advised his draft board that he was going to Canada to complete his education. He returned his green card and flew out in 1967, specifically departing prior to the date he was ordered to report to the army base and thereby hoping to avoid being charged with failure to appear for induction. Leaving the United States was a difficult choice for him. After several moves with his family during his early life, Jürgen had finally begun to put down roots in the United States and build close friendships. Now he was cutting those ties. In Montreal, he didn't know a soul.

> While I would stay out of prison, I thought it would also mean giving up much of my political anti-war activism as well as the relationships I'd established. I thought I'd be walking away from the commitment I'd made to oppose the war. Fortunately, I was able to

continue my opposition in Canada. I felt very privileged to have this option.

Shortly after arriving in Canada, Jürgen received a delinquency notice for his failure to appear for induction. Checking in with the US Consulate to learn more about his situation, he found that he could not go back to the United States for any reason other than to present himself for induction. The US Immigration and Naturalization Act at the time stated that if a non-US citizen left the country in time of war or national emergency, he could not return as a resident or a visitor. Jürgen was barred from reentry because the United States was still technically in a state of national emergency: the national emergency called by President Truman in 1950 over the Korean War was still in effect; it had never been lifted. Jürgen was cut off from family, friends, and a long-term girlfriend—the price he had to pay for leaving the United States.

When he got to Canada, Jürgen discovered welcome opportunities to continue his anti-war activities. He stayed active in anti-war organizations and started his studies at McGill, where he eventually earned bachelor's and master's degrees in social work (and later a PhD from the University of Montreal). While there, he sent dispatches to UPS-LNS (Underground Press Syndicate-Liberation News Service) about how young Americans could seek refuge in Canada. He was coeditor of the *Montreal Free Press* (aka "The Local Rag") and worked with others at the Montreal Council to Aid War Resisters, an engagement revived decades later with the War Resisters Support Campaign in Vancouver in assisting Americans seeking Canadian refuge from the Gulf wars of 1991 and 2003. Although Jürgen was in Montreal, his Selective Service joyride was not over. However, this time it took a good turn when President Carter issued a pardon for Vietnam War draft dodgers. Noncitizens such as Jürgen were included in the order. "Much to my surprise," said Jürgen. "I, a German national living in Canada, was suddenly pardoned by an American president for refusing to fight in Vietnam!" Jürgen headed for the border, eager to see his family. There, he encountered yet another obstacle. His name was in a data bank as a draft delinquent. "I had to show my letter of pardon for the border guards to let me pass," he said. Once back, he contacted the office of the director for the Selective Service in New York and asked them to remove his name from the list. They did.

Although his personal Vietnam War battle is long over, Jürgen remains a vigorous activist for social justice and spends his time supporting a variety of human rights initiatives. In this case, his father's connections did not help Jürgen, but his knowledge of the situation and an awareness of options eventually led him to a satisfactory resolution.

Chapter 14

Facing Jail Time

If you didn't respond to your local draft board's inquiries or orders, didn't show up for your physical, or didn't appear for induction, you could be charged with draft evasion. More than 209,000 men were so charged. If convicted, jail time was a distinct possibility. While almost 198,000 cases were dropped, if your case moved forward and you were convicted, you faced imprisonment. Close to thirty-three hundred men went to prison rather than serve in the military. Most of those men had the option of avoiding incarceration by simply choosing to accept their fate and enter the army when their induction came around. Often, when a draft evader was caught, he would be given a choice: the army or prison—take your pick. For those who opposed the war, this was a lose-lose situation: confinement in a cell or confinement in the army. The men who ardently opposed the war on principle sometimes chose prison, willing to accept the harshness of confinement over participation in wartime activities. Others, feeling that they had taken the game as far as they could and were not willing to accept being branded as draft dodgers *and* felons (violating the Selective Service Act by draft evasion acts or omissions was a felony), chose to be inducted.

Dylan T. Camden was one man who came very close to spending time in a jail cell. Dylan grew up in Southwest Michigan and still lives there, not far from Lake Michigan and its sandy beaches. Friends describe Dylan as a good guy, the kind of person who everyone depends on and who always comes through. I found Dylan to be a thoughtful man, expressive through words, actions, and music; hand him any kind of guitar, acoustic or electric, and he can play it—quite well, in fact. I cannot imagine him being a troublemaker. Nor can I imagine him in a jail cell.

Dylan was a full-time student at Western Michigan University and had a 2-S deferment in 1969. He dropped a couple of classes thinking he'd pick them up later in the year. But before he could return to school, he was reclassified 1-A. To add insult to injury, he then drew a low lottery number. As expected, he was quickly called to Detroit's Fort Wayne for a draft physical that he easily passed. He was told that he wasn't needed right away and sent home.

At the time of his physical, Dylan was opposed to the war. He had taken part in protests and had even placed a silver nitrate happy face tattoo on his rear end, intending to insult the doctors at his physical when he would be asked to drop his pants and bend over. Throughout this period, he wasn't living at home and hadn't advised his draft board of his new address. He ignored forwarded mail and never saw the Selective Service letters calling him for induction. When he finally received his notice, it was in the form of a personal visit from a federal agent.

> I was working late at a local grocery in Kalamazoo. It was around three in the morning, and an FBI man came in and asked for me. He said, "You didn't show up for your induction." I knew I had a problem. He told me they'd been looking for me. I was told I had to report the next morning to the federal building in Grand Rapids for arraignment in front of the judge. The agent was ready to arrest me right there, but I promised I would show up the next day, and the store owner vouched for me.
>
> The next morning I took the bus and went to the federal building, where I spoke with an army recruiter. I found out that if I didn't accept induction, I would go to jail that day. They weren't wasting any time. I didn't argue. There was no point. I didn't want to go to jail. I was drafted, inducted before the day was over.

In Dylan's eyes, he traded one form of prison for another: the army. Once in the service, he was trained as a medic and assigned to Vietnam as part of the Military Assistance Command, Vietnam (MACV), a joint-service command of the United States Department of Defense. The MACV was tasked with operations involving strategic reconnaissance, covert action, and psychological warfare. Part of Dylan's time was spent flying medical evacuation missions back and forth between Lowry Air Force Base in Aurora, Colorado, and Clark Air Force Base in the Philippines and on to Tan Son Nhut Air Base in Saigon—three times a week for six months—airlifting personnel across the Pacific. He avoided direct combat, but he didn't escape the draft, the war, or its aftereffects.

As Dylan put it, "It was the army, and I was a model prisoner throughout my term. I caused no problems and did what I was told, but I was definitely opposed to the war."

When he was discharged, Dylan worked as a nurse and was later employed by the Michigan Department of Treasury. Today, Dylan is retired. When I spoke with him, it was evident that just discussing the war caused him anxiety. There was still anger about his experience and being coerced into the service.

> My attitude is FTA—fuck the army. I harbor a tremendous amount of guilt that I didn't do more to protest the war. It was a bad war. Fifty years later, I'm still assimilating how it affected me and my reaction to it. To some degree, it's like an old wound that is repeatedly exposed.
>
> As I was processing out of Fort Leonard Wood in Missouri, I drove through the gate, stopped my vehicle in the road, and ignited my army travel bag with Zippo lighter fluid and burned it on the spot as a form of protest. Everything in it—pictures, uniforms, keepsakes, decorations, etc.—everything except the dress greens that I was wearing at the time and my original DD-214 to prove that I was again a free man.* I remember the reactions from the MPs at the

---

* Pronounced "dee-dee-two-fourteen," the DD-214 form, the Certificate of Release or Discharge from Active Duty from the Department of Defense, documented a serviceperson's discharge from the Armed Forces. The form listed details of an individual's military stint including time of enlistment and any citations, awards, campaigns, and other notable points. Most important, it indicated the type of discharge a service person received—Honorable, General, General Under Honorable Conditions, Dishonorable, and a few others. The DD-214 was the documentation to provide to employers, schools and universities,

gate as if it was yesterday. They stood there, smiled, and said, "Do you really think that you're the first person to have ever thought of that and actually done it? We see that happen several times a week, douche bag!"

Like so many other men, I immediately went down to city hall to have my DD-214 notarized and placed into a permanent public record, similar to recording land conveyances, titles of ownership, liens, etc. to effectively ensure its authenticity and permanence from alteration by any individual or government authority.

This interview left me in a particularly melancholy mood. I had met Dylan on a few social occasions. Though I did not know him well, I liked him and felt there was great depth to his character with something sad mired inside him that just couldn't seem to find its way out. I realized there was a lot he wasn't saying, maybe couldn't say. PTSD? I'm not qualified to comment, but I have no doubt that serving in the military, for Dylan, was the equivalent of serving penitentiary time, and an experience of that kind almost always leaves an indelible mark.

As his wife said, "His Vietnam experience went straight to his soul. He flew missions out of Fitzsimmons Army Hospital in Colorado—to Vietnam, to the Philippines, and back, over and over, carrying wounded soldiers and Vietnamese civilians. He saw things he will never forget. I love him with my heart and soul."

Dylan narrowly missed jail. Others didn't. Some men found prison, frightening as it was, more palatable than the army. Howard Conner was given the same choice as Dylan but Howard chose jail. "Prison terrified me," he said, "But the army terrified me more."

Howard was a latecomer to Vietnam War awareness. He was immersed in his school and home life, loved music, and was a serious trombonist. He really wasn't paying attention to the conflict

---

and banks and other financial institutions if an individual wanted any type of veteran preference, benefits, or services.

until 1967 during his senior year at the University of Pittsburgh, where he earned a bachelor's in political science and philosophy. He was in the school cafeteria when he saw a group of nuns staring at various photos of civilian war casualties in Vietnam. It struck him instantly that he could not participate in the war.

As he became more conscious of the war and its implications for draft-age men, he became more opposed to the war politically and morally. His position soon hardened. "I absolutely felt the war was wrong. Vietnam was a civil war. Why would I want to kill people struggling for themselves—for their own well-being?"

He also realized his Selective Service board was searching for bodies to fill its quota. Howard believed he had no good options to avoid the draft. He was medically sound and wasn't about to harm himself to fail his physical. As expected, he passed. He couldn't honestly apply for CO status because he wasn't opposed to all wars, only to ones that were not justified, such as the Vietnam War. He decided to let things play out but at the same time applied to and was accepted to VISTA, hoping his service to the organization might count toward some sort of deferment. He was assigned to work with young people in the Bronx. There he participated in anti-war protests and, although sympathetic to SDS and similar groups, couldn't tolerate being around angry people. Accordingly, while he was firmly opposed to the war, his protest profile was low.

Howard's work at VISTA failed to serve as insulation from the draft. His Pittsburgh draft board ordered him to return home for induction and what turned out to be a traumatic experience. At the Pittsburgh center, draftees literally had to cross a line on the floor, accept their induction, and present themselves for service. Howard refused to cross the line. He was repeatedly ordered to cross; he repeatedly refused. "I was shaking and really scared," he said. "I didn't want to cross that line, but what if I had a spasm and accidentally crossed?" Intimidated and fearful, Howard stood his ground—"It was a moral conviction, yet I was frightened"—and was arrested and charged with the felony of failure to submit to induction. He told me he liked the wording of the charge because it signified *resistance* rather than *evasion*. He was released on his personal recognizance and six months later went to trial. While he waited for his court date, army recruiters repeatedly tried to get him to change his mind and enlist, promising him all charges would be dropped. Howard declined their offers.

At trial, Howard was represented by a Pittsburgh-area ACLU attorney he hired for $500—significant money at the time, especially for a student. The attorney helped Howard understand what would happen in federal court. As the trial proceeded, Howard's attorney strongly urged him to change his mind and go into the army, conveying a message, in effect a plea offer, from the opposing US attorney. But Howard again declined. He had decided months earlier that he was not going to revisit his decision. He was firm in refusing induction and was prepared to face the consequences.

The judge found Howard guilty as charged and sentenced him to five years in prison, with four years suspended, and parole as a possibility. (Howard had met his future wife at the end of his year in VISTA and was married six weeks before he was sentenced, a move that the judge excoriated him for as a cheap ploy to obtain a more lenient sentence.) Howard was also fined and forbidden to speak against the government. If eventually released under parole, he could not live within fifty miles of Pittsburgh. Howard's parents, Jews who had become born-again Christians when he was eleven (but still gave Howard a bar mitzvah), were appalled that their son refused to serve, and had to endure criticism from members of their congregation who could not understand his stance. Howard's younger brother and sister were scared about what might happen to him in prison. Howard's wife, a member of the Church of the Brethren, a Christian denomination with a pacifist stance much like the Quakers and Mennonites, fully supported his position.

In 1970 Howard entered the Allegheny County Jail to begin his term. He was the only war resister in the facility and was well known for it. Three weeks into his sentence he got into a fight with another prisoner when he rebuffed the inmate's sexual overtures. Howard is slight in build and didn't fare too well in the confrontation. In the middle of the night he awoke in pain and found blood in his urine. As he described it, he took his steel coffee mug and began rattling it against the bars of his cell to attract the guard "just like in those old prison movies," he said. The guard took him to the infirmary. The next morning, with Howard writhing in pain, the attending doctor examined him, diagnosed a kidney stone lodged because of the previous night's attack, and said, "They got you didn't they? You're the draft dodger." The less-than-sympathetic doctor turned to the nurse and added, "Keep him in restraints and no pain medication." Howard was kept bound to a cot for three days until he passed the stone. "Don't let anybody tell you they don't torture prisoners," he said to me. While in jail, Howard's parents visited once. He asked them not to come again. His wife visited as often as she could. During this time, army recruiters approached him again about enlisting, promising to clear his record if he would accept induction.

After six weeks in the county jail and without explanation, Howard was transferred to a medium-security federal prison in Milan, Michigan. Here too, he was the only war resister. At Milan, Howard had a tenuous relationship with the Black inmates and was hassled by the White prisoners, who saw him as a traitor. Many of the Black prisoners were members of the Nation of Islam. A sort of truce was struck when he began attending a Black studies class with them. He was the only White prisoner to do so. Racial tensions were as prevalent inside the prison as on the outside. Three months into his stay, a new wave of Black prisoners came in and asked if the White guy, Howard, might be an FBI informer. No one stood up for him. To the Black prisoners, he became a question mark.

Inmates had to work in the prison, but Howard refused to work in the laundry or clothing factory (making military uniforms) and was instead assigned to the education department where he taught math. Howard mentioned that there were few human moments he experienced at Milan, but one stood out. "There was a math test prisoners could take for accreditation. When a couple of the Nation of Islam men—my students—passed, they were excited and proud of their achievement. One said to me, 'Man, you're the devil, but if you're ever in Chicago, we got your back.'"

Most of the time, Howard kept to himself. His wife would send him books and the *New York Times*, which he would share with the other men. Every once in a while, Howard would opt for solitary confinement. "I didn't mind, really. I just needed the quiet," he said, so he would refuse a guard's order to clean up or pick up something and would be sent away for a few peaceful days.

Once he was released on parole, Howard was required to get a job within four weeks or return to prison. He was able to find a position in Cedar Falls, New York, at a residence for troubled adolescents. The facility administration was sympathetic to anti-war activists and employed a number of COs. After a few months, Howard quit because of feeling helpless about doing anything that would make a difference in the youths' lives. His parole officer informed him that he now had three weeks to find another job or return to Milan. Howard applied for a position as a pharmacy night clerk at a hospital that is part of the New York state medical system. He was rejected because he was a felon and the consensus was that he could not be trusted around drugs (even though he was not a drug user), but the woman who interviewed him asked, "What about social work?" It was a life-changing question. Howard was hired as an attendant in the hospital's locked forensic unit. The facility was also a teaching hospital staffed by some of Manhattan's most respected psychoanalysts. His experience and interaction with them spurred his interest in clinical social work and led Howard to pursue postgraduate degrees in the field. He went back to school and earned a master's degree from the City University of New York and a PhD from New York University.

Several years later, Howard saw the famous photo taken on June 8, 1972, by Associated Press photographer Nick Ut of naked and badly burned nine-year-old "Napalm Girl" Phan Thị Kim Phúc. She was running toward the camera from a South Vietnamese napalm strike that mistakenly hit Trảng Bàng village instead of nearby North Vietnamese troops. Titled "The Terror of War," the photo won the 1973 Pulitzer Prize and the World Press Photo of the Year award. The image of the young girl horrified Howard and cemented in his mind that despite the hardships he had endured, he had done the right thing by objecting to and staying away from that war.

Howard has worked in the mental health field as a clinician, adjunct and assistant professor of social work at Rutgers, Fordham, and New York University, and as a consultant to medical facilities, schools, and social service agencies promoting the mental health of children. He has been a strong advocate in the struggle for prisoners' rights with groups such as the ACLU and National Association of Social Workers and helped found New Jersey's first county jail mental health program. Howard has also directed development programs and grant-assistance strategies for nonprofit human rights and international health organizations. His breadth of experience includes raising funds from private foundations and individuals as well as from the US and European governments and multilateral organizations including the United Nations, the World Health Organization, and the World Bank. It is a remarkable set of accomplishments for a man who had to endure prison for his political beliefs.

There have been residual effects, however. Howard is still paying a price for his political views. As a felon, he cannot serve on a jury, and getting malpractice insurance is difficult. These may not seem like major inconveniences, yet they are a lessening of his standing as an individual and a citizen. But he can vote, and his marriage is strong after fifty-plus years, two children, and four grandchildren. He points out that he has no regrets.

> It was right for me to do what I did—other people had to do what they did. I don't detest people in the military, but I don't consider them heroes either. You still have choices. Most made the choice to go in or disappear. Thirty-three hundred ended up in prison. We had our position. We're just like anybody else. I believe that both of my children respect and approve of my decision to go to jail. I actually had to talk my son out of refusing to register with Selective Service when he was eighteen and instead submit a statement of his intention not to serve if ever called upon to participate in a US-sponsored war. Three of my four grandchildren now know about my being in prison. My eleven-year-old granddaughter recently asked me to tell her about my experience. She said that if she didn't know me and the details of the Vietnam War, she would have thought I was a coward. This says something about how the military is still glorified in America. Now that she knows my story, she understands why I did what I did. Even an eleven-year-old gets it.
>
> I favor a military draft with no deferments other than medical ones, so all young men *and* women and their families—especially

the vast majority that don't even conceive of military service as an option for their families—will have to think more carefully about their connection to the US war machine and what they should do to act on those beliefs.

Today, Howard lives outside Washington, DC. He's still doing his consultation work and spending as much time as possible with his grandchildren.

While some men hightailed it across the border to Canada to avoid the draft, others went much farther: Europe. And draft evaders were not the only ones breaking the rules. There were also the men who went AWOL or deserted; those who chose to leave the military after they'd already been inducted, in some cases finding it easier to depart once they were in than avoiding induction altogether. Going AWOL or deserting is nothing new, but both are considered much more serious than evasion. It's also important to cite the difference between the two. The Uniform Code of Military Justice addresses the distinction in Article 85, Desertion and Article 86, Absence without Leave. Without going into tedious legal definitions and nuances, it's enough to say that a soldier is AWOL if he or she leaves his or her post without permission and is away for no more than thirty days. If the soldier is away for more than thirty days, the individual is regarded as a deserter. AWOLs and deserters come in all shapes and sizes. And sometimes they have good reasons for leaving.

Tom Nagel is probably one of the last people you would think of as an army deserter. Tom was born in Stockton, Illinois, a rural community of eighteen hundred in the northwestern part of the state, not far from the Wisconsin line.

Tom's father, Harold, was a well-respected county district attorney and Republican community leader. He retired from his public post and went into private practice when Tom was fifteen. Eventually he stepped back into public view and became a county circuit court judge. Tom was inquisitive, bright, and perceptive. Harold recognized his son's potential. When it came time to choose a college in 1966, he wanted Tom to go to Harvard, but Tom opted to attend his mother's alma mater, Denison University, a small liberal arts school in Granville, Ohio. It had an excellent, long-established academic reputation and a good student paper—and Tom was interested in journalism.

At Denison, while working on the school paper as a reporter and feature editor, Tom was attracted to politics and supported the campus Young Republicans organization. One of his writing assignments took him to New York City to cover an anti-war demonstration that ended on the steps of the United Nations. At the protest, Reverend Martin Luther King Jr. gave a searing criticism of the Vietnam War and its relationship to poverty and racism in the United States. A few days earlier, on April 4, 1967, he had come out against the war in his famous Riverside Church anti–Vietnam War speech "Beyond Vietnam: A Time to Break the Silence," in which the war was depicted as immoral imperialism conducted "on the backs of the poor."

Up to that point, Tom had not really paid attention to the war, but King's speech quickly placed that, and more, on Tom's radar. Impressed by King's persuasive presentation, Tom's consciousness was raised and he wrote a news story praising the speech and decrying the war. The school paper, however, wouldn't run the article. On his own initiative, and in sympathy with the civil rights and anti-war movements, Tom started an alternative campus paper that attacked the Ivy League schools and their elite counterparts throughout the country for their hypocrisy in admitting Black students who couldn't afford admission, yet remaining unsupportive of the overall civil rights movement that was gaining steam. With the help of his parents and friends, Tom founded a college scholarship fund for Black students. Amazingly, according to Tom, the school's administration thought his ideals were incompatible with the quality education offered by the traditional institution and asked him not to return the next semester. As Tom says, "In effect, I was kicked out for reporting on the civil rights movement."

Looking for a more palatable and stimulating atmosphere, Tom transferred to McGill University in Montreal at the suggestion of a college friend who believed that Tom would find the school's sophisticated and progressive academic environment appealing. At McGill, Tom met a number of young men, all of whom had evaded the Selective Service by moving to Canada. Tom's move to Montreal, however, was not intended as a maneuver to avoid the draft—he had not yet been called; it was simply a chance to attend an enlightened university. While there, Tom's views evolved and solidified into firm opposition to American involvement in the Vietnam War.

Tom spent the 1968–1969 school year at McGill, then dropped out and lived with a group of people in a communal setting in the Eastern Townships of Quebec. ("It was really cold," he said.) He soon moved to Alberta for work. ("It was even colder," he acknowledged.) Residing in Canada and no longer in school, Tom lost his draft-exempt status. All this time, the Selective Service kept sending him letters about his status and asking, *If you're not in school, where are you?* They also ordered him to appear for a preinduction physical. Receiving no response, the Selective Service began looking for him. If found, he could face prosecution for draft evasion.

During Tom's time in Canada, the Selective Service lottery came up and Tom drew a low number—38, low enough to assure a call-up. Tom also received notice that the authorities were aggressively looking for him and he could face prison if he was found and refused induction. Tom's father, a World War II veteran, did not want him going into the service. He told Tom he knew the local Illinois magistrate and suggested that Tom come home and "we'll get this straightened out." Tom went along with his father's wishes, but things didn't work out as expected. The magistrate was not sympathetic to Tom's views and gave him the choice of two years in jail or two years in the service.

Tom's father had enlisted in the army in 1941, while still in law school, served, and was honorably discharged. He was not, however, an ardent supporter of the military and, according to Tom, believed that the "army is organized anarchy." He did not want Tom going into the armed forces and offered to buy him a ticket back to Canada. Tom declined. Instead of prison or Canada, he reluctantly elected to join the army, but he went with a purpose in mind: he intended "to go in and make a mess of things."

In the fall of 1971, Tom reported for duty in Chicago. He quickly saw that other servicemen were already making a mess of things and doing a fine job of it. There was no need for him to contribute to

Tom Nagel's order to report for a physical examination (courtesy of Tom Nagel)

enhancing the organized anarchy his father remembered. Once he was in, the army flew him to Fort Lewis in Tacoma, Washington, for basic training. "It wasn't difficult," Tom said. "No sweat, I was in shape from hiking and doing outdoorsy stuff."

After basic training, aware of Tom's anti-war leanings, the army assigned him to radio repairman's school at Fort Sill, Oklahoma. He quickly understood that whoever finished at the top of the class would be shipped to Vietnam. He had no intention of being the class valedictorian. By failing to do as well as he could on a variety of tests, he manipulated the system to finish second. Instead of being sent to Southeast Asia, he remained at Fort Sill and was placed in a special computer class with eight other men. Four months later, he came out as a computer expert with a rank of Specialist Fourth Class and was ordered to report to Baumholder, Germany, where he was assigned to the 708th Mobile Maintenance Battalion. When he landed in Frankfurt, he found that his reputation had preceded him. On the tarmac, the base commander, a colonel, approached him:

"Are you the draft dodger, the anti-war guy?"

"Yes, sir."

"And you type sixty words per minute?"

"Yes, sir."

"Then you're working for me."

Tom shared his quarters, a small room, with the colonel's driver, a Black man named Brock. They were the only White-Black roommates on a base of twenty thousand troops. "We were assigned to the room and we were okay with it. But people thought we were either Commies or gays," said Tom. "We were neither."

Tom described his base in Germany as a mobile maintenance division that had no operating vehicles to maintain but did have intermittent electrical problems that wiped out computer memories. In his view, the base wasn't exactly focused on its military mission. There were other priorities: continuous partying and black market activity—selling army supplies, including food and drugs, to the local population. "A bit of corruption?" he asked rhetorically and sarcastically then added as a bonus, "Drugs were everywhere." Although there had been a crackdown on drugs at the base, use was still common. There were also other problems: housing conditions were deplorable with barracks unheated and in disrepair and lack of proper medical care. Overall conditions were unbearable and morale was dismal. However, Tom found a way to cope: "I adapted to the situation like most of the men in my unit. I became a drug addict."

Recognizing the toll the drugs were taking—hashish in the evening, amphetamines by day, Tom turned himself in on the drug amnesty program, which provided rehabilitation through liberal doses of tranquilizers—Valium and Librium—and lectures about taking drugs. Not benefiting from the program, Tom tried to get help from an army psychiatrist in November 1972 and got an appointment date for February 1973. Unable to wait four months, he went without permission to London to see his aunt, a medical doctor, who advised him that while nothing was yet seriously wrong with his health, he should switch to a different duty station as soon as possible. He returned to the base but missed guard duty while away, and was counted as AWOL. Legal proceedings were initiated against him. He was unable to obtain effective legal counsel—his assigned counsel was transferred and immediate replacement counsel was not available. If convicted, Tom was facing demotion in rank, a fine, and thirty days in the stockade. While awaiting court-martial, Tom was given extra guard duty assignments and confined to barracks when not on duty. Within a few days he was told to prepare for transfer to the stockade by six p.m. that day. Following the guidance of a high-ranking enlisted man who advised him about stockade conditions for prisoners and fearing he would be unable to tolerate the situation, Tom immediately went AWOL again and left for France.

It was his second time in Paris; he'd been there during the US bombing of Hanoi, the so-called December raids of 1972. Now, two weeks into January 1973, he was there again. He wrote home to his congressional representative, John B. Anderson (who in 1980 became an independent candidate for president), and Senator Charles Percy of Illinois, calling attention to the toxic environment and corruption at the German base. His unauthorized departure from his unit and allegations about the base culture spurred a congressional investigation initiated by Senator Percy and conducted by Colonel Virgil Warner, director of Investigations and Complaints. Regrettably, nothing changed.

Tom remained in Paris until the war ended. He was now considered a deserter. Tom saw most of the final stages of the war from a French anti-war perspective. During his time in Paris, he stayed with a friend and turned to the Quakers for help with his army situation. At the Quaker Center he found other people in similar circumstances. While settling into life in Paris, he taught English to cover his expenses. He got involved in the international anti-war effort, and with the help of other draft resisters including Jim McKinney (whose account follows) and George Socrates ("Soc") Kazolias, founded a newsletter called *Zero*.

Tom also became aware of the Toronto-based paper *AMEX-Canada: Published by Americans Exiled in Canada*, which was similar to *Zero*, and an amnesty conference, Amex-Canada, that was scheduled for Toronto in January 1977. *Zero* could send two representatives. He and Soc were chosen to attend, but Tom's US passport had been revoked because of his absence from the army, and without a passport of some sort he would not be admitted to Canada. He turned to the United Nations for assistance. Tom and Soc went to the UN office near the Arc de Triomphe where they were referred to the High Commissioner for Refugees of the United Nations and applied for the organization's internationally accepted passport. They were successful and received UN passports—not an easy task—to attend the conference. The passport was a dense, twelve-page, accordion-fold document, but it got Tom where he wanted to go.

When Jimmy Carter won the presidential election in 1976, his first official act after inauguration was to grant a pardon to draft resisters, but deserters were excluded. The Toronto conference, a week later, attracted the interest of the media, and the message Tom and his colleagues focused on was expanding the scope of the pardons to provide "universal, unconditional amnesty" for all deserters, GIs who did not receive honorable discharges, and civilians convicted of protest offenses committed during the anti-war movement. This would include the burning of draft cards and other similar collateral protest crimes. Many people from his hometown saw Tom for the first time in a long time when he appeared on the evening news. Tom and his colleagues also asked that all military discharges be upgraded to honorable if previously issued in a lower category.

Tom Nagel (courtesy of Tom Nagel)

While demands to universally expand the pardons were not met, a month later Carter instituted an amnesty for deserters who did not leave from a combat zone and began a review process for the 432,000 GIs with unfavorable discharges. Tom accepted Carter's gesture and was pardoned in 1977. Many of his buddies in Paris were never granted a pardon or amnesty.

After the pardon, Tom came back home to Stockton and was sent to Fort Benjamin Harrison in Indiana for a physical and to be mustered out of the army. There were hundreds of men in similar situations. Of these, according to Tom, only 1 percent was back from outside the country; most had been hiding in the United States, some under false names. At Fort Benjamin Harrison, they were all guarded by the US Army Band. "Apparently this was what the band did when they weren't playing or marching," Tom quipped. A few years later he received an honorable discharge in the mail. He backs Carter for being sympathetic to draft resisters and granting the pardon even if it wasn't as inclusive as he would have liked. Tom added,

> It's amazing how many people were involved in the Vietnam War resistance movement, went AWOL, or deserted. I'm probably the most patriotic guy ever. I gave up so much for so little. Everyone is mad at me for being on the winning side. Now, even jugheads realize that the Vietnam War was wrong and that Vietnam is a natural ally, even if it's a Communist-ruled Vietnam.
>
> My father was right; I never should've gone into the military. My whole family suffered because I wasn't around. When my grandfather died, they didn't want to tell me. They thought I'd come to the funeral and get arrested.

In Paris, Tom got married and fathered two children. Once pardoned, he returned with his family to the United States. They lived in Madison, Wisconsin, where Tom worked as a typist and computer programmer at the University of Wisconsin. They were there for six years. In 1983 they moved back to Paris, where they still live.

Jim McKinney, a native of Sacramento, California, was one of the men who crossed the Atlantic and avoided the draft, although at the time of his first trip, in 1965, his motivation was simply a desire to travel. The resistance—a direct reaction to the Vietnam War in the form of a self-imposed exile—came later.

Jim graduated high school in June 1964 and dutifully registered with his local draft board. In September, he enrolled at Sacramento City College (SCC) and received a 2-S student deferment. The following July, with his draft board's permission, he and a friend went to Europe. They worked as they traveled, taking jobs wherever they could find them. Jim told me that they were working at the laundry of the Eastman Barracks—an American military post in West Germany that was the Dachau concentration camp during World War II—washing US soldiers' uniforms, when the Vietnam War started to make an impact on Jim's life.

> When I was working in the barracks, several of us were listening to the radio on July 28, 1965, when we heard LBJ make what was to become a historic speech. He announced that he was going "to increase our active fighting forces [in Vietnam] by raising the monthly draft call from seventeen thousand over a period of time to thirty-five thousand per month . . ." despite his campaign pledge on October 21, 1964, when he said at Akron University, "We are not about to send American boys nine or ten thousand miles away from home to do what Asian boys ought to be doing for themselves."

Jim's antenna went up. Shortly afterward, Jim's mother notified him that he had received a notice to report for a draft physical in California. Since he was out of school, Jim had been reclassified 1-A. He went to the US Consulate in Munich to acknowledge the notice and try to arrange for passage home. He did not have enough money and a consulate bureaucrat berated him, saying, "You shouldn't be traveling around on a shoestring," and refused to provide assistance, economic or otherwise. Turned away and warned to somehow get home for his physical, Jim and his friend hitchhiked to Lisbon, Portugal, and eventually scraped together the funds for passage on a US-bound freighter. They landed in New York City, but by the time Jim got to Sacramento in January 1966, his physical date had passed. He was assigned a new date a month away.

Jim returned to SCC, regained a 2-S classification, and then transferred to what is now San Francisco State University (SFSU). During his time there, students organized a sit-in in May 1967, at the office of John Summerskill, the college president. They were protesting the school's policy of reporting students' academic standing to the Selective Service local boards—which used the information to monitor student deferments—as well as advocating for racial and ethnic minorities, victims of discriminatory admission policies at the college.

The sit-in was the start of a series of events that led to a student and faculty strike that began in November 1968 and lasted until March 1969—the longest such school strike in US history. While much of the strike swirled around the discriminatory issues raised by minority group students, the Vietnam War protest was a key catalyst for the walkout. The extended strike was an informative experience for Jim. As he listened to fiery speeches and did some independent reading, his opposition to the war solidified. It was at this time that he went through his physical. As Jim describes it,

> The sit-in came about amid reports of growing military and civilian carnage in Vietnam. There were meetings, rallies, and marches against the war, and the Oakland induction center (OIC) was briefly forced to close. There were also protests to get recruiters from Dow Chemical—maker of napalm—thrown off campus, and to end the college ROTC program. San Francisco Police tactical units were sent in, Governor Ronald Reagan deployed the California Highway Patrol, and student protestors were attacked and beaten.
>
> In 1967, during the summer break between semesters, I went to

work for the US Forest Service as a surveyor's aide and firefighter in the Stanislaus National Forest in the California Sierra Nevada Mountains. I was also ordered by the Selective Service to report for a physical exam at the OIC.

I remember that I went on a bus full of young men from Sonora, California (the headquarters for Stanislaus National Forest). There were a few other guys that I knew from work. They put us up in a hotel, and I recall spending the evening walking around in the San Francisco North Beach/Broadway nightclub district with the guys. I remember the cattle call in the morning and going in for the assembly-line physical. The atmosphere was not too scary, and there was some joking around, but most of the guys seemed to be taking it seriously, at least half-seriously. There was also an ominous unspoken undertone of foreboding, and for me an uneasy Kafkaesque or *1984* Orwellian feeling. I remember they asked us if there was any reason why anyone should be excused from reporting for induction, and I raised my hand and was held back along with a few others, and when it came my turn to explain, I said that I had participated in demonstrations against the war, and that I had gone to meetings of left-wing organizations against the war. I remember the sergeant laughing as if he had heard all that before and then telling me that I would have to stay behind and name names, that I would be held back, and wouldn't be able to get back on the bus with the others. I didn't want to lose my job, so I declined the interview. It was all chaotic in a strange, somehow orderly way, and then I was back on the bus with the others and back to work in the mountains.

In September, I returned to SFSU and I received a notice that I was "found fully acceptable for induction into the armed forces," and an order to report in November for induction.

A draft counselor advised me that applying for CO status could halt the rapidly approaching date of induction, so I quickly put together my application. I also included eight pages outlining my personal spiritual and philosophical beliefs, but I stopped short of calling myself a complete pacifist, even admitting that there were "certain instances in which the use of force might be condoned." I regretted writing that line, as I knew it might result in a denial of CO status, but I was being honest.

238   Chapter Fourteen

> While I (and much of the rest of America) was still in the process of understanding the extent of the illegal, immoral, and genocidal crimes being committed in the war in Vietnam, I was only too aware that my father, three of my uncles, and one of my aunts, had all served in the military in World War II, fighting in the Pacific (Iwo Jima), the Aleutian Islands, and China; and my mother was a nurse on the home front during the war. World War II was considered a "just war," US territory had been directly attacked at Pearl Harbor. As for me, I made sure to go on record that I was against the Vietnam War. I'd attended demonstrations against it and supported anti-war groups including the War Resister's League, the Women's League for Peace, the Spring Mobilization Committee, and the Students for a Democratic Society.
>
> Although I was no longer a practicing Catholic, my motivations for opposing the war were spiritually based, but I wasn't a member of a religion that prohibited its members from participating in war. I felt, uneasily, that I had to concede that I would accept the status of 1-A-O: "Conscientiously opposed to training and military service requiring the use of arms—fulfills his service obligation in a noncombatant position within the military." In December 1967 I was reclassified as a 1-A-O noncombatant [a status that could still subject him to induction].

Jim's induction order was rescheduled for June. In the interim he appealed the rejection of his CO request; it was denied, as was his request for yet another induction postponement.

> When I met with the government appeal agent at the Sacramento Selective Service draft board, he announced that he was not familiar with my file and that he, in fact, did not know what a conscientious objector was. He told me that he "worked with the FBI during World War II, rounding up farmers and hillbillies who simply did not understand why they had to go." When I asked him if they were justified in objecting, he answered yes, that "under the Thirteenth Amendment to the Constitution, the draft system is illegal."
>
> I began to sense that many of the people who were responsible for making the system run did not even know what they were

Jim McKinney during the Vietnam War era (courtesy of Jim McKinney)

doing. My feeling was that the people at the Selective Service office were just doing a job, that they had developed an attitude toward their work during the post–World War II peacetime years that had not really changed much when the war in Vietnam came along. Like most Americans, they continued to see the draft and obligatory military service as a normal part of life for young males. They were bureaucratically efficient and followed their internal rules and regulations with cold, perfunctory precision.

As time went on and my feelings about the war evolved, so did my strategies for dealing with them. That meant consulting with draft counselors at organizations like the Central Committee for Conscientious Objectors to learn ways to follow the letter of Selective Service law (if not its militaristic spirit) to request deferments, to appeal denials, and to delay, postpone, and extend deadlines and orders to report. I moved around frequently and used different mailing addresses, including home, workplaces, and friends, where mail often had to be forwarded. When I did manage to win an opportunity to appear for a hearing with the local draft board in Sacramento and a Selective Service appeal agent, it was quickly apparent to me that they were not sympathetic. They were determined that I was going to be drafted into the military, one way or another.

I remember being at one such meeting with older men, but not older than my father, and so probably not old enough to be World War II vets. One was sitting with his feet up on the desk, and he was asking questions in a cowboy drawl, clearly expressing his disdain for me and anything I had to say about war in general and this war in particular. There were some big differences in attitude between the draft boards in large urban cities, those in small towns, and those in rural areas. I didn't believe that I would ever be able to make much headway with mine.

Jim graduated in June 1969 and received a bachelor's degree cum laude. He had, by this time, undergone two physicals and several induction postponements and appeal denials. He did not report for his induction. Knowing that government agents were looking for him, he attended his graduation ceremony incognito.

But what would follow? One option was to leave the country. Jim had a difficult conversation with his grandmother, who said simply, "Don't go!" Jim wasn't sure what she meant: Don't go out of the country, or don't go into the army?

> I was taken aback, and I didn't know how to react. Only later did I realize that she was giving me permission to say no to the war, she was telling me that it would be okay for me not to go into the army. It was the first time anyone in my extended family had ever indicated that it would be okay if I were to refuse to go to Vietnam.

In September, Jim left for London, England, where his girlfriend, Nancy, was waiting for him. Unbeknownst to Jim, a federal warrant had been issued for his failure to report, yet he had no problems leaving the United States. The Atlantic Ocean was again between Jim and his draft board.

> When I left the country, I was still grappling with how I would handle things if I were ever to be apprehended—would a judge let me off if I agreed to participate in the war in Vietnam? Could I ever agree to participate, even as a noncombatant? Would I be able to steadfastly refuse? Would I go to prison? In January 1970, my mother forwarded the last of the Orders to Report for Induction. An officer had written, "your delinquency flows from the automatic circumstance of your never having complied with any of your induction orders. We would appreciate being advised of your plans with regard to your compliance with your outstanding induction order."

I had always kept in communication with my draft board, although I must confess, not in a timely fashion, and I intentionally wanted to give the impression that I was trying to comply, but I had seen and heard enough by now to know that my government's war in Vietnam was illegal, immoral, and unjust—the war was cruel, the military was guilty of crimes against humanity, and it was inflicting untold suffering upon millions of people, Vietnamese and Americans alike. There was now the indisputable fact that I had become an outlaw, that I was alienated from my family and country. Only later would the truth behind the lies about the Gulf of Tonkin incident and the false pretenses for the congressional resolution authorizing military action come out—war was never officially "declared" by Congress, the sole branch of government empowered by the Constitution to do so. When the lies about the body counts, the bombings of the dikes and civilian targets, the civilian casualties, the war crimes and wartime atrocities finally began to surface, enough people became convinced that the war was wrong and what I had done was right.

The preceding paragraphs, written more than fifty years after the war, elucidate the anger, bitterness, and disgust, along with the angst, relief, and liberation that Jim felt at the time. Back then, he had come to believe that the war was a fraud perpetrated by the US government on the Vietnamese and the American people. He resented it and could not get far enough away from what he believed was a sham war.

After Jim met Nancy in London, they traveled throughout Europe before settling in Paris, but he was still wanted by the authorities.

In Greece, I received a letter from my mother saying that the FBI had visited my parents and warned them that if I didn't report for induction within thirty days, I'd be in serious trouble. Nancy and I were out of money, but we heard about work in Germany, so we traveled to the Black Forest and took jobs at a Canadian air base where I worked in construction; Nancy was a kitchen helper. We rented a room above a bakery. I received several letters from home while in Germany. One said that my diploma from SFSU had arrived and my brother had left for Vietnam after being home on leave for Christmas. Another letter came, again ordering me to report for induction, this time on January 27, 1970. In February my mother wrote that the FBI paid a second visit to the house and the sheriff's office had delivered a warrant for my arrest. My passport was about to expire, so I traveled to the US Consulate in Stuttgart for a new one. To my surprise, the application went through and I received a new passport [something he might not have been able to do today, given current computer technology that in all likelihood would have caught his outstanding warrant].

We then made plans to move to Paris, just in time, as it happened, because the baker's family alerted us that the German police had come looking for me while we were at work. We quickly fled over the border into France and found our way to Paris.

We found an apartment, and I was soon able to start work teaching English as a second language [ESL] at a private language school in Paris. Nancy found work as a secretary for a small import/export company.

Jim and Nancy also enrolled at the Alliance Française to learn French and began studies at the Sorbonne. For the first few months, life was quiet. Then one day the police came knocking.

Two detectives appeared at our door. Nancy and I were taken to what was then called the Bureau de Sûreté Nationale, or French National Police station. We were placed in an ugly gray room and the detectives brought in a huge telephone-book-size binder. It was filled with reports of my anti–Vietnam War activities in California. I couldn't believe how much was in there and wondered how it was gathered. What was it doing in the hands of the French police? Had the German police also seen it? We didn't know what was going on or what to expect. We started asking questions. At that point the two detectives went to a corner in the room, had a conversation, returned, and said, "We are not fighting in this bloody war" and offered us political asylum. We were very surprised. Suddenly we were political refugees.

France, under President Charles de Gaulle, did not agree with US actions in Vietnam. When US soldiers began going AWOL from American bases in Germany and other European countries because of the war and draft resisters found their way to France, they were given asylum with little or no publicity. But there were conditions. Those placed on Jim and Nancy were threefold: (1) They could not take part in political activities; (2) they had to report every two weeks to the local police; and (3) they had to pay their own way—no financial support from the French government. Other war opponents who received political asylum did so under similar conditions. The young couple agreed to the terms and headed back to their sixth-floor walk-up apartment, elated at this development but sobered at the prospect that Jim might never be able to return home.

While Jim and Nancy earned their keep and reported to the police as required, Jim didn't stay away from political activities. At one point the ESL teachers at his Paris school went on strike, and he inevitably became involved. Over time, he took on increasing responsibility in the teachers' union and helped organize strikes for better pay and teaching conditions. He became known among his fellow teachers and friends for his opposition to the Vietnam War. At a gathering of striking teachers at the Bourse du Travail (Paris labor council), Jim walked into a meeting and received a standing ovation. "Why are they clapping?" he asked, puzzled. "Because they know you're against the war," he was told.

Jim's political activities increased. He was soon involved with PACS (Paris American Committee to Stop War) welcoming deserters from American military forces in Germany. He attended expatriate meetings about the war and founded, along with Tom Nagel and George "Soc" Kazolias, *Zero—Paris American Exile Rock-Bottom Newsletter*, an underground political newssheet. Today, the three men refer to themselves as "the troika" and are still close friends. *Zero* was distributed stealthily on the streets of Paris. The newsletter was illegal and routinely confiscated by French authorities. After the Ford amnesty in 1974, the paper was no longer considered a political risk and was sold openly. When Jim and Nancy weren't working or involved in teaching or politics, they both managed to complete their bachelor's degrees (Jim's second) at the Sorbonne, which qualified them to teach in French public schools.

Throughout Jim's time in Paris, he corresponded with his mother and grandmother. His brother, an army helicopter mechanic deployed as part of President Nixon's secret invasion into neutral Cambodia, sent letters that never arrived. And there was an interesting letter that did arrive from Jim's sister. She wrote, "Some FBI jerk called . . . said you were a fugitive of the law . . . I told him that you were my brother, that I loved you, and that I felt whatever you did about the draft was your own business. After all, you're a big boy and can wipe your own ass."

His parents had initially been upset with Jim's position regarding the war. There had been a lot of tension. His brother had joined the army in 1969 and thought he would see Jim in Vietnam once Jim was in the service. That never happened. Cousins had also enlisted and gone to Vietnam. But they all knew that Jim was against the war. When his brother returned from Vietnam, he was addicted to heroin, and after two decades of personal turmoil, committed suicide. His cousins also had serious drug problems when they returned home. The family came to realize the damage the war was doing.

In Europe, Jim had kept in touch with members of anti-war organizations and draft counselors as well as members of exile groups in Canada and Sweden. He eventually joined a legal campaign led by lawyer Michael Tigar, who was working pro bono on behalf of draft resisters in exile. Jim was one of the forty-four hundred draft resisters specifically excluded from the clemency program initiated by President Ford. In the summer of 1976, Jim won his draft resistance court case in absentia; his indictment and the warrant for his arrest were dismissed. Tigar sent a welcomed telegram: "You can come home."

Jim returned for a visit that Christmas. To ensure that he would encounter no problems at the border, he obtained a document at the US Embassy in Paris, purportedly from Secretary of State Henry Kissinger, approving his reentry to the United States. Yet, federal agents interrogated him for hours upon his arrival in Bangor, Maine. He finally reached Oakland, California, at three a.m., at which point his family greeted him warmly and the healing began.

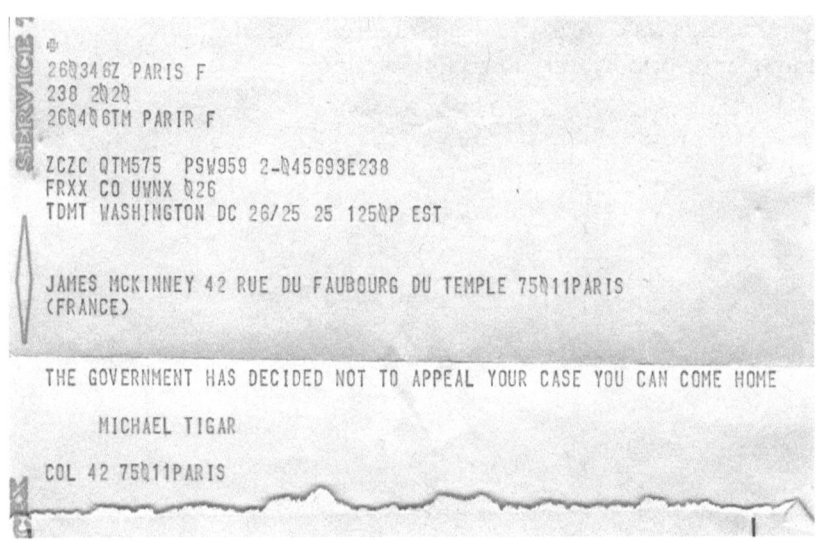

Telegram from attorney Michael Tigar: "You can come home" (courtesy of Jim McKinney)

Soon after the holidays, Jim and Nancy went back to Paris and stayed until 1978. Upon returning permanently to the United States, Jim began teaching ESL at City College of San Francisco. He retired in 2012, after thirty-four years at the school.

Jim McKinney (courtesy of Jim McKinney)

While time has softened the past, and some of the anger has ebbed, the Vietnam War still weighs heavily on Jim's mind. The strong feelings linger.

"I wish I'd done more and had come out much earlier and more forcefully against the war," he said with some regret. "Not going into the army was the best thing I ever did. I'm now a pacifist. Wars never solve anything."

Jim's sentiments remain

solid to this day. He expresses no regrets over declining his invitation for the opportunity to go to Vietnam.

Chapter 15

Perspectives

The administration asserts the right to fill the ranks of the regular army by compulsion. . . . Is this, sir, consistent with the character of a free government? Is this civil liberty? Is this the real character of our Constitution? No, sir, indeed it is not. . . . Where is it written in the Constitution, in what article or section is it contained, that you may take children from their parents, and parents from their children, and compel them to fight the battles of any war, in which the folly or the wickedness of government may engage it? Under what concealment has this power lain hidden, which now for the first time comes forth, with a tremendous and baleful aspect, to trample down and destroy the dearest rights of personal liberty? Who will show me any Constitutional injunction which makes it the duty of the American people to surrender everything valuable in life, and even life itself, not when the safety of their country and its liberties may demand the sacrifice, but whenever the purposes of an ambitious and mischievous government may require it? Sir, I almost disdain to go to quotations and references to prove that such an abominable doctrine has no foundation in the Constitution of the country.

—Daniel Webster, text of a speech delivered in the US House of Representatives on December 9, 1814*

This impassioned statement by Daniel Webster, politician, lawyer, and orator par excellence, in opposition to the use of conscription in the late stages of the War of 1812, is often quoted by draft resisters. The Thirteenth Amendment of the Constitution is also noted. Its prohibition of slavery and involuntary servitude is frequently construed to include a ban against the draft. Historically, there has always been—and in all likelihood will always be—resistance to conscription for war. The degree of resistance will depend on the

---

* Daniel Webster, "Webster's Speech against Conscription," in *The Letters of Daniel Webster, from Documents Owned Principally by the New Hampshire Historical Society*, ed. C. H. Van Tyne (New York: McClure, Phillips, 1902).

nature of the war, who is advocating it, who will profit from it, and who will suffer for it.

While being drafted into the armed forces during the Vietnam War era had an obvious and direct impact on a young man's life, just having the draft lurking in the background had an equally significant bearing on critical life-changing decisions. Pursuing an education or learning a trade, launching a career, getting married, and starting a family were complex matters all by themselves. Factor in the possibility of unwanted military service and the equation got more complicated. Yet, as almost every man I interviewed told me, all those life complications could be cast aside in response to a call for manpower in a *just* war that genuinely threatened the security of the United States—World War II was the example cited most frequently—not the Vietnam War.

Many of the men who shared their stories for this book came from families with a history of military service: they had fathers, grandfathers, brothers, or uncles who fought in World War I, World War II, or the Korean War, even the Vietnam War. In some cases, the men's resistance to the draft caused schisms within the family or embarrassment and shame in the community because young men are not supposed to resist when their nation calls them to fight. But this was a questionable war at a tumultuous time in an America that was rampant with political conflict, social unrest, and youthful muscle-flexing—a significant part of it precipitated by the war. It shouldn't have come as a surprise that young men and women rebelled; considering the nature of the times, it was practically a given.

During the Vietnam War, the draft was staring us in the face. It was never far from my thoughts, and much of what I did in terms of school or career was affected by my efforts to minimize my exposure to the draft. I had to submit to the machinations of the Selective Service and my local draft board, which was managed by a gruff bureaucrat whose chief purpose was to fill a quota. In the eyes of the Selective Service, each of us was simply a number, interchangeable with any other guy they could find; in the end, cannon fodder.

Once the draft was no longer a factor in my life, I went on to

Eli Greenbaum (author's collection)

finish law school in 1972. I also kept working in advertising and ended up doing both—practicing law and creating advertising campaigns—in the years since.

But I've often wondered what would have happened and how I would have been affected if I had gone into the army and to Vietnam. As a young man untested by life, like many of my peers, I was anxious about induction and what would follow. Basic training was an unknown: Could I meet the physical demands? Would I survive life in the barracks and the abuse or intimidation from equals and superiors, all of which are part of the military initiation and hazing process? I had always thought of military service as an alien concept, one in which my possible personal shortcomings could ultimately create a dangerous situation on the battlefield for the men around me as well as for myself. Would I be an asset or a liability? I did not believe it would work out well for my fellow soldiers, me, or the army.

I couldn't see where I'd fit in. And given the army's reputed penchant for frequently mismatching people with their assigned roles (I would've been a great clerk, so I probably would've been trained as a paratrooper, or, even worse, because of my slight build I'd wind up as a totally inept tunnel rat), I had no confidence that I would be properly used. "Used," definitely. Properly, no.

Once I was 4-F, my life changed. No more mail from Local Board 179. No more Miss Modelski. When the war was over, I stopped carrying my draft card. I was free to pursue my career and go about my life without having Vietnam weighing over me. However, that did not dismiss my concerns. I was still troubled about the guys who wanted to say no but didn't know how, still upset about the men the government was throwing to questionable fates.

Consider this anecdote about conscription (and desertion) from Aaron Lansky's *Outwitting History*, referencing author Mendele Moykher Seforim's book *The Travels of Benjamin the Third* and the explanation the characters Benjamin and Sender give in Yiddish at their interrogation in Russia as they try to avoid execution for deserting after being conscripted into the tsar's army:

> "Your honor," Benjamin vociferated. "Trapping people in broad daylight and selling them like chickens in the marketplace—that's permissible? But when the same people try to escape, you call it a crime? . . . Speak up Senderl [sic]—don't stand there like a golem! Come out with God's own truth . . . and say together with me: 'We want to tell you that we don't know a thing about waging war, that we never did know, and never want to know. We are, praised be the Lord, married men; our thoughts are devoted to other things; we haven't the least interest in anything having to do with war. Now then, what do you want with us? You yourselves ought to be glad to get rid of us, I should think!'"*

Lansky adds his own comment regarding the excerpt and the men's situation:

> We lose something in the translation. What Benjamin actually says about the "arts of war" is this: *Zey geyen undz afile gor in kop nisht*— They don't even go into our heads. In other words, militarism lies outside their cognition: beyond their interest, their ability, or their comprehension. Their position, as political activist Abbie Hoffman would have appreciated, is radical to the core, for it challenges not only the legitimacy but the very *premise* of military culture. And the incredible thing is they get away with it. Roaring with laughter, the assembled officers set our Jewish heroes free on grounds of insanity.†

---

* Aaron Lansky, *Outwitting History* (Chapel Hill, NC: Algonquin Books of Chapel Hill, 2005), 163.

† Lansky, *Outwitting History*, 163.

As Lansky's literary example illustrates, the concept of military service, for some men, is impossible to fathom. Many of the people I interviewed fall into this category.

The entire Selective Service experience saddened me. The Vietnam war machine destroyed the trust many members of my generation had in our government. I believed my country was better than this. I thought my country was above turning its men into anonymous numbers and ultimately into war statistics *without just cause*. Like so many of my peers, I had grown up thinking that we, the United States, were the good guys in the white hats, that my country would not lie to me. My country would always tell me the truth. Was I naive? Apparently. Too trusting? Yes, that too. It was during the Vietnam War era that I realized that we might not be such good guys after all. I understood that it wasn't always clear as to who was wearing the white hat. When my draft board dismissed me and I was finally fortunate enough to get my chance to backpack across Europe, I learned quickly from my encounters with young people in hostels in Amsterdam, cafés in Athens, and parks in Copenhagen that we were perceived as "ugly Americans" primarily because of the war (although civil rights and racial issues also played a part in the judgment). Vietnam had diminished our international image. We were definitely not wearing the white hats then.

We now know more about that war, its gestation, and the manipulations that drew us into a conflict that destroyed hundreds of thousands of American and Vietnamese lives. In part, we can thank Daniel Ellsberg and the release of the Pentagon Papers, returning GIs who had stories to tell, and the media that showed the country what was happening. Vietnam introduced the baby boomers to the politics of war. By forcing that war down our throats, I believe the military changed the way Americans perceive conflict and our response to it.

There was fallout in the war's aftermath too, particularly in the less-than-ideal treatment of Vietnam veterans. Consider the message sent by singer-songwriter Bruce Springsteen in his song "Born in the U.S.A." Springsteen, who was 4-F during the draft, was an early supporter of Vietnam War veterans. "Born in the U.S.A." came out of his conversations with the veterans. The song was originally titled "Vietnam" and after several iterations was released in 1984 under its now well-known name. The song's high-energy refrain seems to exude pride in being an American, but if you read Springsteen's lyrics, another message comes through. The song describes the negative effects of the war and the despair of a working-class Vietnam War veteran returning to a less-than-welcoming America. With its rousing chorus, the song was often referenced at political events to rally the crowd. But what so many listeners hear as a patriotic anthem could be interpreted as an anti-war song sporting an unrestrained chorus.* Its popularity endures today.

The destruction resulting from any war is horrendous. The damage done by the Vietnam War and the Selective Service was particularly difficult to accept because, for many people, it was not a war that could be justified; nor was war ever declared by Congress. According to Michael Beschloss in his book *Reaching for Glory*, even President Johnson questioned the war effort he was overseeing. When he ordered Secretary of Defense Robert McNamara, on February 26, 1965, to bomb North Vietnam with the launch of Operation Rolling Thunder, Johnson reportedly said, "Now we're off to bombing these people.... I don't think anything is going to be as bad as losing, and I don't see any way of winning."†

Was it worth putting our nation and our young men and women through that? Were the human and economic costs warranted—for us and for the Vietnamese? Or was the war simply a field test for new weapons systems, experimental military equipment, a trial run of nontraditional war tactics, a way for defense companies to be awarded lucrative government contracts—or a way for ambitious political figures to secure and wield power? All these questions led

---

* "What Does 'Born in the U.S.A.' Really Mean?" https://www.npr.org/2019/03/26/706566556/bruce-springsteen-born-in-the-usa-american-an them; Kurt Loder, "The Rolling Stone Interview: Bruce Springsteen on 'Born in the USA,'" *Rolling Stone*, December 7, 1984.

† Michael R. Beschloss, *Reaching for Glory: Lyndon Johnson's Secret White House Tapes, 1964–1965* (New York: Simon & Schuster, 2002), 194.

to a key point made by the men I interviewed: Were we going to put our asses out there because some politician in Washington who wasn't hesitating to send other people's children into a war said so? The short answer was a resounding *no*.

The men I interviewed were focused on avoiding military service in *this* particular war at almost any cost. Nearly all said they wouldn't hesitate to enlist if the war posed an existential threat to the nation, but, as they noted, Vietnam was not that war. What was the security threat to America? Many of the men referred to our leaders of that time as "egomaniacal morons" and "idiots"—those are the more polite references—for involving us in someone else's fight, someone else's civil war, one that came at great cost to our nation. More than once, the interviewees shared their concern and respect for the men who went to Vietnam in their stead but expressed no regret for avoiding the war.

The draft-eligible men who contributed to this book refused to become cannon fodder in the Vietnam War. They each asked themselves when, where, and how does one draw the line and refuse to take part in something perceived as not our country's fight? Admittedly, we have obligations to our country, but reflecting on our individual morals and ethics, we found there are limits to those obligations. We asked ourselves, when do we have the option to refuse and, more important, when do we have an *obligation* to refuse? Individually and collectively, we rejected and turned away from blind obedience. We believed—and still do—that we have the moral responsibility to decline to serve our country when we believe its course is wrong. It was our *duty* to refuse.

The Selective Service was messing with a generation that didn't want to be messed with, a defiant generation willing to stand up, ask questions, and oppose policies—and a war—it believed were wrong. Consider too, that if a war is worth fighting, is justified, is a real threat to the nation, there may not be a need for a draft. People may volunteer as they did in World War II; they will come forward to defend the nation, but that was not the case with Vietnam.

We now have a volunteer army comprising people who should know what they are getting into when they enlist; men and women who should understand up front about the potential dangers and hardships of serving. The military is a viable and honorable career option and a good opportunity for many people. The professional military provides its members with a collective and important purpose: the defense of our nation, a mission the people of this country understand, appreciate, and rely upon. That purpose inculcates confidence, pride, loyalty, community, and honor among its members. But if the armed forces are improperly directed, engage in questionable conflicts, or participate in atrocities, then their honor and service to the nation come into question.

If there was an active draft today, would the Iraq and Afghanistan wars have gone on for as long as they did? If our young people were being plucked from their everyday lives and conscripted to fight in distant wars, would there be protests? I think the outrage would be palpable, and we'd have been out of those wars years ago or never gone in, 9/11 notwithstanding. In a situation where no one is (allegedly) fighting against his or her own will, where there is no draft lurking to alter your life, where you have stepped into it on your own with eyes open, the right to protest has been effectively waived and neutralized.

The threat of conscription made life difficult, with repercussions that frequently lasted long beyond draft age. When the Vietnam War was over, just because someone avoided the draft didn't mean there weren't lingering effects.

In the five decades since the Vietnam War, perspectives have evolved. Hindsight reigns. Eventually, many of the parents who were initially embarrassed or enraged by a son's resistance came around to understand, accept, and even approve of and support the younger generation's view of the war. Yes, there is still anger and disdain from some quarters in the United States directed at the men who resisted the war. But those who resisted held on to their ethical principles, at times acting as the nation's conscience and making significant personal sacrifices to avoid participating in what they saw as an immoral war.

However, not everyone sees it that way. The men who resisted are also frequently called cowards or traitors accused of shirking their duty to the country, for taking part in protests that supposedly prolonged the war, for compromising soldiers' morale, for running away and abandoning the nation, for soliciting the help of complicit doctors, for daring to know better than our political or military leaders. The men and women I interviewed challenged those defamatory charges. Some of the people I spoke with were catalysts of change before the war; others became activists *because* of the war. Because of the war and the draft they found themselves on a trajectory that upended their lives.

It took guts to say no to the Vietnam war machine, to a government and its systems that were geared to use you. It took courage to say no to the power of the military, to bullying bureaucrats, to the coercive nature of law enforcement, to the politicians with their dubious motives and manipulative strategies, and supportive lobbyists that fed self-serving desires. It was brave to leave families, to leave the country, not knowing if or when loved ones would be seen again. It took nerve to risk prison and the threats it held from other inmates and staff, and to confront a blemished future. It was bold to challenge the concept of cannon fodder, to refuse to become a statistic, to battle a war process that had the power to kill you. It took guts to protest, face an angry authority, and hold picket signs that read "Hell, no, we won't go!" In short, it took extraordinary strength for these men and women to stand firm, to say *no*, and to face the consequences. The men and women I spoke with were not cowards. They were not traitors. They stood up for what they believed in and understood and accepted the cost: some were ostracized, some were embraced. Anyone who said no paid some sort of price.

We who declined to fight did so because we loved our country and did not want to condone or legitimize its actions in Vietnam. We made a choice: hell, no, we didn't go!

Acknowledgments

Hell, No, We Didn't Go! could not have been written without the cooperation and contributions of the men and women I interviewed. They gave me their time and trusted me with their stories. They were patient and polite, no matter how often I pestered them with questions. Their personal accounts are the heart of this book. I am deeply grateful to them all.

No writer works completely alone. In the end there are others whose talent, knowledge, and experience will elevate a work and take it to completion. In my case, I thank Eric Keller, Gail Salenbien, Janis Rossman, and Fred Lonidier for their creative muscle. The late Esther Broner was an early champion of the book, validating its premise and purpose. Jennifer Burke, public affairs specialist at the Selective Service System headquarters, answered all my questions quickly and completely, giving me pause as she put the agency in a new, friendlier light. Peter Werbe, editor of the *Fifth Estate*, offered his newspaper's archives. Susan Ehrenrich, Amy Rutenberg, Tom Grace, and Mel Small provided intellectual perspective and constructive criticism to make this a better book. Michael Kehoe, former University Press of Kansas (UPK) marketing and sales director, pointed me in the right direction to Joyce Harrison, editor in chief of UPK. Her immediate understanding of this book, her consistent encouragement, and her sharp pencil played a huge role in shaping the manuscript. Historian John Prados, a true scholar, fact-checked the manuscript and gave it the thumbs-up. UPK's Derek Helms, director of marketing and publicity, Erica Nicholson, production editor, and Karl Janssen, art director, and their teams were instrumental in bringing this book to life. If I have overlooked someone, my sincere apologies; the omission was accidental.

Thanks, too, to Beeps, my wife, editor, and muse, for guiding this project from start to finish and, as you say on your Bloom Ink website, for "helping me put my best narrative forward."

I also thank my sister, Ilana Tauber, for her encouragement and support. And I thank my parents for introducing me to books, libraries, and the joy of reading. I wish they were around to read this.

Appendix 1

Selective Service System Statistics, Classifications, and Chain of Events

The information in this appendix is from the Selective Service System website, www.sss.gov. The material has been lightly edited.

INDUCTION STATISTICS

The following shows the number of men who were inducted into military service through the Selective Service System during major twentieth century conflicts.

Conflict and Number of Inductions

World War I (September 1917–November 1918)	2,810,296
World War II (November 1940–October 1946)	10,110,104
Korean Conflict (June 1950–June 1953)	1,529,539
Vietnam War (August 1964–February 1973)	1,857,304

Vietnam Inductions by Year

1960	86,602
1961	118,586
1962	82,060
1963	119,265
1964	112,386
1965	230,991
1966	382,010

1967	228,263
1968	296,406
1969	283,586
1970	162,746
1971	94,092
1972	49,514
1973	646

The last induction call went out on December 7, 1972. The last man inducted entered the US Army on June 30, 1973. The Selective Service System's induction authority expired on July 1, 1973.

CLASSIFICATION

Men are not classified now. Classification is the process of determining who is available for military service and who is deferred or exempted. Classifications are based on an individual registrant's circumstances and beliefs. A classification program would go into effect should Congress and the president decide to resume a draft. At that time, men who are qualified for induction would have the opportunity to file a claim for exemptions, deferments, and postponements from military service.

During the time of the Vietnam War, local boards determined classification in accordance with regulations and guidance issued from the Selective Service National Headquarters. Deferments were available for students, some fathers, farmers, and other occupations that supported the national interest. It was the duty of the registrant to provide information required by local boards to ensure proper classification. However, deferments granted at the time lacked nationwide uniformity.

Conscientious objectors were required to serve twenty-four months contributing to the maintenance of the national health, safety, or interest as their local board deemed appropriate. COs could select a suitable alternative service job or be assigned one. (See Alternative Service Program below.)

In 1971 deferment policies were established in the *Registrants*

Processing Manual to enforce the uniform application of Selective Service regulations. Student, fatherhood, occupational, and agricultural deferments were phased out.

The following is an edited list of the more commonly used Selective Service classifications from 1948 to 1976. (Classifications changed over time. Not all the classifications presented here were used throughout the Vietnam War era. Some of the classifications listed may not be applicable if a draft is reinstated.) Roman numerals I, II, III, IV, V were sometimes used:

Classification — Description

1-A—Available for military service.
1-AM—Medical specialist available for military service.
1-A-O—Conscientious objector—conscientiously opposed to training and military service requiring the use of arms—fulfills his service obligation in a noncombatant position within the military.
1-A-OM—Medical specialist conscientious objector available for noncombatant military service.
1-C—Member of the Armed Forces of the United States, the Coast and Geodetic Survey, or the Public Health Service.
1-D—Member of a Reserve component or student taking military training.
1-H—Registrant not currently subject to processing for induction or alternative service.

Selective Service System note: With the cessation of registrant processing in 1976, all registrants (except for a few alleged violators of the Military Selective Service Act) were classified 1-H regardless of any previous classification.

1-O—Conscientious objector available for civilian work contributing to the national health, safety, or interest.
1-OM—Medical specialist conscientious objector available for civilian work contributing to the national health, safety, or interest.
1-S—Student deferred by status—(H) high school; (C) college.
1-W—Conscientious objector performing civilian work in the national health, safety, or interest.

1-Y—Registrant qualified for service only in time of war or national emergency.

Selective Service System note: The 1-Y classification was abolished December 10, 1971. Local boards were subsequently instructed to reclassify all 1-Y registrants by administrative action.

2-A—Registrant deferred because of civilian occupation (except agriculture).

2-AM—Medical specialist deferred because of critical community need involving patient care.

2-B—Registrant deferred because of occupation in a war industry.

2-C—Registrant deferred because of agricultural occupation.

2-D—Ministerial students—Deferred from military service.

2-M—Registrant deferred for medical study.

2-S—Registrant deferred because of activity in study.

3-A—Hardship deferment—Deferred from military service because service would cause hardship upon his family.

4-A—Registrant who has completed service; or sole surviving son.

4-B—Official deferred by law.

4-C—Alien or dual national—Sometimes exempt from military service.

4-D—Ministers of religion—Exempted from military service.

4-E—Conscientious objector opposed to both combatant and non-combatant training and service.

4-F—Registrant not qualified for military service.

4-FM—Medical specialist not qualified for military service.

4-G—Sole surviving son—Son or brothers in a family where the parent or sibling died as a result of US military service, or is in a captured or MIA status, are exempt from service in peacetime.

4-W—Conscientious objector who has completed civilian alternate service.

5-A—Registrant over the age of liability for military service.

A college student could have his induction postponed until he finished the current semester or, if a senior, the end of the academic year. A high-school student could have his induction postponed until he graduated or reached age twenty. A man could appeal his classification to a Selective Service appeal board.

RETURN TO THE DRAFT

If the United States were to return to the draft, the sequence of events would be as follows:

1. Draft Authorization: Congress and the President

A national emergency, exceeding the Department of Defense's capability to recruit and retain its total force strength, requires Congress to amend the Military Selective Service Act to authorize the president to induct personnel into the armed forces.

2. Activation of Selective Service System

Selective Service activates and orders all personnel to report for duty. Reserve Force Officers, along with selected military retirees, begin to open area offices to accept registrant claims. Local, district appeal, and national board members are notified to report for refresher training.

3. The Lottery

A publicly attended, nationally televised and live-streamed lottery is conducted. The lottery, a random drawing of birthdays and numbers, establishes the order in which individuals receive orders to report for induction. The first to receive induction orders are those whose twentieth birthday falls during the year of the lottery. If required, additional lotteries are conducted for those 21, 22, 23, 24, 25, 19, and finally 18.5 years old.

4. Orders to Report to Military Entrance Processing Station (MEPS)

Induction notices are sent and registrants may now make claims if desired for a postponement, deferment, or exemption. Inductees report to a local MEPS for induction. At MEPS, registrants are given a physical, mental, and moral evaluation to determine whether they are fit for military service. Once notified of the results of the evaluation, a registrant will either be inducted into military service or sent home.

5. Activation of Local and District Appeal Boards

Local and Appeal Boards begin to process registrant claims for classification as conscientious objectors, dependency hardships, ministerial and ministerial student deferments, and appeals.

6. Induction of First Draftees

According to current Department of Defense requirements, Selective Service must deliver the first inductees to the military within 193 days from the onset of a crisis and the law being updated to authorize a draft.

ALTERNATIVE SERVICE PROGRAM

The Alternative Service Program affects those persons whose conscientious objection encompasses both combatant and noncombatant military training and service. The program allows men who have been classified 1–0 by their local boards to fulfill their service obligation in a civilian capacity contributing to the maintenance of the national health, safety, or interest.

The Alternative Service Program is administered by the Alternative Service Offices that will be located in forty-eight major cities in the United States. There is also a District Appeal Board composed of no less than three civilian volunteers. It is their responsibility to review certain appeals of job assignments by the Alternative Service Workers.

A major part of the contingency planning for Alternative Service is to identify agencies and associations that could assist the Selective Service in placing conscientious objectors in suitable alternative service jobs. Examples of alternative service work are conservation, caring for the very young and the very old, educational projects, and health care.

Conscientious objectors who are to be placed in the Alternative Service Program will be asked to describe their skills, aptitudes, and interests in order to facilitate their placement. An attempt will be made to match the objector's skills and aptitudes to an eligible job, while at the same time ensuring that his service makes a meaningful contribution to the national interest. All assignments will be made within thirty days of reclassification to conscientious objector status.

Employers will be asked to describe their job openings and the qualifications of persons required to fill them. The employer may interview conscientious objectors before deciding to hire them, or he may leave the placement decision in the hands of the Alternative Service Office. In all cases, the employer and the Selective Service must execute an agreement for the employment of conscientious objectors before any work assignments are made. All assignments will be made within thirty days of reclassification to conscientious objector status.

It is the policy of the Selective Service to treat persons in the Alternative Service Program fairly and with dignity and to assign them to positions that will make genuine contributions to the national health, safety, or interest.

Appendix 2

Items Received from the Selective Service

Upon registering with their local Selective Service System draft board, most men were given a two-sided fact sheet and an informational brochure to help familiarize them with the conscription process.

SELECTIVE SERVICE FACTS
SELECTIVE SERVICE SYSTEM
LANSING, MICHIGAN

1. **Registration:**

   a. Every male is required to be registered at a Selective Service Board on his 18th birthday, or within five days after that date.

   b. Registration is required even though you are enlisted in a Reserve or National Guard Unit. Men on active military duty who have not previously registered must register within 30 days following separation. All males born after August 30, 1922, must register.

   c. Following registration, you will be mailed a Registration Certificate which you must have in your possession at all times. Alteration of your Registration Certificate is a Federal offense involving severe penalties. Apply for a new Certificate (SSS Form No. 2) at your Draft Board if yours is lost or destroyed.

   d. The residence address you give at the time of registration determines the Local Board which will always have jurisdiction over you.

   e. Notify your Local Board of any change in your mailing address.

2. **Classification:**

   a. A Questionnaire will be mailed to you some time after your 20th birthday. The confidential information you supply will be used by your Local Board to determine your classification. The law provides that all men must meet their military service obligation unless the board determines that deferment is essential in the national interest. Most deferments are temporary and extend liability to age 35.

   b. When you receive your Notice of Classification, you will have ten days in which you may ask for a personal appearance before your Local Board to discuss your case or you may file an appeal for further review of your case by a Board of Appeal.

   c. You are required to notify your Local Board of any change that may affect your classification. In addition to reporting changes of address, you must advise your Board of changes in physical condition and in occupational, marital, family, dependency and military status.

   d. Plan to complete your education or training before entering active military service. Normally you can expect to complete your college education before being called for induction. Keep your Local Board informed of your college or technical training plans and any changes in student status.

(Over)

The Selective Service Facts sheet provided information registrants needed to know about the draft (author's collection)

3. <u>Selection</u>:

   a. If you are in Class I-A or Class I-A-O you will be ordered to report for physical examination at about age 21 to 22 to determine your physical, mental and moral acceptability for induction into the Armed Forces. Currently less than two out of three men can qualify.

   b. Qualified men will be selected in sequence of age and ordered for induction into the Armed Forces for two years of active duty at about 22 to 23 years of age. Normally, induction calls will be filled first by volunteers, followed by non-fathers under age 26 selected in age sequence, the oldest first.

   c. Nine out of ten qualified registrants enter service before age 26.

4. <u>Voluntary Induction or Enlistment</u>:

   a. While your obligation for military service is mandatory, you may choose <u>when</u> and <u>how</u> you will meet that obligation after you have completed your education and before you are ordered for induction.

   b. From age 17 to 26 you can volunteer through your Local Board for two years active duty in the Army.

   c. From the time you register at age 18 until you are ordered for induction at about age 23, you may enlist in any of the Armed Forces for two to four years of active duty. There are also many opportunities in the Ready Reserve or National Guard requiring six months of active duty followed by reserve service in your home community.

   d. College students can meet their service obligations in the various officer candidate and ROTC programs open to them.

   SELECTIVE SERVICE CLASSIFICATIONS (In sequence of consideration)

   I-A.....Registrant available for military service.
   I-A-O...Conscientious objector available for noncombatant service.
   I-O.....Conscientious objector available for civilian work.
   I-S.....<u>Student deferred by law.</u>
   I-Y.....Qualified for service only in time of national emergency.
   II-A....Occupational deferment.
   II-C....Agricultural deferment.
   II-S....Student deferment.
   I-D.....Qualified member of reserve component.
   III-A...Extreme hardship deferment, or registrant with a child.
   IV-B....Official deferred by law.
   IV-C....Deferment of certain aliens.
   IV-D....Minister of religion or divinity student.
   IV-F....Registrant not qualified for any military service.
   IV-A....Registrant with sufficient prior military service.
   V-A.....Registrant over the age of liability for military service.
   I-W.....Conscientious objector performing civilian work.
   I-C.....Member of the Armed Forces of the United States.

   CALL YOUR SELECTIVE SERVICE LOCAL BOARD FOR FURTHER INFORMATION

"Selective Service and You . . .," a second pamphlet offered additional information (author's collection)

YOU SHOULD KNOW

Your primary obligation is to keep your local board informed of your mailing address at all times.

REGISTRATION

1. The *residence* address you have given will determine your local board.
2. If you move to any other location, this board will remain the board of jurisdiction.
3. You will be mailed a Registration Certificate. Sign it and have it on your person at all times.
4. In all correspondence to your local board refer to your Selective Service Number shown on your Registration Certificate.
5. It is a violation of Selective Service Law to alter your Registration Certificate, or to have a certificate which has been altered.

CLASSIFICATION

1. A Classification Questionnaire will be mailed to you.
2. From information submitted in this questionnaire the local board will determine your initial classification.
3. Report *all* changes in your status (such as: Marital Status; Births of Children; Student Status; Occupation; Physical Condition) to your local board IMMEDIATELY—IN WRITING.

SELECTIVE SERVICE CLASSIFICATIONS

CLASS I

- **Class I-A:** Available for military service.
- **Class I-A-O:** Conscientious objector available for noncombatant military service only.
- **Class I-C:** Member of the Armed Forces of the United States, the Coast and Geodetic Survey, or the Public Health Service.
- **Class I-D:** Qualified member of reserve component, or student taking military training, including ROTC and accepted aviation cadet applicant.
- **Class I-O:** Conscientious objector available for civilian work contributing to the maintenance of the national health, safety, or interest.
- **Class I-S:** Student deferred by law until graduation from high school or attainment of age of 20, or until end of his academic year at a college or university.
- **Class I-W:** Conscientious objector performing civilian work contributing to the maintenance of the national health, safety, or interest, or who has completed such work.
- **Class I-Y:** Registrant qualified for military service only in time of war or national emergency.

CLASS II

- **Class II-A:** Occupational deferment (other than agricultural and student).
- **Class II-C:** Agricultural deferment.
- **Class II-S:** Student deferment.

CLASS III

- **Class III-A:** Extreme hardship deferment, or registrant with a child or children.

CLASS IV

- **Class IV-A:** Registrant with sufficient prior active service or who is a sole surviving son.
- **Class IV-B:** Official deferred by law.
- **Class IV-C:** Alien not currently liable for military service.
- **Class IV-D:** Minister of religion or divinity student.
- **Class IV-F:** Registrant not qualified for any military service.

CLASS V

- **Class V-A:** Registrant over the age of liability for military service.

APPEALS

1. You, your employer, or dependent may appeal your classification. This request must be submitted in writing to your local board.

2. An appeal must be taken within *10 days* after your local board mails you a Notice of Classification, except when a longer period is allowed as stated on that notice.

3. Additional information on appeals will be on each Notice of Classification mailed to you.

REMEMBER

1. Report a change of address to your local board at once.

2. Keep your board informed of your current status at all times.

3. Classifications are subject to change by the local board at any time.

4. If you are away from your local board and you are in doubt as to your obligation to Selective Service, GO TO THE NEAREST LOCAL BOARD and request assistance.

5. Failure to comply with an order from your local board may make you subject to fine or imprisonment.

```
MICHIGAN LOCAL BOARD NO. 179
         WAYNE COUNTY
      1050 WEST FORT STREET
      DETROIT, MICHIGAN 48226
```

(Local Board Stamp)

Selected Bibliography

"ACLU Blasts Draft as Punishment." *Fifth Estate*, November 19, 1965, 1.

Anderson, Dave. "How a Clerk Spared Ali from Prison." *New York Times*, December 17, 1979.

Baskir, Laurence M., and William A. Strauss. *Chance and Circumstance: The Draft, the War, and the Vietnam Generation*. New York: Knopf, 1978.

Beschloss, Michael R. *Reaching for Glory: Lyndon Johnson's Secret White House Tapes, 1964–1965*. New York: Simon & Schuster, 2002.

Clay v. United States, 403 U.S. 698 (1971).

"Draft-Defying Doctors." *Time*, November 16, 1970.

Ellsberg, Daniel. *Secrets: A Memoir of Vietnam and the Pentagon Papers*. New York: Viking Books, 2002.

Gillette v. United States, 401 U.S. 437 (1971).

Gregory, Hamilton. *McNamara's Folly: The Use of Low-IQ Troops in the Vietnam War*. Conshohocken, PA: Infinity Publishing, 2015.

———. "McNamara's Morons: Salvaging the Deficient for the War Effort." *VVA Veteran* online newsletter (May/June 2016). https://vvaveteran.org/36-3/36-3_morons.html.

Grossman, Dave. *On Killing: The Psychological Cost of Learning to Kill in War and Society*. New York: Back Bay Books, 2009.

Hunter, Margaret. "Ford Offers Amnesty Program Requiring Two Years Public Work; Defends His Pardon of Nixon." *New York Times*, September 17, 1974.

Lansky, Aaron. *Outwitting History*. Chapel Hill, NC: Algonquin Books of Chapel Hill, 2005.

Loder, Kurt. "The Rolling Stone Interview: Bruce Springsteen on 'Born in the USA.'" *Rolling Stone*, December 7, 1984.

Oestereich v. Selective Service System Local Board No. 11, 393 U.S. 233 (1968).

Potter, Paul. "Naming the System." Speech delivered during the March on Washington, April 17, 1965, Washington, DC. Available at the website of the Students for a Democratic Society. https://www.sds-1960s.org/sds_wuo/sds_documents/paul_potter.html.

Prados, John, and Margaret Pratt Porter, eds. *Inside the Pentagon Papers*. Lawrence: University Press of Kansas, 2004.

"Proclamation 4483—Granting Pardon for Violations of the Selective Service Act, August 4, 1964, to March 28, 1973." National Archives, Office of the Federal Register. https://www.archives.gov/federal-register/codification/proclamations/04483.html.

"Resistance and Revolution: The Anti–Vietnam War Movement at the University of Michigan." Michigan in the World, University of Michigan, accessed November 2, 2023. http://michiganintheworld.history.lsa.umich.edu/antivietnamwar/exhibits/show/exhibit.

Ross, Daniel. "'Unknown Territory': Canada and American War Resister Identity in the Pages of AMEX, 1968–1971." In *Canada-US Borderlands Colloquium*, 8–9. Toronto: York University Library, 2010.

Selective Service System. "Changes from Vietnam to Now." Accessed August 2, 2023. www.sss.gov/history-and-records/changes-from-vietnam-to-now/.

———. "Conscientious Objectors." Accessed August 3, 2023, https://www.sss.gov/conscientious-objectors/.

Sheehan, Neil, Hedrick Smith, E. W. Kenworthy, and Fox Butterfield. *The Pentagon Papers: The Secret History of the Vietnam War*. New York: Racehorse, 2017.

Smith, Bryan. "Sudden Impact." *Chicago Magazine*, June 20, 2007.

United States v. O'Brien, 391 U.S. 367 (1968).

United States v. Seeger, 380 U.S. 163 (1965).

"The Vietnam War Statistics." Shmoop.com. Accessed November 1, 2023. https://www.shmoop.com/vietnam-war/statistics.html.

Webster, Daniel. "Webster's Speech against Conscription." In *The Letters of Daniel Webster, from Documents Owned Principally by the New Hampshire Historical Society*, edited by C. H. Van Tyne. New York: McClure, Phillips, 1902.

Welsh v. United States, 398 U.S. 333 (1970).

"What Does 'Born in the U.S.A.' Really Mean?" NPR, *Morning Edition*, March 26, 2019. https://www.npr.org/2019/03/26/706566556/bruce-springsteen-born-in-the-usa-american-anthem.

Wolff and Shortt v. Selective Service Local Board No. 16, et al., 372 F.2d 817 (2d Cir. 1967).

"Women Against Daddy Warbucks." In *Sisterhood Is Powerful*, edited by Robin Morgan. New York: Random House, 1970.

For Further Reference

For additional information concerning the Vietnam War, the military draft, resistance to both, and the social climate of the time, interested readers may consider the following sources:

Abney, Wesley. *Randon Destiny: How the Vietnam Draft Lottery Shaped a Generation*. Wilmington, DE: Vernon Press, 2018.
Appy, Christian G. *Patriots: The Vietnam War Remembered from All Sides*. New York: Viking Books, 2003.
———. *Working-Class War: American Combat Soldiers and Vietnam*. Chapel Hill: University of North Carolina Press, 1993.
Burns, Ken, and Lynn Novick, dirs. *The Vietnam War*. Written by Geoffrey C. Ward. Aired September 2017, on PBS.
Cortright, David. *Vietnam War Almanac: An In-Depth Guide to the Most Controversial Conflict in American History*. Chicago: Haymarket Books, 2005.
Elmer, Jerry. *Felon for Peace: The Memoir of a Vietnam-Era Draft Resister*. Nashville, TN: Vanderbilt University Press, 2005.
Flynn, George O. *The Draft, 1940–1973*. Lawrence: University Press of Kansas, 1993.
Foley, Michael. *Confronting the War Machine: Draft Resistance in the Vietnam War*. Chapel Hill: University of North Carolina Press, 2003.
Gitlin, Todd. *The Sixties: Years of Hope, Days of Rage*. New York: Bantam Books, 1987.
Gottlieb, Sherry Gershon. *Hell No, We Won't Go! Resisting the Draft during the Vietnam War*. New York: Viking Books, 1991.
Hagan, John. *Northern Passage: American Vietnam Draft Resisters in Canada*. Cambridge, MA: Harvard University Press, 2001.
Halberstam, David. *The Best and the Brightest*. New York: Penguin Press, 1993.
Heineman, Kenneth J. *The Peace Movement at American Universities in the Vietnam Era*. New York: NYU Press, 1993.

Hunt, Andrew E. *The Turning: A History of Vietnam Veterans Against the War*. Revised. New York: NYU Press, 2001.

Kasinsky, Renee. *Refugees from Militarism: Draft-Age Americans in Canada*. New Brunswick, NJ: Transaction Books, 1976.

Levine, Mark L., George C. McNamee, and Daniel Greenberg, eds. *The Trial of the Chicago Seven: The Official Transcript*. New York: Simon & Schuster, 2020.

Lewis, Penny. *Hardhats, Hippies, and Hawks: The Vietnam Antiwar Movement as Myth and Memory*. Ithaca, NY: ILR Press, 2013.

MacPherson, Myra. *Long Time Passing: Vietnam and the Haunted Generation*. Bloomington: Indiana University Press, 1984.

Morrison, Joan, and Robert K. Morrison. *From Camelot to Kent State: The Sixties Experience in the Words of Those Who Lived It*. London: Oxford University Press, 1987.

Nicosia, Gerald. *Home to War: A History of the Vietnam Veterans' Movement*. New York: Crown Publishing, 2001.

Prados, John. *Vietnam: History of an Unwinnable War, 1945–1975*. Lawrence: University Press of Kansas, 2009.

Rutenberg, Amy. *Rough Draft: Cold War Military Manpower Policy and the Origins of Vietnam-Era Draft Resistance*. Ithaca, NY: Cornell University Press, 2019.

Satin, Mark. *Manual for Draft-Age Immigrants to Canada*. 1968. Repr., Toronto: House of Anasi Press, 2017.

Simons, Donald L. *I Refuse: Memories of a Vietnam War Objector*. Trenton, NJ: Broken Rifle Press, 1992.

Ward, Geoffrey C., and Ken Burns. *The Vietnam War: An Intimate History*. New York: Knopf Doubleday, 2017.

Weiner, Tom. *Called to Serve: Stories of Men and Women Confronted by the Vietnam Draft*. Amherst, MA: Levellers Press, 2011.

Willbanks, James. *Vietnam War Almanac: An In-Depth Guide to the Most Controversial Conflict in American History*. New York: Skyhorse, 2013.

www.ingramcontent.com/pod-product-compliance
Lightning Source LLC
Chambersburg PA
CBHW030529230426